Michael Kreiser

JEFF PORTER is the author of *Lost Sound: The Forgotten Art of Radio Storytelling*, the memoir *Oppenheimer Is Watching Me*, and coeditor of *Understanding the Essay*. His essays and articles have appeared in several magazines and literary reviews, including the *Antioch Review*, *Northwest Review*, *Shenandoah*, *Missouri Review*, *Hotel Amerika*, *Wilson Quarterly*, *Contemporary Literature*, and the *Seneca Review*. He loves cameras, dogs, and guitars—though not in that order. He lives in Iowa City and teaches English at the University of Iowa.

Catherine Sebastian

Planet Claire is the second title from **ANN HOOD's** nonfiction imprint with Akashic, **Gracie Belle**. Modeled after her experience writing the memoir *Comfort: A Journey Through Grief*, and named after her daughter Grace, Hood's imprint reaffirms for authors and readers that none of us is alone in our journeys. She is the author of the best-selling novels *The Obituary Writer*, *The Knitting Circle*, and *The Book That Matters Most*. Hood was born in West Warwick, Rhode Island, and currently lives in Providence, Rhode Island. She is the editor of *Providence Noir*.

Planet Claire

SUITE FOR CELLO AND SAD-EYED LOVERS

a memoir

JEFF PORTER

GRACIE BELLE

ALSO AVAILABLE FROM GRACIE BELLE
an imprint of Akashic Books curated by ANN HOOD

Now You See the Sky by Catharine H. Murray

〜

Published by Gracie Belle/Akashic Books
©2021 Jeff Porter

Paperback ISBN: 978-1-61775-846-1
Hardcover ISBN: 978-1-61775-907-9
Library of Congress Control Number: 2020935825

All rights reserved
First printing

Gracie Belle
c/o Akashic Books
Brooklyn, New York
Twitter: @AkashicBooks
Facebook: AkashicBooks
E-mail: info@akashicbooks.com
Website: www.akashicbooks.com

For Claire

*I have never been here before: my breath comes differently,
the sun is outshone by a star beside it.*
—Franz Kafka, *Aphorisms*

TABLE OF CONTENTS

PROLOGUE

One fine morning, without having done anything wrong, my wife Claire died. She sat in her favorite chair drinking coffee and shortly after collapsed in her study. Young and resilient, the needle on her life span hardly past midway, Claire died abruptly, as though I had been absentminded or had left the gas stove on or the door open. I looked up from the morning paper and she was gone.

That was a year ago. A year earlier my dog died. Claire's death was sudden, unexpected. Milo's was a slow death. We watched him go. I'll never be the same, Claire said. Me either, I said. And we weren't. My wife and I were together for twenty-seven years. Then she was gone, in medias res. To say I was broken into pieces, that like Humpty-Dumpty I had fallen apart, is not entirely accurate. Nor is it entirely wrong. *Entirely* is a word that no longer works for me, if truth be said. That word no longer works either, because of its proximity to the other. Claire died and a part of me flew off somewhere else. To this day I've been looking for both, my wife and runaway me. Loss upon loss.

I'm lost without Claire, I said, why go on? My mind is a

graveyard. Darkness and devils! Hyperboles sprung at me from everywhere. And yet here I am as alive as the next baffled soul. What followed her death was a year of profound gloom and heartache, obviously. But it didn't feel obvious. Grief is mysterious, bewildering, painful. I was miserable, still am. It was as though I'd been slit open, stabbed by a large knife, and I savored the pain. There was blood everywhere, even in my dreams. One by one, I said to myself, we are all becoming shades, returning to the dark and wormy earth. I dragged my bones through the empty, tortured space of my life, a fugitive, my mind filling up with quotes from Shakespeare, Joyce, and Beckett. I am like a cork upon the tide, I thought, as if I might find solace in eloquence.

Claire was never fooled by eloquence. She was too keen to be tricked by a pretty sentence. Not that I didn't try. A meticulous scholar, she lived with tremendous focus. She was rarely distracted and never failed to settle unfinished business. Her planner was a work of art, each week precisely detailed with meetings, chores, events, birthdays, appointments, deadlines, passwords, expiration dates, account numbers, memos. *Milo's annual rabies shots* (February 16). *Dad's b-day* (March 25). *JP Atlanta trip* (March 29). *See NYT hearing aid article + comments* (July 20). *Use UN Mileage Plus to book flights to France* (September 18). *Findlay Market: Blue Oven bread + English muffins* (January 2). This was the work of a nimble mind. There was so much chaos in the world it was foolish to live without intention, and so Claire lived life scrupulously, more than anyone I know. To be caught off guard by death, with so much left undone, was worse than death itself. That was not in the plans. We looked forward to growing old. We would do this gracefully together. We would sip coffee in a Portland café and watch the hipsters pass by. We would make fun of our eye wrinkles. Claire would learn how to play the mandolin.

What was in the plans were gardening, a new dog, travel, book projects, some well underway. There was always yard work. The lilac, damaged by early snow, had to come out. The smoke bush: trim back or remove altogether. There was the Beauchamp Pageant project, an illustrated biography of the Earl of Warwick, dating to the reign of Richard III. Another book on tragedy (ironically). So much to do and so little time. As a writer, Claire was graceful and sharp-witted. I loved her work, loved watching her write, pen in hand, bent over her yellow notepad, quietly in her study, at school, in the British Library. An efficient, unrelenting researcher she was, deciphering strange medieval texts with mysterious patience and insight. Her mind was a thing to wonder at, her coherence singular. I always felt I was her cognitive other, the guy whose feet went one way and whose brain went another. I am so distracted, so nonlinear. Wrong-way Charlie, she called me. Perhaps my unruly gestures will get a rise out of her, but that's not likely to happen. The dead rarely come back anymore—but who knows. Really, we know so little.

We know this. A typical human being possesses about eighty-six billion neurons. It's hard to do an exact calculation because neurons are so densely packed together, but right now I count only forty-four billion in my brain, barely half. The other half has gone missing. I'm not exaggerating. People on TV exaggerate. People on TV talk endlessly, but I'm tallying unique neurons in the Jell-O between my ears—one hemisphere at a time—and coming up short. Is it possible to live even a subnormal life with only half a brain? There's the case of Jody Miller, who suffered life-threatening seizures as a young girl and had half her brain surgically removed. Jody not only survived the procedure (a hemispherectomy) but won a ton of awards and scholarships before graduating college. The left side of her brain was able to take over the role of the missing hemisphere. I haven't entirely given up hope.

Anyway, I use the word *entirely* all the time—I need to stop. It imparts a sense of wholeness to things I can't experience anymore. In its place another adverb—*anyway*. *Anyway* is an elliptical word. It doesn't add anything but subtracts. It's subtractive, able or tending to remove. When I say *anyway* at the beginning of a sentence, I do not initiate a full-scale launch of meaning. On an existential level, *anyway* is a surrender to the economy of being, assuming that being likes to cut costs now and then.

Anyway, when your partner dies, everything around you seems to collapse. You look deep within yourself, not for courage, just for the wherewithal not to lose your car in a parking garage. Please don't let me lose my car tonight in the hospital parking garage. The bigger question, which you don't dare ask yourself, is how to keep the nothing that is now you from exploding into bits and pieces that spiral out into space. My hair crackles with static electricity even as I write that sentence. *Nothing is more real than nothing*, wrote Beckett. Nothing is a word that sticks around, like flies in August or shadows in October. Like an awful taste in your mouth.

It's very complicated to write about death. Wish I didn't have to. Can you ever not know again? Not knowing about death is really good. To be so naive—maybe innocent too. I don't think I can do this alone. I don't think you can either. Sooner or later it comes to death. Love flirts with grief every hour of the day.

Outside my study a road worker in brown overalls is breaking up my street with a T-shaped jackhammer and is making ear-shattering sounds. Better that, though, than silence. Silence is scary. When the lamb broke open the seventh seal, says the Book of Revelation, there was silence. Now that's spooky, like dead air on the radio. Life is deafening.

In the Bergman film *The Seventh Seal*, Death follows a medieval knight returning home from the Crusades. He is a bitter man, weary and disillusioned, troubled by the silence of God in the face of so much dying. He meets a stranger who doesn't look too chirpy. Who are you? asks the knight. I am death, says Death. You have come for me? asks the knight. I have been at your side for a long time, says Death. The knight is worried that life is nothing more than senseless terror, so he asks Death to play a game of chess, to extend life just long enough to find some answers. If death is the only certainty, what else is there? Death shrugs his shoulders and accepts the challenge. The knight suddenly feels inspired. "I, Antonius Block, am playing chess with Death," he says. Death doesn't really care one way or another. He just looks bored in his ominous black cloak. His indifference is beyond terror.

The crazy jackhammer pounds the street, bashing through concrete. Bone-jarring steel on stone, bits of rock flying off. How does the road worker survive that commotion? Bang, crack, whack. Things are always flying off, more than we know, I think, sometimes disastrously. It's the law of centrifugal force. Everything is in flight from an imaginary center. Dragonflies, beetles, turtles, swallows, desert nomads, comets, asteroids. Asteroids are the worst because they're rocky and bulky.

The Kuiper Belt is teeming with asteroids, short-period comets, and icy bodies. Also dwarf planets and little moons. A hundred years ago an asteroid from the Kuiper Belt exploded over Siberia. It just flew off into space. It had no business crashing in Siberia but there it was, a large flying rock. The fireball wiped out two thousand square miles of taiga forest. There was a mighty boom. Eighty million trees went up in flame. The explosion rocked the earth, split the sky in two.

The jackhammer has stopped. The peonies are exhausted and there hasn't been rain in weeks. I'm wearing a black sweatshirt, blue jeans, and Converse sneakers. I look like a man who is quietly at work, but in my head asteroids are crashing into earth with the force of atom bombs.

As I write, a stink bug crawls over my notebook, across my jottings. Complicated grief can wreck a person's life, I've read. Drinking disorders, post-traumatic stress, increased risk of cancer, dementia, manic depression. The grief-struck sometimes drop out of life altogether. That doesn't sound good. It's not that I walk around like a zombie. No one has said to me, Jeff, you need to get your life back in order. The effects of grief, I find, are more subtle. The unconscious impulse to forget is keen. The brain wants to protect itself, what's left of it, even if that means wandering off topic or ignoring facts. I fight back. I try to remember everything about Claire with vivid directness. Her face, her presence, her blue eyes, her voice, the way she walked, how she sat at her desk, her laugh, her frown, her exacerbation. Claire keeps me alive—even now. Why can't a man keep himself alive?

An impression that won't go away, though, is that it's all wrong. My life is all wrong. How can anything ever be right again? How do you write a sentence when it's all wrong? It all seems wrong.

I've been to the emergency room with knife wounds twice, blacked out and suffered a concussion, crashed my bike into a tree, rear-ended a pickup truck at a stoplight, pulled my lower back yanking weeds. Life is suddenly perilous. Over six thousand deaths occur annually from falls at home. I can detect a menacing soundtrack to the left of my ear, as if I'm in someone else's dark, weird film. I take deep breaths. In through the nose, out through the mouth. Julian Barnes writes that the bereft cross over into an alien universe after the loss of a spouse, a world without any familiar logic. No kidding. I never once wondered what I might do if something really bad happened. Never once did I imagine that my wife would die unexpectedly. Me, yes. But then I wouldn't have to pick up the pieces. I am in the house that Claire and I built, in the life we made, naked in the bathtub. I'm shivering. I feel like a wet rug. If I pull the plug maybe the water will drain away.

Runaway me, by the way, left in a hurry. Just couldn't take it. I call him Space Boy, because he's airborne. The real world is elsewhere, he hinted. Maybe he preferred not being boiled to death in melancholy. He's a can-do sort of fellow, doesn't like moping around. He went looking for her. I admire that. Stress can take a tremendous toll on our bodies, he said before leaving. Downward spiral and all. You're on earth, he added, there's no cure for that. And just like that he left. He set off to find Claire and left me to pick up the pieces. He radios home from time to time, from outer space no less.

Doesn't space take a tremendous toll on *your* body? I radioed back. Unimaginably, he said. His messages can be strange. The Boomerang Nebula? What's that? I radio back. A very cold place, he says. Five thousand light-years away. Jesus! I say. It's a preplanetary nebula, he says. I look up the Boomerang Nebula on my laptop. It's colder than empty space, it says here, a glowing shell of ionized gas. It's actually a very interesting nebula, I'll give him that. That's where I'm going, he says. The Boomerang. I think she's there. For some reason, he can't say Claire's name.

Obviously the dead don't need or want our grief. They're busy with other things, have a whole new set of rules. It's the living—we poor naked wretches—teeming clueless over this planet. Death always seemed so imaginary. How utterly it rips apart our lives. It leaves nothing behind, maybe some memories, and those you had better keep safe or else. Most of us think neither of death nor nothingness. It's just not in our bones. But one day, as the knight says, you stand at the edge of life and face darkness. Who are you? I am death, Death says.

This is not your usual memoir but I doubt any book about loss is really typical. When death comes a-knocking, all trivial fond records are wiped clean away as if by the impact of a mile-wide asteroid. The crater inside your chest feels awfully deep. Dust blots out the sun. One starts from scratch, and then with only half a brain. Invariably, you lose a part of yourself. There are consequences to being torn asunder. How the mind works under these constraints is a thing to behold.

CHAPTER ONE
PLUTO (THE SEPARATOR)

~~

*Pluto is a dwarf planet in the Kuiper Belt, a ring
of bodies beyond Neptune. Pluto is very, very cold.*

—NASA

You lie motionless as the respirator lifts your chest up and down. You have been here for seventy-two hours and I haven't seen your eyes in three days, not since you collapsed. Blue eyes—I've fixed their color in my mind. Blue-gray. Already I've begun the work of remembering. You seem so restful you could be sleeping but you're not. The paradox is messing with my mind.

Before you died, this is what I dreamt. In the dream, I can't take my eyes off yours, your closed eyes. Like Superman, I want to see through your eyelids, beneath the subcutaneous tissue. I want to see your blue eyes once more. Just a thin fold of skin, your eyelids seem unnaturally opaque and won't let me in. The dream nurse follows her routine, replacing IV bags and resetting devices.

Other dream nurses stop by. Everything is procedural for them, especially dying. They observe the monitors, obsessed with your numbers. I'm watching, keeping an eye on your closed eyelids. Suddenly, they open. It's a dream but it seems so real. Your eyes open and they're not blue. What happened to your blue eyes? I think, alarmed. Your eyes are dark and their vitreous body is cloudy with black ink, as if these new eyes are still evolving. I'm shocked. Inky black eyes! The nurse says this is common. I say no it isn't. My wife has blue eyes. This isn't normal! My wife has turned into a black-eyed angel, I tell the dream nurse who thinks I'm nutty. But why doesn't Claire recognize me? At first you don't recognize me—Who are you? your eyes say—but then maybe you do, I think. I'll never know and I'll always remember those sublime, spooky eyes— eyes that hold all our pasts and futures.

But here you are in this awful moment, docked in room seven of bay one in intensive care. Monitors, wires, blinking LEDs keep a watch on you. An oxygen tube runs into your mouth, and beside it a smaller tube which brings in fluids. You can't pee so another line runs to the foot of the bed where a urine bag hangs. Methodically, a nurse comes by to empty that bag every fifteen minutes, reloading the IV pumps with drugs to stabilize your blood pressure and manage your carbon outtake. There are six rows of squiggly lines on the Philips monitor above your bed, all different colors. Heartbeat, carbon dioxide level, drainage of fluid from the brain, body temperature. I keep an eye on the screen. I want the yellow, green, blue, and pink numbers to mean something. There's so much invested in pumping air into your still-warm body it's impossible to think you won't open your eyes. But you aren't here.

I close my eyes. Out the kitchen window a chipmunk has leapt up into a pot of basil and is nibbling on my leaves, my aromatic leaves. You like my pesto, despite all the garlic. Are you putting *four* cloves of garlic in the pesto? you ask. I'm sure *two* will do. I'm preparing some right now. Flashbacks make me hungry. You're keeping an eye on me, suspicious, as I'm a garlic fiend. Good food is unthinkable without garlic, I say. In moderation, of course, you say. Here they are, four fat garlic cloves on the cutting board. I just stare at my darlings like a madman. A minimum of four, I say. I'm so stubborn. More if I could but I'm being regulated. You give me a wry look. I toss in a few extra pine nuts and a bit more Parmesan to take off the edge, a concession to my charming wife.

I haven't made pesto since your collapse. That's what I'm calling this catastrophe. Collapse. I don't know what else to call it. The *unnameable*. In the yard, meanwhile, big pots of basil are going to seed. This is pesto-making season. Instead, I'm reading your last book, a study of the post-Chaucerian poet John Lydgate. I want to tell you this before you go. It's really a terrific book. Medieval drama. Not poetry but popular theater. Teaching Chaucer the poet was fun, you told me, but he had been rendered elite by the profession. You're a coal miner's daughter and like digging in the remote spaces of the archive. You have a nose for that, overlooked things. In the case of medieval literature, that's popular drama, especially the nonliterary type—mummings, wall hangings, tableaux, ceremonies, seasonal games—the kind of performances and displays that were ephemeral in nature and rarely documented. To the modern eye, these are marginal creations undeserving of critical attention. Even if we wanted to recoup them, we couldn't, since they are, for the most part, unrecoverable.

You like to rescue things: dogs, furniture, houses, cars—even husbands. You rescued a baby squirrel once. What's that in your hand? I ask. A baby squirrel, you say. It's alive? I think so. Where did it come from? It fell from the tree out front. That's a long fall, I say. How did it survive? A cushion of pine needles at the base of the tree must have broken its fall. The squirrel's eyes are still closed. You sure it's alive? Yes, you say. We call it Waldo.

I'm thinking about Waldo as I read your Lydgate, how quickly things of this life come and go. That's not entirely true, though. It's funny how the world you describe, which vanished long ago, is so alive in this book. It's more alive than Waldo ever was in his brief tumble through pine cones and air. It's evident in the way you reconstruct seasonal rituals and fleeting events. A Corpus Christi pageant in Dungate Hill with skinners (dealers in fur) carrying wax torches, followed by singing clerks and priests. Behind them, with beaming smiles, the mayor and alderman, accompanied by winged minstrels. What a scene—what a racket! It's vividly recreated on the page, the processions, feasts, pageants, dances, mimes. The way you mix ethnography and literary history is pure art.

The nurses in the ICU have pretty suburban names, like Kelly, who returns to your bedside every twenty minutes. She's reloading the IV unit with muscle relaxant. You do seem deeply relaxed, but that is because you are comatose, your eyes closed, it seems, evermore. Kelly is brushing your eyelids with a clear moisturizing gel. She does this very delicately, as if tending to her own mother. There's a clear plastic housing in your mouth that allows the oxygen tube to slide left or right. Kelly moves the hose to the right, but this forces your mouth askew, as though punched in the face. The illusion of tranquility is broken. I don't say anything, but this troubles me. Kelly turns your body on its side, checking your back and bottom for bedsores. I remember Pedro Almodóvar's *Talk to Her*, a movie we saw together, when the male nurse Benigno turns the comatose Alicia on her side, massaging her body with rosemary alcohol. Benigno's care of Alicia is extremely devoted. He talks to her continually, even attends movies he thinks she would have liked and tells her what he saw. He says to Marco you have to pay attention to women, talk to them, be thoughtful. Caress them. Remember they exist. It is good to think of comatose patients as alive and even as aware, medical people say. They speak of an intimacy beyond words.

Medieval culture was more mutable than we think, and rediscovering that mutability is a kind of quest that runs through all of your work. I'm realizing that now as I read your book. The modern urge to categorize the uncategorical is a dynamic you oppose with gusto. How do we read a battle narrative stitched on a tapestry hanging in a drafty castle where the winds howl in January? An epic poem, a performance, a painting, a fancy carpet? And what about mumming, goofy music-and-dance scenarios set to verse? I don't imagine this was any kind of congenital skepticism on your part but a hard-earned suspicion. I like that: you are not one to jump to conclusions. Me, I leap on conclusions from a great height.

I can't help thinking that you are also on guard against the hubris of male intellectuals. Another hard-earned suspicion. Or to put it another way, you are trying to protect the otherness of the past from the arrogance of the modern. In your work, it seems like a moral and intellectual imperative. These fragile traces of early English culture, like a mumming from 1427 that barely exists in manuscript form in a library in Cambridge, a poetic pageant that, in performance, lasted all of two hours. Commissioned but performed only once. There is more than a hint of sadness in this. We are both melancholy. We never forgot Waldo.

I remember asking you once: what's mumming all about? Sounds like fun. Can I do it? Sure. It's not hard, you say. It's a lot of guys in masks prancing around and making noise. They drink a lot too. Very frat-boyish. How is that interesting? I ask. How is anything interesting? you reply. The reason for this discussion, you may remember, is a proposition. You want me to come to Philadelphia with you and film the Mummers Parade on New Year's Day. It sounds cold, I say, as in icy cold. Your puffy jacket, you say, will come in handy. Does it take all day? Probably. I look up Philadelphia's weather. High of twenty degrees, low of six degrees. Don't know if my gear can take it, I complain. The camera might freeze. Can't you cold-proof your gadgets with a muffler or something, like a dog? That makes me laugh, but I'm dragging my fanny. I really don't like bitterly cold weather. It will give you a chance, you say, to check out the Dock Street Brewery downtown. Hmm, I say.

The nurses hear me whispering in your ears. The late-night shift is puzzled at first but then understands I'm talking to you and not myself. I lift your right leg up and massage your calf, kneading your muscle like bread dough. And then I rub each toe, squeezing your warm flesh over and over. The pathos of the body. Here we are, the living and the dying. Between sleep and death you lie perfectly still. From the continued reports of doctors, those dark messengers, little or no blood flows to your brain. There is no sentience, there is no awareness in you. A tiny glow radiates from under your fingers, though. In your warm hand you are clutching a glowing red light, a secret heat. The smoldering embers of a life lived well, I think to myself, because my mind is so full of sentimentality, as if to make up for your unconsciousness, thoughts you yourself would never think. But the glow, just the glimmer of a medical device, is suggestive. It can't be otherwise. Through the vessels on the back of your hand blood runs, a normal flow of life, feeding the tendons in your fingers which cling to the red light. You can't see this, but your body is carefully wrapped in a gauze-like covering. Under your right leg a white towel is folded, elevating your calve to improve circulation. Other parts of your body are propped up on pillows. The nurses are under orders to make sure your blood circulates on schedule to each organ. They want to harvest as much of you as possible.

Your Lydgate study won a prize, as did your previous book, and I can see why. The writing is deft and the thinking so complex that I can't resist your prose, even though my head hurts. There's not a clunky moment here. The elegance of your sentences is matched by the cogency of your mind. Such a mind. There are these remarkable passages of painstaking observation, as in Chapter 1, where you discuss the scribe John Shirley and his efforts to copy Lydgate's dramatic entertainments, followed by a close reading of Shirley's manuscript, but not in the traditional way. There is no hunting for literary meaning. Instead, you track Shirley's peripheral jot-tings, his performance-oriented notes, in order to see how Lydgate's ephemeral pieces have been remediated in manuscript form. You are curious about the way Ly-dgate's "dramatic" output was absorbed by his contempo-raries. You care less for authors and texts than for readers and audiences. To a nonmedievalist's eye, the analysis is so rigorous and informed, the logic so precise, as to seem surreal. And all the footnotes. How do you medievalists do this sort of thing? Unlike most academics, you people actually read one another's books and go out of your way to keep them in circulation. It's really astonishing how collaborative your field is. I always feel like Ahab when writing, a crazy lonely bastard.

I remember slipping into your study one afternoon while you sat at your laptop writing the Lydgate book. I tried to look over your shoulder—I was curious—but you waved me away. You were guarding your book against my sarcasm. Not before I stole a peek. Porosity of representa-tional borders, I say out loud in a snarky tone. You shoot me an anguished look. That's some noun phrase, I go on. *Porosity.* What's wrong with *porous*? I ask. Boy, that kind of flak would really piss you off. Can't blame you. It was a cheap shot. It's not difficult to deflate academic writing. It's much harder knowing how the inflationary style ac-tually works in this business—because it does work. You evicted me from your study, banned me for two whole weeks. Milo gave me his *I told you so* look.

Massive blood clot, they originally thought, a possi-ble effect of transatlantic flight, as we had just returned from Dublin. But the medical people were clueless. By the time they scanned your brain and found blood it was far too late. They sent your lifeless body to the neurological unit at the university hospital. That's where I found you later in the day. I was taken to you outside the scanning room, just lying there on a gurney. A Middle Eastern neurologist approached me grimly. They had run a complete scan on your brain. He described the results in technical detail, how the bleeding surrounded and inflamed your brain, how the fluids compounded the effect. The inflammation was exerting extraordinary pressure on the brain, choking off blood and oxygen supplies to vital regions. He showed me the CAT scans of your traumatized brain, pointing out the dark-gray areas he identified as evidence of bleeding and other areas that seemed to be dying out. The dark spots were sinister. They multiplied. They were in my eyes and then my brain. I felt shaky, speechless, dopey.

The gist of his awful story was that your mind was brain-dead. Even if we were able to bring her back, he said, which is highly unlikely, she would never be the same. Serious brain injury. Every story the medical people told me about you was darker and more disheartening. Not one of these people held out a thread of hope. And there you were, on your gurney with an oxygen mask and tubes running into your mouth. You were alive but not in any way that was meaningful to the people who loved you.

The intensive care doctor said it was best to gather in one of the meeting rooms. The nurse-slash-social-worker was there and the attending RN. I was unsteady, but being surrounded by medical people only made me feel worse. It seemed like a conspiracy. They wanted me to surrender. The IC guy rehearsed the technical details of your aneurism, only now he called it an *unrecoverable brain injury*, repeating the scenario that had silenced your mind. By now, I was familiar with the story line. The IC guy provided the distressing details in a grim and attenuated voice. I didn't like that voice. He seemed to be hiding something, eager to get to the next step: declare you brain dead and prepare your body for diagnosis. As you signed on for organ donation, your body parts would have to be analyzed for reliability.

According to the EEG monitor, however, you seemed to be producing slight residual brain activity. The IC doctor was annoyed by this, since it meant the neurologist possibly would not certify your brain death, at least not until the squiggly lines on the EEG could be dismissed. An inconvenient complication. The IC guy took pains to assure me that what looked like activity was nothing more than noise, that he was *confident*—yes, he used that word—your brain had conked out, that you were *finis*. He admitted that it was up to me to decide whether or not to honor your commitment to organ donation. An instinctive dislike grew between us, and I was tempted not to comply. This fellow seemed too eager to lay his institutional hands on your body. His pale shifty blue eyes, his boyish good looks, preppy getup, his University of Wisconsin degree. His ward had already done enough, it seemed to me, with the bundles of wires and tubes, all to no effect, beyond keeping your organs fresh and robust for someone else. He seemed too young and untried to be weighing in on life and death. Beyond repeating the obvious details of your case, he seemed a bit helpless, maybe clueless.

Your face is so still today. The EEG nurse is here. Before attaching two dozen scalp nodes to your head, she draws an X to mark the spot and numbers the electrode placement: F8, T4, A2, O1, C3, and so on. F for frontal, T for temporal, O for occipital. Even numbers refer to the right hemisphere and so on. I'm telling you this because you might be interested to know that your head is now crowded with electrodes, which are taped to your scalp rather perversely, if you ask me. Over twenty of them. So bizarre. It's startling to see how small your waveforms are on the EEG monitor. F3, for instance, is almost flatlined. So is F4. T4 and T6, though, reveal more active squiggles. Eighty-six billion neurons sparking such a weak signal in a mind that once produced so many thoughts. These things should be impossible. But hold my tongue or break this heart.

I don't know if I ever shared this story with you (I'll tell you now before you leave), but in the middle of my dissertation I tried to switch to fancier prose style, as Nabokov would say, stealing locutions from Lacan and Derrida, those snazzy Frenchmen. I couldn't pull it off, alas, but I really wanted to sound more showy. My reward was a whopper of a nightmare. The next night I dreamt I was wandering through the mythical labyrinth built by Daedalus of Crete, the master inventor, and came face-to-face with a monster—the Minotaur. I'm not kidding. The Minotaur was really spooky, ghastly, greasy, and ruthless. He stood before me like a giant and held a huge ax in his hand, and then he split me in two, right down the middle. I woke up stunned. Well, so much for a fancy prose style.

My borders, if truth be told, are very porous. The world pours through my dura mater like water. Every way I turn the universe is enticing me. It seduces me. My middle name is Porosity. For instance. I'm at my laptop writing about my grandfather, a cagey Sicilian immi-grant. The sentence goes, *Raven-minded Joe knew in his dark heart he would never return*, but does not end because I'm struck mid-sentence by the expression *raven-minded*. What on earth is that? I know it came from my brain but that doesn't mean anything. Meanwhile, you, Claire, are downstairs making dinner. Winter vegetables, tofu, and bok choy. Yum.

I know a little but not much about ravens, so online I go, and that's when the trouble starts. First of all, I want to tell the difference between a raven and a crow; next I'm learning about ravens in Native American folklore. That's when you give me the first dinner call. DINNER! My eyes are glued to the screen. I read that the raven is symboli-cally associated with trickster figures in Native stories—the examples are fascinating. If I were smart, I'd call it a good day's work and head downstairs for dinner with my honey. Joe is a kind of trickster guy—how true—move on. That's when you give me the second dinner call. DIN-NER!!! Okay, I yell, I'll be right down.

I'm lying. I won't be right down. I've just stumbled on an article about crows and necrophilia and I can't stop reading. It's like porn. That's when you give me the third and last dinner call. This one is an angry scream. I leap out of my chair and run downstairs. Boy, am I in trou-ble. Your look is daggers. "I am poured out like water, and all my bones are out of joint." That's what I should have said. (When in trouble, quote scripture.) Instead, I tell you about the perverted crows. You're silent. That's how angry you are. The birds don't get a rise out of you, not even an eye roll. The winter vegetables are cold, and so is your shoulder.

It's no big deal, of course, but it kind of stinks that I had fun playing the adolescent one in the family because that meant you had to perform the role of serious adult. I know that upset you. At times, it was a point of tension. Who wants to be an adult? You had better things to do. I'm confessing. It's my sadness talking, reaching out to you in ways that were impossible when we were together. It's so sad to see people alone in the hospital.

Even now my mind is butterflying across the page. I really think if you were here, if you weren't leaving me, I'd toe the line much better. I would even make a bargain with the so-called devil never again to digress—never ever again.

Where was I? Lydgate.

I love the stuff about Lydgate's mummings in Chapter 2, where you describe his commissioned pageant for the powerful Mercers' guild in London honoring the new mayor, who was himself a Mercer. I had to look up Mercer (merchants). The ceremony begins with a long introduction in elaborate verse, you explain, that ushers into the hall three mock ships carrying mummers disguised as merchants from the Far East. This is followed by dancing, music, costumed actors casting nets and so forth, and finally gift-giving to gratify the new mayor. It's like a scout jamboree.

Another nurse has just arrived to reload the automatic IVs. I don't know her name but she is friendly and goes about her business quietly. I watch her closely as she applies the gel to your eyelids and repositions the ventilator tube, assesses hydration. She drains the urine bag and shifts your body, making sure your head is elevated thirty degrees. Touch and talk is also recommended. The nurses call you by your name—"Claire"—when disturbing your trachea, explaining the procedure. "I'm going to put pressure on the ventilator tube, which should cause discomfort." They do this to check for a reaction. If you were to cough, well then, you'd be back among the living. I'm learning the routine by heart. Should the IC unit be abandoned in a global panic, I could load the IV bags myself, apply the ointment, reposition your limbs, check for back sores, but I wouldn't disturb your trachea. I know you're not here. It's just your body, your sad body, which you have deserted. If not for me, you would be a stray.

This morning I found a black and yellow quilt that had been stitched together by volunteers affiliated with the IC unit. *May you be cradled in hope, kept in joy, graced with peace, and wrapped in love,* read the card attached to the quilt. The quilt is lovely, with floral patterns, polka dots, and chevrons, a relief from the banality of beige. I thank the volunteers of intensive care for the two of us. Better this your shroud than gauze and oatmeal.

No one would call Lydgate's mumming great literature, but its literary qualities are hardly relevant. As a historical document, this particular pageant is a treasure chest, especially in relation to xenophobia, arguably manifest throughout the country. London, like any other big city or port, had a large immigrant population. Aliens and foreigners made up a significant community of others. Dressing up as gift-bearing merchants from the Far East was no doubt a significant gesture. This is how you explain the whole picture:

Anti-foreigner sentiments, which animated the polemics of the late 1420s, are submerged in these performances under a glowing patina of openness, amiability, and generosity—virtues in short supply on the streets of London outside the Mercers' and Goldsmiths' halls. But if these foreign merchants are welcomed into London's guilds, they are at the same time placed in a clearly subordinate position of submission, as gift bearers come to pay tribute to the mayor, the crowning symbol of London's civic might. What underscores civic power is the mummings' emphasis on the literary; Lydgate's verses not only present an example of the poetic arts but also serve to instruct Londoners in a literary aesthetics grounded in a specific use of written English. In so doing, the mumming creates a vision of cosmopolitan vernacularity in which foreign culture is made native.

I'm not going to say anything about *vernacularity*, even though it's a doozy, because the writing is smart and elegant and the thinking so graceful, subtle, and informed. The way you wrap your mind around the larger picture—with such precision—seems so effortless it turns me on. It is frankly kind of sexy, your clarity (forgive me). It's impossible not to be taken in by the integrity of your mind. There is an energy that binds the content of each sentence together, as though the strength of your style were electromagnetic. You were like that in life too, staying on topic, immune to distraction like no other, binding things together. Constantly binding things together. Life seemed vivid and sharp by your side, always in focus. Now it's just delirious. I feel like a child lost in a vast city seething with strangers. There's a moral force in your clarity, in your precision. A force that speaks of a will to live. Why was that not enough?

I return home for the night feeling utterly lost. I lie down with your book. It's not Lydgate that draws me to this work but your mindful way of writing. You did your best to confer on me, Mr. Digressio, some of your magic. Every once in a while I will surprise myself with a flash of clarity, thanks to you. I hope I'm not embarrassing you, by the way. I know how self-conscious you are. This book was not a career move. You were already an accomplished medievalist with a national reputation. You could have easily switched gears and written a book about noise and hearing, as you planned. I was all for that. It's time for a fun book, I said. No more footnotes. Write a memoir about your ears—your deafness is marketable. Disability studies are big. You are a creative person.

You were tempted, maybe a little, but you wanted to see your commitments through. You had published an edition of Lydgate's mummings a few years ago, and so it made sense to complete the project by reclaiming the guy, chiefly regarded as a major fifteenth-century poet, for early modern drama. That would mean rethinking medieval drama history and challenging the priority of poetry in canon building, but that made the project even more essential. Such big ambitions.

Confession: last time I wrote an academic book I put in extra footnotes just to impress you. Tons of footnotes. I went nuts. One reviewer called the book *erudite*. That got a good laugh out of me.

Your last research visit was to the British Library in early July 2016, just weeks before you died. A flare-up of archive fever. It's what you do best, parsing the delicate

script of a scribe's six-hundred-year-old handiwork. It
was a three-day stay in London while I taught in Dublin.
One more look at John Rous's illustrated *The History of
the Life and Acts of Richard Beauchamp, Earl of Warwick.*
This would be the subject of your next book, a rough draft
of which awaits its next turn on my thumb drive. This late
medieval book is an illustrated biography (presented as
a drama) of Richard Beauchamp, earl of Warwick from
1382–1439. It's made up of fifty-three line drawings with
brief comments on each illustration. Beauchamp was a
contemporary of Henry V and lived through the Hundred
Years' War, but somehow managed to keep his head. The
twenty-eight-page manuscript depicts the earl as a model
of pious and chivalrous behavior, as you would say. What
seized your attention was the mingling of media and the
blurring of genres: narrative, illustration, performance.
As such, this text sat squarely within your vision of the
medieval as a culture of mutable forms.

I'm looking now at your notes from that archival visit,
clinging to all that's left of your mind. You spent hours in-
specting every line and curve in the *Beauchamp Pageant*,
as it's called. You note:

> *On F. IV pages have been cropped: see chopping of
> ascender of H in "Here" and elsewhere in the MS.
> Another note: light coloring in brown of alternating
> tiles on flooring in f. 2. Pencil framing of page—
> border, and separate space for picture and caption—
> can be seen (except near top where upper border
> has been cropped). Note that the artist has allowed
> a piece of architecture to protrude into the space
> lined-out for words. F. 10: again, drawing intrudes*

on text, so much so that only 2 lines can be written freely across top of page, with others truncated into left 2/3rds. f. llv: see horses faces.

My favorite note—*see horses faces.* In all, nearly two dozen carefully written pages of scrutiny (in pencil—no pens allowed in special collections) comprising well over one hundred carefully observed details.

All that attentiveness. It makes me wonder.

How did you begin this day of research? At Gail's Artisan Bakery in Bloomsbury where, at eight thirty in the morning, you ordered a small cappuccino and pain au raisin. £5.30. Among your notes is a receipt. Your server was Lucyna Sobanska from Poland. If I remember right, this was just two weeks after the UK's surprising Brexit vote. I'm guessing you chatted with your server about that. Lucyna, of course, has a Facebook page where she lists Gail's Artisan Bakery as her place of employment. She's now manager. Your British Library password is 402899. I offer you these details as a reminder that you, Claire, are now the subject of a book—a wife observed.

Speaking of which, remember watching the TV show *Fringe* together? *The X-Files* for the twenty-first century, you called it. Our favorite character was dubbed "the Observer." This was a strikingly bald guy in a black suit and fedora with no eyebrows. He was a time traveler from a vague future keeping an eye on things. Always taking notes. You liked that part best. He was stoic, attentive, thorough, and took terrific notes. You said it's a shame the Observer is gendered male because the truth is women are more observant than men. I didn't argue. In our own lives this was obviously true. I said you're right. In fact, I went on, you remind me a little bit of this guy, except that you're not bald and your eyebrows are intact. This made you laugh. You have a notebook just like the Observer's, a little black Moleskine journal. Whenever you visited the British or Trinity libraries, you returned with oodles of notes. It's where your books started. Had you stayed around a little longer, I would have bought you a fedora. In fact, I did.

Your brain has sabotaged itself and here is your body, warm and tender to the touch. A body without a mind. The nurse inserts needles in your wrists and near your ankles. None of these devices keeps me from rubbing your hands and feet. I stroke each finger. How delicate and fine your hands are, warm and limber. I stand up and place your hand between mine like an expert and trace the curves in your fingernail and the creases in your joints, I track the lines in your palms. Hardly a wrinkle anywhere. Such smooth hands, such exquisite fingers. If this hand could talk it would say beautiful things, and I would listen all day to the words of your fingers. Your calves had not been tampered with so I massage these too, imagining that your unresponsiveness is a sign you have fallen into a deep and pleasurable trance only my hands can produce.

Out for a morning walk. Typically warm in late July but much cooler today, the wind blowing through the trees. Here and there, yellow leaves are swirling down. Soon the changes will be upon us. You would be at my side now, but you're not present so I will tell you what I see and hear. I stop to listen. The wind whooshes through the trees. A cicada, resting in the shade of butterfly weed, wings its way to the white pine across the street. Just be-

yond, an orange tabby saunters along the curb and scurries after noticing me. On the other side, a dark-brown
and white collie observes all of this quietly from his front
porch. Three glossy black ravens swoop low from perches
in the tall maples. Everywhere I glance black-eyed Susans
look back. On the corner, a mass of zinnias sway to and
fro like seagrass. The universe is vibrating with life, I say
to you. I know that you aren't present, but I feel you close
by, just as alive as the cicada and the tabby and the birds.
But your body is stock-still right now as I rub your pretty
fingers. The forced air heaves your chest up and down, as
though you were only sleeping.

I'm walking Toby, the neighbor's dog, and bump into
folks who live nearby. The kindness of others. A strange
sight, they say, me walking alone down Fairchild Street.
Always together, walking side by side, chatting and smiling—you and your wife—they say. We seemed inseparable
to others. Funny how we never said that out loud but we
both knew. We were indivisible until we died, we thought,
and death was far down the road. Toby is happy out and
about. But wait, better circle back. I left the weedwacker
battery in the charger downstairs. Might overheat. Not
taking any chances. I circle back around the block, confusing Toby, and return home. I pull the plug on the charger. Not overheating, it turns out, but I'm not taking any
chances. Don't feel lucky. Have to keep an eye on me,
that's what I'm thinking. Too inattentive at times. What
you had to put up with, surrounded by inattentive people
up and down the ladder, for whom you covered. You had
to offset the world's inattention. Toby poops. More hugs
from kind people. Death is very humanizing, even for me.
Pass by Bill the rat terrier. I hate to break the news to you

but there's a large Trump sign in the window. Would not have guessed.

I'm kissing you on your forehead, the only area free of wires, tubes, or nodes, just beneath your bald spot. I didn't want to tell you this but the neurosurgeons shaved a section of your blond hair. Like me, you are partly bald. They drilled a hole into your skull to insert a drainage tube. A measure of last resort, the procedure was meant to relieve the fluid buildup in a portion of your besieged brain. Too much cerebrospinal fluid from the trauma of bleeding. From the moment you passed out, the pressure on your brain worsened. A ventriculoperitoneal shunt is the absurd name of the thing.

On my walk this morning I see a wolf. He is sitting on a large area howling at the sky. The roof of his mouth is red. Very lifelike. Nearby are two lovebirds and a hawk, and across the driveway a family of fox and dear. Kitschy yard art. The older fox is howling at the sky too. So many animals fixed in place, like a fairy tale, stopped dead in their tracks by some wand-waving crone. Life-size, the wolf seems deep into his howl. I find myself in perfect empathy with him. I understand the meaning of his posture, how he focuses his whole being on this howl. The sound of a wolf can carry as far as six miles in the forest and even farther in open space. The small fox is howling too, encouraged by the wolf. With heads bent back, the animals point their snouts toward the sky, broadcasting their howls to the next town.

I was told a 911 call was dialed from my office yesterday at school. Surprised, I called the department. Who dialed 911? I asked Joelle. The official reported the call came from your office, she said. Two policemen here to investigate. I told them you weren't on campus, she said. No, I wasn't there. I was by your bedside. Spooky. The reports of phones dialing 911 on their own are rare but they do happen. "Dying" phones have been known in the past to call 911 by themselves. It's a headache, said one phone official I talked to. We get thirty or more calls a month from phantom dialers. Cordless phones have this tendency, he said, when their batteries are low. They dial spurious numbers on their own. It's right out of the movies. My office phone is corded, I told the phone guy. Well, then, I don't know, he said. Never heard of that before. While I'm on the topic, someone turned over the birdbath in the backyard. I hardly think a rabbit or a squirrel did that. You were the only one I knew who routinely rolled the concrete birdbath over to prevent mosquitoes hatching in standing water. Did you do that?

But I did dial 911 for real just the other morning. You were lying on your back, gasping for air. No light in your eyes. No sign of life but that horrible nonhuman growling, gasping for air. No one can prepare for such a nightmare. I couldn't find you behind those pale-blue eyes, now suddenly lifeless. Only your body clinging desperately to the singularity of life, the last-resort jerks of a body left behind. Were you gone already? I screamed at the 911 operator. I couldn't form any sentences, only pieces of thought. Not breathing! My wife, not conscious. Send someone. Hurry. Please. Not breathing! Gasping terribly! And then I tried to breathe into your mouth but this only terrified me more because I didn't know what I was doing. The 911 operator tried to give me CPR instructions over the phone but I only screamed at her to send an ambulance. Please, now! Not breathing! Send someone! I screamed. I was hysterical. To see the most aware being in my little world so inert, so irreversibly knocked out. I had you in my arms but knew you weren't there. The fireman and the ambulance came quickly, alarming neighbors. Flashing lights and shrill sirens on a peaceful, pastoral late-summer morning. We were to leave soon for Cincinnati, once I had spoken with the plumber, who arrived exactly when you collapsed, lying on your study floor with your arms spread out in the middle of a yoga exercise. There was no thud. Your brain just exploded.

The cicadas have stopped singing. Most are dead by now, their six-week cycle having ended. The Iowa cicada is known as the scissor-grinder. A lot of rubbing of membranes. I miss their singing. Its passing is the first sign of autumn, the most melancholy of seasons. Summer is when we play at being free of time and all its dire implications. Glimmering sunshine, fireflies, the smell of mown grass, and flowering hydrangeas. Life goes on—until it doesn't. Then nothing makes sense. Very hot and dry today. The garden looks parched. It feels strange tending the yard without you. I keep waiting for you, behatted and begloved. That's not going to happen, but this won't sink in for some time. At any rate, I watched the sparrows prancing under the rain of the sprinkler, and also noticed the sudden appearance of surprise lilies. So erect and pink. Large, naked, two-foot-tall stems burst up with several funnel-shaped flowers. They are sometimes called *resurrection lily*. I know they are a favorite of yours. That they appear suddenly in the dog days of summer with a splash of paint seems a thing of perfect whimsy. Everywhere reminders of life and death. Ostrich fern, I've never heard of that. I read that surprise lilies go well with ostrich ferns.

A new locator has just arrived in a white Ford pickup. All the watermen drive white pickup trucks and he has just marked up the front lawn with exotic symbols and colorful flags. A diamond between two parallel lines (there are several of these) indicates buried phone lines. Some are more elaborate like miniature crop circles. One looks like the astrological sign for Pluto, a little person with its hands up in the air. All refer to what is below the surface, to underground cable and wire lines. They remind me of markings on the shaved parts of your head where two dozen nodes are placed to monitor your brain waves, to search for signs of life inside your failing brain.

The diggers are coming in the morning to excavate, looking for the leak in our waterline. Somewhere it's leaking. Want to mow the grass before they make a mess. Walked up to Russ's for gas. Hot and humid. These basic home-care routines are very comforting. Focus on something that does not threaten my grip on life. A nonexistential outing. The mower came a little too close to a bunny warren in the front lawn. One of the bunnies panicked and fled into the street. Ran after the little fellow, circled behind it, scooped it up in my hand. It let out a sharp, terrified squeak. I chucked the bunny back into its hole firmly enough it decided not to come out again. Its mother turned the corner of the house to take a look. Noise of the mower must seem deafening. Began Weedwacking (autocorrect wanted to change this word to *medevacking*) but ran out of spool. Good, I thought to myself. One more little thing to concentrate on. Was glad to prolong the chore. Calming to sweep the sidewalk and porch. I did this very slowly, like a handicapped person hired out of charity. It's the big events that show you how easy it is to lose your mind, like an abrupt death. I'm finding it's little things, like replacing the string spool on a weedwacker, that are keeping my wits together.

It's a perfect day for digging a hole, Doug says. He's here with his brother Kenny, a deputy sheriff. Doug is in his early fifties, lean, semibald, with a cheerful mustache, blue eyes, cracker-barrel style. Doug exudes competence. Kenny is younger, squatter. Both have clean, honest faces. The Midwest male at his best. Kenny is operating a small backhoe with rubber track pads, digging two precise holes, one at the stop box by the curb and the other above the sidewalk. Doug turns off the stop box. The good news is that the sound of running water stops, which means the leak is on our side of the curb. Doug will "snake" out the entire line of old steel pipe with chain and backhoe, and then slide in the new blue plastic water pipe. Doug's teenage daughter drops by on her moped to lend a hand. I have to clear out the corner of the basement where the water valve turns off and lay down old rugs and tarps. The basement now belongs to Doug and Kenny.

This is what they told me about your brain aneurysm, what happened to you Wednesday morning at nine a.m. While you were lying on your back, a balloon-like bulge formed in the wall of your brain artery. Who knows how long that bulge was there, but on Wednesday morning, just as you raised your toes off the ground, the bulge tore open and bled profusely, damaging nearby cells. A brain aneurysm can occur in any artery wall that is weak or has a defect. In most cases, a brain aneurysm has no symptoms until it tears. Blood from a torn aneurysm can block cerebrospinal fluid circulation, leading to fluid buildup and increased pressure on the brain. I am told it is often associated with hardening of the arteries, high blood pressure, heredity, or a head injury. Did you suffer from any of these? Not that I know of. Did you suffer from any brief blackouts while we were in Dublin? Any neck stiffness, confusion or sluggishness, nausea or vomiting?

About thirty thousand people in the US suffer a brain aneurysm rupture every year. One in fifty people have an unruptured brain aneurysm. That's one every eighteen minutes. They are fatal in 40 percent of cases. Of those who survive, about 66 percent suffer a permanent neurological deficit. Four out of seven people who recover from a ruptured brain aneurysm will have disabilities. The median age of an aneurysmal hemorrhagic stroke is fifty years old. There are typically no warning signs. An estimated 50 to 80 percent of all aneurysms do not rupture during the course of a person's lifetime. You, my dear wife, were one of the unlucky few. One last gruesome factoid, and then I'll rub your toes. There are almost 500,000 deaths worldwide each year caused by brain aneurysms and half the victims are younger than fifty.

If only I could pile up numbers until numb. It doesn't work that way.

Doug and Kenny have finished repairing the watermain leak without tearing up the sidewalk or the burning bush. Ironically, the two holes they've scooped out resemble recently dug graves. One for you and one for me. It's plenty warm but the holes look mighty cold.

You and I by the lake. What a beguiling idea. It's dark and chilly out. That summer in the Adirondacks, just before we married, we took the canoe out late at night, drifting across the smooth lake. You, me, and the cat, Ulysses. We listened for birds and watched the dark sky. The yodel-like cry of loons and shooting stars, every night. The cat had a thing for canoes, wouldn't let us embark without him. You marveled at the vastness of space. Where is everyone? you said. Must be elsewhere, I replied. Can you imagine hurtling through that emptiness in a rocket? I asked. So unimaginably alone out there, you said. Makes me dizzy.

Pluto is now called a *dwarf* planet after being shunned by astronomers. Pluto, they said, didn't dominate its neighborhood. It was too small. Besides, its orbit is messy. Here one moment, there the next. When Pluto was originally discovered eighty-some years ago, it was thought much bigger, several times larger than earth. As a matter of fact, Pluto is smaller than the moon. Not that any of this matters—but I do feel a twinge of sadness for Venetia Burney, the English girl who at the age of eleven named the newly discovered planet "Pluto" in 1930 after the Roman god of the underworld. She was having breakfast in Oxford one morning when her grandfather described the new discovery. "I think Pluto would be a good name for it," she said, because Pluto dwelled in a place where sunshine couldn't reach.

She finished her muffin and thought no more of it. In 2006, the year astronomy demoted Pluto, Venetia's husband died—a double whammy. I mention this because Venetia's dad, like you, was a classicist. I have a strange affinity for classicists. Don't know why—just do. Even before we met. The American astronomers in Flagstaff, the site of the discovery, had no idea what to call the new planet—Planet X, perhaps—so they were glad for advice. In Hindi, Pluto is know as Yama, the god of death.

Gustave Holst composed *The Planets* between 1914

and 1916, several years before the discovery of Pluto, and so that planet was missing from the original work. Earth was missing too, since Holst was primarily attracted to the astrological aspects of the planets. This might explain the curious naming scheme for the seven movements: Mars, the bringer of war; Venus, the bringer of peace; Mercury, the winged messenger; Jupiter, the bringer of jollity; Saturn, the bringer of old age; Uranus, the magician; and Neptune, the mystic.

What an odd way to think of the solar system. Rather anachronistic for a modernist. Holst, we are told, was an avid reader of Alan Leo, a theosophist and modern astrologer. The chapter scheme of his 1912 *The Art of Synthesis* (Mercury, the thinker; Venus, the unifier; Mars, the energizer; and so on) obviously spoke to Holst, who imagined his suite as a spiritual journey, the order of the planets symbolizing life from youth to old age. He wasn't really interested in the actual dynamics of the solar system, like gamma ray bursts and galactic drift.

In 2000, British composer Colin Matthews was commissioned to rectify the omission of planet nine from Holst's work by adding another movement to the original. He called the new suite "Pluto, the Renewer," and— voilà—Holst was astronomically correct. Or so everyone thought. Just days later, however, Pluto was deplanetized and Holst's work was in error again.

The *Renewer*?

After 45,000 years of dying, we still don't know what death is, what it points to. We only know its signifiers, the stink of corpses, the stillness of flesh, closed eyes. Your death will disturb every part of me. I want to throw things at it. We throw symbols at death. No sooner is the

loved one gone than we send frantic messages. We over-
whelm the dead with messages. The deeper the pain, the
greater the frenzy. I will heave planets at your death, big
ones like Jupiter and Saturn, giant symbols. Who cares
what they mean—as long as they're big. That's lame but
it's all I can do.

A strange thing occurred when you lost conscious-
ness, when you let out that horrible gasping sound. That
inhuman sound coming from you, nothing I'd ever heard
before. I went blank and a strange darkness flickered between my eyes—and stars, faraway stars, I think. Just a
fraction of a second but I saw distant stars and dark space.
When I opened my eyes I knew a part of me was gone. It
was like I'd run away from myself. Where did I go?

Dreamt of you last night. You're in a new apartment
with up-to-date furnishings, the minimalist modern style
you've always liked. Nice sofa, coffee table, double bed.
Lively colors. No walls, though. Unbounded space. You
show me around, but you don't know quite how things
work here. You stop to look over a slim manual. I want to
help but you say not necessary. You're still in your white-
striped exercise outfit with a dark top, the one you wore
on that terrible morning. Neither of us knows what's really
going on, why we are both here. Seems perfectly ordinary, though, as if you're away on fellowship somewhere,
maybe North Carolina, and I've come for a visit. I look at
the manual. I don't really understand it. And then you say,
I am here a whisper away. I look up, surprised. We were
inseparable, you continue. I guess such happiness comes
at a price.

The dream stays with me through the next day. I want
to hear your voice again but it's just me alone. I feel like a

Viking, put out to sea with only his sorrow, who must sail past the dead to some kind of beach landing. If this were a film you'd hear only the sound of creaking wood and the distant cries of storm petrels, and the groan of hands on rope. You are full of tubes and wires and your brain is slowly, quietly dying. I am terrified. I begin babbling, as we often did on walks, telling you how pretty your fingers are and that the plumber has not dug up the burning bush, as you feared. Last night, a ticket lady at the movie theater offered me a senior citizen discount. Worried now I will fall into sudden old age. I feel untethered. I could float into orbit. What keeps me grounded if not you?

CHAPTER TWO
CHARON (THE BORDERMAN)

*Charon, foul and terrible, his beard grown wild
and hoar, his staring eyes all flame, his sordid
cloak hung from a shoulder knot. Alone he poles
his craft and trims the sails and in his rusty hull
ferries the dead.*

—Virgil

*I*t was the surly Romans who named the first five
planets (those visible to the naked eye) after their
gods. Modern astronomy continued doing so long
after. And so in June of 1978, an American discovered Pluto's first moon and named it Charon. Charon is the ferryman who conveys the dead across the River Styx on their
way to the underworld. This bleak journey actually costs
money, and so the ancients buried their dead with a coin
in the deceased's mouth to pay Charon his fee (Charon's
obol). Nothing's free.

On the day Charon was discovered, June 22, you were
touring Corinth in Greece, snapping a photo of the hilltop acropolis. Just a kid, twenty-four years old, but one

who loved to fly across the sea. An astute classicist, you traveled to Europe and Greece nearly every summer. I'm peeking at your photo album from that trip. You began in Munich, then on to Venice, Florence, and finally Greece. Your photos are organized meticulously, each one labeled with a typed caption on green paper. Here's a photo of the ferry that took you, Toni, and David Price across the Corinth Canal, says the caption. Another one of sheep by the road in Mycenae. How come I never saw this photo album until now?

I myself am in the middle of the book *Triste Tropiques* on this same day in June. Here in the rainforest of the Northwest, I'm a long way from home, surrounded by tall, blue-eyed blondes. *Tristes Tropiques* provides some relief from the Nordics, but I keep nodding off. On every other page, Claude Lévi-Strauss crawls into his hammock and wraps himself in mosquito nets. He's somewhere in sultry Brazil. The air is so languid. I feel drowsy. It's only the piranhas, dangerous to the unwary bather, that keep me turning the page. This is what I do in Oregon, get lost in books. But you're in Corinth, you lucky ducky, where the sky is pellucid, the air dry. Little do we know what awaits us. Me you, you me. And so much more.

I'm getting used to the intensive care ward. I know exactly where to park and how to find my way through the medical maze. I'm right here beside you now. I trust you hear me, my never-ending voice. As I watch the respirator raise and lower your chest, I wonder what you're thinking, wherever you are. Are you grieving too? The lead doctor drops by and rehearses his Grim Reaper spiel. Your wife lacks brain stem reflexes, is suffering from severe intracranial bleeding, and has no respiratory drive, he says without intonation. But you look fine, I think. You are warm to my touch, breathe regularly, have a good pulse. I can't reconcile these two things in my mind, and mining your body parts—they are waiting for you more impatiently now—sounds so gothic to me. Organ donation is lifesaving, I am reminded, so I should be less morbid. The folks here think I'm a brooding husband who won't face reality. But I'm a Sicilian, I'm tempted to say out loud, and don't forget these things lightly. Lucky for them I'm not from the old school, like my grandfather. By the way, the etymology of the word *hearse* has something to do with wolf teeth—go figure.

Mike the undertaker keeps dropping by, though I'm not sure why. Maybe it's good business to keep an eye on survivors. I'll soon be part of his trade. The undertaker is robust; I'm sure he'll outlive me. *Robust* is a word that has fled from my vocabulary, like *entirely*. Anyway, Mike knows you're on life support and feels obliged to run by me the worst-case outcome, which is really the most likely scenario. We both know this but pretend otherwise. Your body will be stored in his mortuary refrigerator. I should tell you that transferring your body from the hospital in his death wagon will cost five hundred dollars. That's about a hundred dollars per mile. I don't mean to sound cheap, but golly.

Then again, the work of fetching and moving a dead body is more elaborate than many think. I looked it up. You need a vehicle with an airtight compartment and a stretcher. You need to select the correct body—check those name tags—and make sure the appropriate paperwork is complete. Who knows how many corpses lie waiting in the hospital morgue at any point. There could be fifty or more. Is the paperwork filled out properly? Has it been signed? Is the name of the deceased spelled correctly (Claire with an e)? You will be zipped up in a body bag, which will be placed on a stretcher and moved into the back of the van. That's as far as this thought can go. My mind will not let me think of you as that corpse in a blue body bag zipped tight, even though my fingers are typing this sentence. I close my eyes and see stars in a dark universe streaming backward toward a starting point.

It took four days but I gathered a hundred photos snapped since we married. Photos from the Yukon, Santa Fe, Portland, New York, southern France, Tokyo, Rome, Sicily, London, Dublin, Melbourne. Photos of yard work, with the dog, beside the mother-in-law, at family events, in arroyos, up mountains, along fast-running rivers, above the sea, in medieval churches, raking leaves, grooming Milo, reading the *Times*—photos neither of us ever saw, scattered across acres of disk space. What good is an unviewed photo? Does it even exist? I printed each photo on four-by-six glossy paper. A photographic chronicle of our life together emerged with surprising clarity. I'm looking at these now, photos that each tell a different story, but how can I not tear up? Roland Barthes wrote that death haunts every photograph of a loved one. But that isn't so here. No forewarnings of your death in any of these pictures, no lingering shadows, just the simple ease of someone so at home in her life.

In this one, you are standing in the Yukon near Destruction Bay, just off Haines Highway, beside a rocky stream that runs into Kluane Lake. Snowcapped Dalton Peak looms up in the near distance. You are running your hands through your hair, grimacing slightly from direct sunlight. Sunshine is not your friend, you of the northern clime. A mild frown on your face. You have on olive-green khakis with a drawstring and a black long-sleeve crew-neck T-shirt. Your right foot levitates above the smooth round river stones. Dwarf fireweed shoots up between the rocks, behind you the gray bubbling stream running toward the lake. Boreal Blue spruce. The magenta flowers. Summer in the Yukon—such a vast space—and just the two of us alone with eagles, bears, and prairie dogs. What are you thinking along Quill Creek? For the life of this photo, you will always be floating above the fireweed with the beauty and grace that came so naturally to you. In my besotted mind, there is a hush as each element of the scene composes itself around you. How I long for that presence.

That summer, we drove up the Haines Highway across the Canadian border, up along the Chilkat River, following the trail through the Chilkoot Valley used by the Tlingit long ago. The ruin of the bark beetle was everywhere, the yellowed-out Sitka spruce trees, the pale needles, the beetle-killed forests nearly as spectacular as the high peaks, glaciers, rivers, lakes, and ice fields, as we meandered—all by ourselves—through the wide alpine valley. At Haines Junction we stayed at the Raven Hotel, owned by a German couple who arrived years ago but never left. A strange place, filled with dour middle-aged Europeans. You had scallops, me pasta with bison meatballs. In the lobby was a life-size porcelain great heron. I later ran frantically after a brown grizzly bear swimming across the lake—it's a bear!—snapping pictures with my camera (all of them out of focus), you behind me with a forgiving smile. Ever the keen teenager, your eyes said.

You the shrewd adult. The Raven Hotel is for sale, by the way.

On a ferry, we coasted back to Juneau down the Gastineau Channel, like crossing over into another realm. Who knew we had reached the midpoint of our marriage already? It seemed we had only started. In another photo, you are looking out the ferry window at the Chilkoot range, enchanted by the fantastic seascape. You turn to me suddenly with a far-reaching look in your eyes. I feel as though you are looking at me across time, between worlds, here in this moment, in my space-time. The clarity of the photo is startling, if not disturbing. But who in love doesn't think this? Who in love does not see continuity where this is only empty air? On the other hand, you may simply be showing annoyance with my pestering camera.

They tell me your body is scheduled for organ donation soon. Your brother and sister came to say goodbye, Beth and Jay. There were tears of sorrow and disbelief. The tubes, the wires, the partly shaved scalp frightened them. You seemed centuries older. They hadn't expected this. You were young and sprightly just two months ago, but now you seemed stricken, as though racked by pestilence. How can I console them? We hug. It's lame but it's all we can do. I try to see you as they do but can't. You are glowing. Why can't they see it? Your lovely body all alone—abandoned even by you—drawing on a reserve of poise, as if the body knew all by itself, without any help, this untimely end was not just that but some inscrutable change that only now, in life's final breath, began to flower.

I apologize for the lyricism. It's like a virus. You're rolling your eyes, wherever you are, I can feel it. It's time for your fluids and neuro assessment. Everyone has left but me and the nurse, who bends over your face and lifts your left eyelid, shining a light into your pupil. I blink rapidly myself. The pupil should constrict, she says. Fixed pupils are an ominous sign. She repositions your ventilator tube in a painful way so as to cause gagging. She says this is a *noxious stimulus*. She is looking for any kind of response that might suggest you are still in there. If you gag you are there. But no gagging. I could have told the nurse you weren't here. I've known this for two days. You're just not here. That your body persists without you astonishes me.

On a walk I came across a cicada lying on its back, its arms folded. It seemed to be dead, but given that a black and yellow wasp was perched on its belly it may have only been paralyzed. Cicada-killer wasps are known to paralyze the insect with their venomous sting and then carry the crippled bug to a burrow. The female wasp lays her eggs just under the second leg of the cicada. Once the egg hatches, the larvae begin eating the cicada from the inside, but taking care to keep it alive. Matt brought by homemade bread this morning. Yesterday, Gemma dropped off a pan of enchiladas. I babble on when friends come by with meals. Must be fear of silence, having no one to talk to. When your partner goes, there's nothing between you and the void. Silence means that.

If truth be said, I don't want to let you go. Maybe this is a kind of madness. We are both possessive, me and the IC doctor. We want your body, as though you are a Hollywood hottie: he to harvest your organs, me to rub your toes. I've held firm, like Antigone. I won't abandon you. The IC guy is stubborn. We are locked in some ancient battle over your comatose body.

I'm rattling on now—can't help myself. Remember the rainbow over Dublin Harbor? It was our last week in Ireland. We had joined friends at the Pakistani place across from Bull Island. Walked all the way from the Clontarf train station to the Wooden Bridge in the pouring rain. My feet were soggy—I was a mess. The umbrellas weren't much help. I wanted to duck into the coffee shop but you wondered what the point of that was. We still had a mile to go, and the rain wasn't letting up. I just wanted out of the bloody downpour. Water, water everywhere. The Woodenbridge seemed miles in the distance and I was exhausted. But you soldiered on, always, never gave up. No one perseveres like you. Such a fighter—how can you be silent now?

By the time we left the restaurant the rain had finally stopped. And over Dublin Harbor, reaching from beyond Bull Island past the Pigeon House, was a colossal rainbow, the largest either of us had seen. Our first rainbow. It was too much for my phone camera and left us mostly speechless. It lingered for almost thirty minutes. At the end of every rainbow sits a pot of gold. Not this one. Maybe rainbows are just tricks of light and moisture. Still, it seemed like the end of something, our summer in Ireland maybe, and the beginning of something else. I don't know if you felt that way. We never talked about the rainbow. There was too much on our minds. Birds fly over the rainbow, why then oh why can't I? Happy little bluebirds.

Mike the undertaker will transfer your body from the hospital morgue to his facility. He has the appropriate refrigerator. Mike does not come cheap, however. I can't quibble with him, of course, because no one wants to be trite at a time like this, when death in all of its grandeur has slipped onto the stage, cape and all, as they say. All of these thoughts are wearing on my mind the way wind, rain, and snow batter a headstone. And that is why I won't let go of your body right now. The stillness of your warm toes, how your fingers curl around the glowing red LED— these are the signs of life I can touch, caress, rub, massage, hold between my nervous fingers. Time is running out. The organ snatchers are watching me secretly as I speak to you, and Mike the undertaker is warming up his doomsday van.

But here I am all alone again. You are here too, that's true, cute as ever, no matter the twisted tubes and wires and partly shaved scalp. I see you as you are, in all of your heartbreaking beauty. And even though I know your mind is gone, has taken leave of this place, I won't let go, which is totally perverse. The presiding doctor keeps looking at me like I'm a nutcase. Funny how you had what Poe called a sense of *strange impending doom*. It lasted all year. You even had panic attacks—ever since Milo died. Doting dog owners we were, but his untimely death unsettled us, as if Milo had been a lucky charm against disaster. Now that he was gone, we were vulnerable. Catastrophe lingered around the corner. The fact that I had a premonition of his death didn't lessen the sense of doom. I've inherited your dread, a ground-rumbling sensation that my existence is so temporary I might not make it to the weekend.

On my walk today, I couldn't help but notice an old Honda motorcycle resting in a driveway on Davenport. It was a black and candy-gold 1972 CB350, one of Honda's best-selling models. In 1972, over sixty-eight thousand were sold in America. We were still under the influence of the Peter Fonda and Dennis Hopper movie, when the idea of sheer motion seemed radical. I was one of those sixty-eight thousand American kids who purchased a café racer, as they were called. Mine was burgundy and black and I bought it brand new, squandering my graduation money. It cost $833. It was an impulsive thing to do, especially just before going off to graduate school. A year of tuition! I can't imagine you throwing caution to the wind like that. I could be reckless. But being a daredevil— remember Evel Knievel jumping across the Snake River Canyon in his rocket-powered bicycle—was part of our zeitgeist. With a CB350 Honda of his own, Knievel staged the oddest stunts during his heyday, leaping over rattlesnakes, mountain lions, pickup trucks, double-decker buses, crazy deep canyons, and broke every bone in his body in the effort. Still, he outlived you, the most cautious person on the planet, by seven years. Of course, I didn't leap over any canyons or save the day. All I got were hemorrhoids from motoring up and down I-95 at eight thousand rpm. What a grind that was. Should have taken a bus.

Every time I hear the sound of your desperate gasping for air, I lose another part of my brain. I'm slowly giving myself a lobotomy. Little chunks of gray matter falling on the hardwood floor. It's thundering violently outside. It remains obnoxiously warm. More hard rain. I'll have to check the basement for pooling water. This has always been my job, to keep alert for home disasters. It's something I do well. I think our oven is on the blink. With the broiler on, I melted the plastic coffee press on the stove top. Too much heat was escaping. Google says this is normal. I can't imagine how terrible it would be if Google were the only contact I had with the world, but it would be easy to lose touch. Loneliness, the *New York Times* just said, has become a *quiet devastation*. Emily Dickinson is oft quoted in such conversations: as when she calls loneliness *the Horror not to be surveyed but skirted in the Dark*. She reserves the upper case for her big themes. Henrik Ibsen too: *The strongest man in the world is he who stands most alone*. That sounds a little silly, frankly, but it's Ibsen. And Tennessee Williams: *We are all sentenced to solitary confinement inside our own skins, for life*. None of this is true.

Death is coming and I need to speak with more urgency—against your encryption. The dead are always encrypted, buried deep in the ground, sealed up, cast out, unattainable, barred forever from the loving touch, from these fingers that tickle your feet. How can I prevent this? I may fall into fits of melancholy—it can't be helped—but please understand there's a method to my delirium. I need to whisper these thoughts in your ear one last time, and I know you can hear me, because we have come to this baffling moment, so utterly unthinkable, when I must say goodbye to your body. The presiding doctor has built a case against you, and the neurologist will soon be here to sign the certificate. They have clear etiology of brain dysfunction, as these people say, and will test one more time your failure to respond to painful stimuli. Next, you'll enter the organ-donation phase, as you requested, but I'm sure you're not sticking around for this. Mike the undertaker will then come for you, and I'll next see your body at his place. It won't be the same. It'll never be. But I promise to keep talking, endlessly, if that's what it takes. I've read that death means you are in the third person. I won't let that happen.

ħ

CHAPTER THREE
SATURN (THE COGITATOR)

〜

I came into the world under the sign of Saturn,
the planet of heaviness, detours, and delays.
—Walter Benjamin

I am writing this at my desk in a small room in the middle of the night. Out the north window hardly any sign of life. Most have turned in. From the south the faint glow of streetlights. An overgrown dogwood scrapes the side of the house. At my back is a bed and a pair of night tables. Scattered about are books, papers, and magazines. There's a camera on a small glass stand. Always a camera nearby. I have no desire to leave my writing desk and sleep in an empty bed. Time does not allow much leeway, though. I rise up in the morning heavy, like a sack of rocks, dragging my awkward body through its paces.

I will myself forward. Begin, I say. Embark, I say to myself. No zest, no alacrity. I feel ponderous. Pay attention, I say to myself, impatient. Pay attention and move with quickness. Life is too short for gloominess, for shuffling your feet. I don't like brooding but that's all I want to do, fret, worry, sulk, mope. I feel a terrific reluctance, so much gravity. We're on the earth—no remedy for that. Who said that? Be careful, I warn myself, you're turning into a Beckett character. God forbid, I say. I wander through the living room. Without you the house seems larger, and each footstep is harder than the last. The incalculable force of sorrow. My arms and legs are turning into stone. The Medusa syndrome. The entire world is turning into stone, and you are not here to ease my fear.

One should be light like a bird, writes Italo Calvino, if only to resist the heaviness of this world, the unbearable weight of living. Baron von Munchausen traveled to the moon on a cannonball. Gulliver Jones to Mars on a magic carpet. Space fantasies, such a relief from earthbound gravity. A radio message from Space Boy, another fugitive. It's nighttime here, always, and cold, he says, but the solar system is awash in light and color. Surprisingly, it's not exactly quiet out my portal. Meaning what? I ask. My headphones are picking up a faint whistling sound, he says, that comes and goes in melodic radio bursts. A bit eerie, as if I'm not alone out here. Who knows, I radio back, maybe you're not.

There's a stink bug in the antenna housing, Space Boy continues. Your first stowaway, I message back. Space Boy keeps in radio contact as he goes about his thing, hurling himself into nothingness with uncanny savoir faire. I'm glad to hear from him, though I try to conceal my enthusiasm. He's such a ham. Maybe Space Boy is right. I know you're out there somewhere amid the space dust and ionized gases. It's a feeling I can't shake, even marooned on this troubled planet.

Once I was like Space Boy myself, hurling my body across vast distances. You too, come to think of it. It was the "Space Age," after all. We were college-age kids then, young Claire and young Jeff. You were off to London, Berlin, Paris, Rome, Athens, summer after summer. I always envied your transatlantic adventures. I was such a rube in comparison. A teenager, I drove to Toronto with my family once—it was colder than Buffalo, so we turned around and drove home. You never went into detail about your time abroad, not that I didn't inquire, but you weren't interested in your own past. Now that I remember, I was hardly more forthcoming. I never told you about my cross-country treks, nor did I say much about grad school or college. I read a lot of books, I told you, and was lonely. I strummed my guitar, I said. What kind of songs did you play? you asked. Leonard Cohen and later John Prine. Once, you asked me to play a song by John Prine, so I got out my guitar and played something. *I hate graveyards and old pawnshops, for they always bring me tears*—I sang. You joined me in the chorus: *Memories they can't be boughten, they can't be won at carnivals for free.* That was fun. We both loved John Prine and pledged to play more songs when old, you on the mandolin, me on the guitar.

Everyone played guitars back then, it was the thing to do, and ride motorcycles. I once drove a motorcycle from New York to Florida, my first trek. This was a totally nutty thing and for that reason I never told you about that trip. Plus, I feared it would not compare well with London and Paris and other exotic locales in your travelogue. Thirdly, it wasn't a glamorous motorcycle. I wish I could say I rode a Harley-Davidson through the Badlands of South Dakota, as that would have been the manly thing to do, but I left Buffalo for Florida on an under-sized Honda in a March blizzard. That's right, Evil Kniev-el's Honda 350. That's like embarking across the Atlantic in a dinghy against a gale force of twelve on the Beaufort scale. I was not traveling alone, happily. My pal Gary was just as nutty as me and he too was riding a pint-size Honda. It was all we could afford.

I'm emboldened to tell you that story right now. Ours was an inauspicious start. It was twenty-two degrees and howling winds battered road signs and trees. It was mid-March in Upstate New York, no time for outdoor barbe-cues, fly-fishing, or a carefree ride on a motorcycle. The sky was homicidal. Before we crossed the Pennsylvania line, fifty-mile-per-hour gusts stripped the backpacks off of our sissy bars and protective wear off our backs. Blow-ing snow pummeled our headgear. I lost my five-dollar motorcycle gloves in Salamanca. If we were smart, we would have turned around. We should never have seen *Easy Rider*, I said to myself. The romance of the open road and everything, the call to adventure, had taken us in.

Gary was more crazed than I—he pressed on. I wanted to hole up in a cheap motel until the weather broke. He was determined, like Ponce de León, to set foot in Flori-da. I admired Gary's resolve but I was looking for some-thing vaguely more soulful. Maybe smoke pot and cruise down small, forgotten, out-of-the-way roads. Maybe meet eccentric folks in rural America. I wanted to tell my pal that it's not the destination that matters but the change of scene, as I was a big fan of Brian Eno (who said that). My mind was full of clichés. On we rode past Harrisburg, Baltimore, and Washington—it was so frigid—without a break. My Honda was grinding at eight thousand revolutions per minute—it was redlining—for eleven hours a day. That's a lot of shaking. The vibration was surreal: my whole body was aquiver. The area between the anus and the scrotum, in particular, didn't like this. My pelvic floor muscles felt compressed. By the time we arrived in Richmond, where we stayed with my cousin, fatigue from wind blast and sore bums had got the better of us.

But we had escaped the Northeast in winter on motorcycles, and that was something. Here the air was aromatic and the trees leafy. We changed the oil in our bikes and took my cousin's kids for rides; they were spellbound by these two strangers on motorcycles (no matter they were Hondas). To them, we were rock stars, even if my fanny hurt and Gary seemed more stooped than usual. We were surprised by our newfound charisma, which we took to Atlanta. There I made out with a Scandinavian au pair from whom I caught mononucleosis, and then journeyed on to the sacred waters of Florida, guarded by snakes, crocodiles, and angry old people. After numerous adventures too embarrassing to recount—Gary and I got so stoned one night we wound up in a snake-infested campground beside a canal cluttered with dead animals—I returned home and sold my Honda for more than I paid. With that money, I ponied up for my first year of grad school.

Zen and the Art of Motorcycle Maintenance wouldn't come out until the next year, and by then I would be in Oregon. I read the book a few years later, searching for clues about my own cross-country experience. Nowhere does Pirsig say anything about hemorrhoids, which to me is the inner truth of motorcycles. That and the fact that it's always cold on a bike, even in the Everglades. I had thought of my trip as a rite of passage. If it was that, it wasn't the start of something new but the end of a way of life. It was sad to say goodbye to that life, believe it or not.

The funny thing is that the moment I returned home I had to leave. Something inside me was accelerating but I couldn't say what. I had traveled four thousand miles on my motorcycle and it was time to leave again. The world spun around too. The Vietnam War officially ended (not that anyone believed this), Nolan Ryan pitched another no-hitter (that's incredible, my dad said), *The Godfather* won an Academy Award (but Marlon Brando was a no-show), Picasso died (Picasso who? Uncle Tony said), and the Watergate story broke. I felt fidgety. It must be a guy thing, I thought, restlessness. Worse, I was having trouble dating. Maybe I have a personality disorder, I thought. I would go west this time, all the way to Oregon. Mountains and sea. It was 1973 and I was about to become a nerd. I was going to graduate school, a sanctuary for misfits. No more motorcycles. No more baseball. No more TV. A lot of books and writing. This was new.

I crossed the Rockies in a 1967 Mercury Montclair four-door hardtop. It was a last-minute purchase ($160) after realizing that hitchhiking 2,700 miles to Eugene wasn't a good idea. I wasn't sure the Mercury would go the distance, though. The bearings in my differential went bad a week before my big adventure. Such a giant car—so many things could go wrong, my sister said. Yeah, I know, I said. I stifled my misgivings, packed the trunk, and said goodbye to my family. So long, folks!

Soon I was driving under a dark Western sky, the Mercury's dashboard lighting up brilliantly. Nothing but stars and the total eeriness of horizontal space. I was in the middle of a *Star Trek* episode, banking left and right over Rawlins, Wyoming. Captain's log, stardate 42973.2. I have no idea why I'm doing what I'm doing, but here I'm in the vast plains of Wyoming, am only twenty-two, and know diddly-squat about anything. Captain's log supplemental: most kids have a plan at this stage of their lives, because they're obsessed with Beat poetry or mitochondrial dysfunction. Or like you, medieval drama. Not me. My mind is as empty as Wyoming.

Tell me more, you say. Certainly. Once in Eugene, I settle down with back-to-nature types not far from Ken Keasey's home in the hovel-town that is Springfield, a bleak blue-collar community that lies in the shadow of the Weyerhaeuser pulp factory. I had never met a Californian before; there were none back home in Buffalo. Ron is from Irvine, Mary from San Bernardino, and both are eccentric. Together they strip from their small stick-frame house every modern electrical convenience I have grown up with. Whatever required an outlet—clocks, stoves, lamps, radios, TVs, stereos, egg beaters, blenders—was out the door. They were confirmed Luddites. They banned hair dryers, irons, electric typewriters. (I found a used Royal Futura mechanical typewriter in a pawnshop on Main Street.) They didn't stop there. Ron raised ceilings, built lofts, exposed walls, carved out exterior windows in interior spaces, even cedar-shingled his bedroom floor and walls. He was turning into a hobbit. Without television, there was nothing to do in the evening but read or sing (electric guitars were banned). That's how I learned John Prine songs.

I'm reading so many books I'm catching up to you. That's all I do, read and write and walk through the drizzle. It's always raining so everyone sits down with a book and drinks coffee. My hair is long now. I'm changing. On visits home I sound different. I don't talk normal. My sentences are absurd. I try to correct myself but this change is irreversible. I sound like a book. When I speak to my sister, writing comes out of my mouth, not speech. She looks concerned. My dad thinks I sound educated. My mom wants to know when I'm coming home. It's been four years, she says, isn't that long enough? Besides, you look skinny. I'm making my family read *The Book of Thel* by William Blake. My sister wants to see *The Shining*, but instead I read Dylan Thomas stories out loud. This is getting a bit out of hand, my mom says. Everyone can't wait until I go back to Oregon.

How we defied gravity back then. On an early evening walk, darkness everywhere. The moon is gone and the humidity is inky black. The stars are pinpricks in a nighttime sky so vast I want to faint. I turn right onto Reno Street, where I see Bill the rat terrier's people smoking cigarettes in the dark. You remember them, Mike and Mickey. I could hardly see them in the dark, just the embers of their fags. They asked—I hoped they wouldn't— "Where's your wife?" I stopped in my tracks and felt a tremendous downward drag on my organs, as though the pull of the earth had increased by a factor of five. I didn't want to speak, I didn't want to say any of it, but I couldn't move away. How do people move on this planet? My mouth had become so small no words came out. I tried to say your name but, as in a nightmare, there was no voice, just a downward pull. My lungs, my heart, my eyeballs, my kidneys—all seventy-eight organs—were plummeting at thirty-two feet per second squared. Blood was pooling at my feet. I became light-headed. Mike and Mickey puffed on their cigarettes, waiting for me to speak. Words failed me. Later, as I struggled home, confused and bewildered, I felt as though I'd fallen out of a plane and somehow survived the plunge, though every bone in my body was broken.

I've begun plans for your memorial service, with the help of Judith and Perry. There'll be music (Bach—how solemn) and Chris Merrill's daughter will sing Melody Gardot's version of "Somewhere Over the Rainbow." That will keep the tears flowing. I drove to Grinnell yesterday, westward bound. Forced motion. Once out of Iowa City, dark clouds filled the sky. Near Victor, population of 893, I saw clusters of sunflowers in the grassy meridian, waving in the wind. The lovely sunflowers, *sorrowing ladies,* you once called them as we drove through Iowa. The rolling cornfields are nearly harvest-ready, fields of green and gold, snug and warm. The dark tunneling cornrows, flowering ragwort and chickweed, the circling ravens. To share such beauty is all we need for a flash of a moment to be at home in this world. But you weren't there.

I feel pretty weird. It begins in the pit of my stomach and radiates outward. Different parts of my body twitch. I watched my calf muscle spasm for several minutes, rapid involuntary contractions, as though someone with a remote control were pranking my body. Anyway, Grinnell hasn't changed since last time. Some things never do, small towns in the Midwest. Before returning, I stopped at Candyland Station on Route 6 for a chocolate shake. Remember the diner-themed soda fountain with the Mobil gas pumps out front? The retro interior décor, black and white–tiled floor, red-vinyl stools, chicken salad and grilled cheese sandwiches. Roberta was behind the counter, as usual, with comforting small talk. Rain's coming, she said, by six, they say. Wonder if they'll call off the football games. What games? I asked. Grinnell and Oskaloosa, she said.

A group of septuagenarians sat at the white laminate table by the door chatting and eating chicken salad. Time turned back on itself. One old-timer has mayonnaise pooling near the corner of his mouth. Roberta's eyes are dark brown, her hair blond-colored, and she smiles vaguely, as though keeping something from us. Such a striking tableau I hear the voice of Rod Serling in my head: Portrait of a woman at work, Ms. Roberta See, age fifty-two, across the counter from a lonely man, age indeterminate. The place is here, the time is now, and the journey into the shadows that we're about to watch could be *your* journey.

It's not dark yet but I will myself to leave this place, Roberta and her pies and her sandwiches, to turn back to the highway. Beyond Candyland is an immensity of empty space and gathering clouds.

Loss, they say, is not just an emotional disturbance but physical too. It is like an electromagnetic shock to the widowed brain. Science has put its finger on a specific hormone triggered by the sudden loss of a partner— corticotropin-releasing factor. The sadness chemical. It's a neurotransmitter involved in stress response and is elevated in extreme cases of loss. This was determined by a study of prairie voles, known for pair-bonding. The animals were misled into thinking their lifelong partners had been snatched by predators, by weasels, hawks, and snakes, or something like that. What a cruel trick. Scientists separated the bonded pairs who immediately began grieving. Prairie voles mate and affiliate exclusively with each other for most of their lives, thanks to oxytocin and vasopressin, which means the male voles stay around to help raise the kids. Only 3 percent of all mammals behave this way. Once artificially separated, though, the voles' corticotropin-releasing factors spiked, which led to depression and other related forms of unhappiness. Dark dreams, morbid thoughts, fatigue, feelings of unworthiness, insomnia. When scientists gave the prairie voles a compound that blocked the sadness chemical's signaling ability, the widowed voles stopped feeling depressed. They played cards, drank, and partied.

Better living through chemistry. I guess these guys are looking to treat bereavement with drugs, disable the sadness chemical. The odd thing about grieving is that, like spirit possession, it wants to achieve full expression. It wants to run its course and won't be denied. I'm just reporting from the field. When I grieve for you—and it's around the clock—I feel as though I am in the company of someone else, a presence of sorts. It begins as a knot in my stomach and seems to mirror my shape, like a second body, a spectral body. It is the interface between me and death, and somewhere in between there is a residual you. Death is a tear in time, and grief with its strange body hears that wound.

There I go again. Sorry. On my walk today, I passed by Oakland Cemetery. Who doesn't like a good cemetery, so scenic? You were fond of graveyards yourself, one of our favorite walking routes. I once took a nap on a grave in a very old cemetery. It was a sunny day. I was in the middle of a Henry James novel and nodded off. The next day my grandfather died—raven-minded Joe.

They say death comes in threes. First Milo, then you. I'm next. Today, I took my phone out and snapped a photo of two old tombs. The headstones were those of Fred and Margaret Blum. Fred died in 1895, Margaret in 1897. Early settlers in Iowa City, I guess. The headstones were marble so the worse for wear. Still, the Blum name was legible after nearly 120 years. Smatterings of a name. A stranger from the future—that's who I am—musing over the last discernible traces of Fred and Margaret. Not quite blotted out yet but on the brink of oblivion. The erasure of time. It's not lichen or discoloration. Marble simply is not the hardest stone. It decomposes. Rain, snow, wind, atmospheric gases.

Acid rain has erased more names from headstones than you'd think. Another decade or two of this and Fred's and Margaret's bones will be unnamed. Who were these people? passersby will ask. Other headstones are already unreadable, tombs of the unnamed, inside the graves soldiers on the long march toward oblivion. The hollow spaces in the letters have lost their form. Fred's headstone is still plumb, but Margaret's is listing to the left by twenty-five degrees. She is leaning toward Fred. Do the bones chatter at night or whisper in the rain?

None of this matters to you, in principle, as it was your wish to be cremated, and though the idea of persistence interests me, I won't talk about that now because I know how little patience you have for such nonsense.

I am such a spectacle. If you could only see me now, my mistakes, mishaps. I'm afraid of embarrassing you, frankly. I feel hideous. But I know what you'd say—the dead are everywhere so don't exaggerate—that's what you're thinking. Most things look different in a state of grief. You begin to pay attention to people's faces, the sadness lurking behind the worry, the hurry of clouds, the hubbub of birds, things in nature, trees and woodpeckers and milkweed. All the changes, so many. You become attentive, even watchful. This is not how you remember things when the world is familiar and life steady, when a stable set of knowns is like money in the bank, when the end of summer is a habit of mind and the first snow a chore. Now it looks so different. I listen to what is here, lingers, witness what belongs here. It's a kind of attunement. To my surprise, death belongs here and so too hideous nothingness, right beside the fragrant magnolia. I owe the world this, I realize. I am willing to be here, whatever this being here means.

Some cultures are better than others when it comes to death. Buddhists, for instance, believe in rebirth. When you die you will be reborn again, until you are wise enough to escape the cycle of death and rebirth. They also believe a person's state of mind at the point of death is important. On the morning of your collapse, I was unnerved by the water leak. They'll have to dig up everything, I said. You were unfazed. I was anxious about traveling east. The traffic will be obnoxious, I warned. You were serene. I was rattled by the new semester soon to begin. I was unprepared. You shrugged school off. What was that all about? I asked myself. So unworried. Typically we shared one another's phobias but your serenity was bizarre. You seemed in touch with something I didn't understand. Readiness is all.

The Maori believe the spirit persists after death and is welcomed to the spirit world. For the Maori, the end-of-life phase of a person includes visitations and conversations with those beyond the veil, conversations about a spiritual journey to the next place. I wonder if the Maori are familiar with the Boomerang Nebula—you never know. Even mourning has its differences. In many cultures, extravagant displays of grief, from wailing and hair-pulling, reflect the love for the deceased. Tormented tears are tolerated. In Bali, however, mourners are under orders not to weep, as in Japan, where death is viewed not as a tragedy but as the great escape. In China, professional wailers are available for great shows of grief. Not only that but Chinese mourners often hold conversations with dead relatives, which is thought to be curative.

As I was about to say, I have of late lost all my mirth. I can't eat and I can't sleep. Oatmeal makes me cry and even peanut butter. Scientists explain that sorrow is a form of stress, like anxiety, and that with it come bodily changes. That's because certain stress factors, like the hormone cortisol, shoot up. The immune system takes a hit and so does your sleep life. Anyway, grief comes with loss of appetite, palpitations, even hallucinations. I've even read how grieving men and women see things. They see their dead spouses, maybe as they knew them, but also as metamorphosed creatures, butterflies, caterpillars, sparrows, rabbits, cats, turtles. I haven't yet encountered any unusual messengers but speaking to an empty chair can't be normal. With coffee cup in hand, I'll pass the time of day with you. It's early in the grieving process but I figure I may as well get used to it. Shakespeare helps. I've had some scary moments too, if you must know, bizarre instances of *somatic distress*, as they say, where I've felt breathless and bewildered. But more than anything else I feel restless, and when I'm not restless I feel like I weigh a ton. I can't sit still—or I can't get up. I walk aimlessly around the house, searching for something to do. I am thy husband's spirit, doomed for a certain time to wander around the living room.

But aren't we all designed to grieve?

On my walk today a flock of seagulls, hundreds of them, soaring high in the midday sky, whirled up and down, turning 180 degrees as one, like a school of herring. They moved in a mesmerizing pattern, synchronizing their flight at the same speed and direction. At such a high altitude the gulls resembled ghostly shades of gray, barely visible, but when turning abruptly southward they reflected sunshine in brilliant flashes of light, like a constellation of little stars. I followed their slow random movements for fifteen minutes. The sheer thrill of flight, riding upward currents of air.

You may not know this but migrating birds will sometimes form a "kettle" to exploit a current of rising air. In tight formation, they seem to be "boiling in a cauldron." I looked that up. The gulls will gain altitude before leaving the rising current to glide to the next updraft, using as little energy as possible. Gliding, not flapping, swirling around in lazy circles, no rush to go anywhere. Their flight is unpredictable. Up and down, swirling this way and that, clockwise and counter, hypnotic under the midday sun, entirely free of gravity. Of the body but beyond it, nearing the edge of space. They are like fish swimming through the sky, their silver underbellies radiating flashes of bright light. I wish you had been there. My neck hurt from craning my head backward for so long.

I've become suspicious of my lyrical impulses since you left. I wonder if this isn't just a cover for something opposite in my nature. I have a history of being contrary and difficult, not lyrical. It worries me that I've lost touch with that self, that he's buried in the past. I can hardly be blamed for becoming more softhearted, but I'd like to remember him better, the contrarian. I'm trying to hold onto myself.

Here's a photo of eleven-year-old me. I'm with my mom, dad, and sister. Pat and Herb, still in their thirties, look like the Kennedys. An attractive couple they are, the wavy-haired Italian woman and her debonair husband. Judy has a winning smile. She's a little giddy, in fact. The scene is Niagara Falls. We are this close to the rocky precipice. Behind us, rumbling water tumbles below. We are a poster of the nuclear family. Here's a surprise that would make you laugh. A Kodak camera dangles from my neck. I don't remember that. Was I taking pictures so young? I always thought my camera fetish came later, after meeting you, not that you were the instigator but that being with you simply opened my eyes. It's a cute camera, a Kodak Brownie Starlet, but who is actually taking this picture? It's nicely framed. Jeez, we're so close to the edge! I have on black Converse sneakers and don't look nearly as dorky as I remember. Another surprise: I don't see a smart-alecky smirk on my face. I would have imagined it was there from the start. A revelation.

It will turn up soon, though—the insolence, I mean. I can feel it coming. Just ask my mom. She could tell you about that Saturday morning three years later when, late for work, she begged me to look after Judy and maybe pick up around the house. A more empathic son would have said, Sure, Mom, especially as I see how frazzled you are. Instead, I produced a contemptuous grin, as if to say . . . Well, I can't even write it. This was too much for my mom, an explosive Sicilian. She screamed at me in Italian—something like, *Si credi a questa cazzo di merda*—which means, I think, Can you fucking believe this shit? And then she picked up a magazine rack crammed with issues of *National Geographic* (which are heavy) and hurled it at my head.

I was a bad boy but I don't know where my badness came from, especially this contempt for authority types. It drove my parents nuts. I was grounded more than I can remember. Go to your room, Jeffrey, my dad would say. Busted for being snide and defiant. I blame it on the Cold War, on Khrushchev. I remember vividly how Khrushchev poked fun at Vice President Nixon in Moscow. It was on TV. We had just built an exhibit in Sokolniki Park, a so-called model American home of middle-class luxury. Touring the exhibit, Nixon said to Khrushchev, Look at this kitchen, will you? It's terrific. We have houses like this all over California. And how about that built-in washing machine? We have such things, Khrushchev answered. What we want to do, Nixon went on, is make life easier for our housewives. Look over there, that's what we call a blender. These modern devices make life more trouble free for our moms. That's when Khrushchev, bald as an egg, flashed Nixon his devastating smirk. I was just a kid but I'll never forget it. We do not have such a foolish attitude toward our women, Khrushchev said derisively. He had a point, even a kid like me knew that, and to see the embarrassment on Nixon's face. Well, that made an impression.

I try to remember what it was like to be me before I met you, but it's not as easy as I would have guessed.

Those other Jeffs are evasive. Here's one. This is teenage Jeff, slightly perplexed. His weekends aren't his own. He's been recruited to work for his dad on Saturday mornings delivering clothes. He doesn't like the job but what can he do? He is a lazy teenager and now he has to get out of bed unreasonably early. The odd thing about this, as I remember it, is that he woke before his dad, who was hungover from the previous night. Herb was an active musician before you met him and spent every weekend downtown at a gig. A talented bass player and singer, really. I'm sorry you never heard him. He was a hipster too. That's why my mom married him. He was unquestionably cool. Sadly, none of this has rubbed off on young Jeff or me. Anyway, this Saturday situation wasn't a father/son thing so much as forced labor. Herb drove the truck, young Jeff hauled the dry cleaning to its destination.

My dad was so worn out from his late-night carousing he didn't talk, but he looked miserable. Something was eating him up inside or maybe he just felt lousy from a hangover. My mom was on his case that morning. He obviously felt guilty. It was a bad habit, returning home at four thirty a.m. His chronic boozing on weekend jobs made everyone tense. But he seemed clueless about how he might reconcile musicianship, as he called it, with the demands of family life. The musician and the father were two different guys. My dad was a riddle to me. He kept everything inside and it got the better of him. (Note to self.)

The van was cute, though, and when an older Jeff would drive it himself he would feel unshackled. Right now he's only fourteen and lugging two suits, one dress, four shirts, and one woman's gaudy overcoat up the steps of a newly built split-level on Wurlitzer Drive. The plastic bags flutter in the wind. He rings the bell and waits impatiently. It's December and cold. The frigid air stabs through his cheap parka. He rings the bell again. A round-faced blonde in a white terry-cloth robe opens the door, Mrs. Sacco. Her husband Frank owns a booming pizzeria in the city. They just moved to the suburbs. In her early thirties, Mrs. Sacco is friendly and vaguely attractive. Young Jeff has a crush on her. Frank Sacco is friendly too, but he is a short, dangerous wop. He could pass for Joe Pesci. Once Frank caught young Jeff staring at his wife. It was midsummer and Mrs. Sacco wore tight-fitting Bermuda shorts. Jeff knew Frank was waiting for this moment, waiting for Jeff to gaze at his wife's shapely legs, but he couldn't help himself. The wop and the wasp, Jeff thought, holding the neatly pressed garments over his shoulder. Sharklike—that was Frank's smile. But Jeff liked Frank. He was energetic and rolling in money. Italian Americans are very effusive when rolling in money and Frank was no different. He even let the naive fourteen-year-old flirt with his wife. Jeff vowed to visit Frank Sacco's pizzeria, but Herb advised against it as the joint was in a bad part of town.

My dad had good ears, perfect pitch in fact. He could identify any note I played on my guitar. Your hearing, alas, is a catastrophe. One morning as we ate breakfast, I asked if you'd like another waffle. Belgians waffles with pecans and strawberries. Quite good. Remember? You looked at me, smiled, and nodded vaguely, as though I had asked a theoretical question, as if I had asked you about the accelerating expansion of the universe. By then I knew the signs of your generic head bob, a gesture designed to feign hearing. So I asked what you heard me say, and you replied, Do you like Simon and Garfunkel?

Before you left, I massaged your ears. I've longed to rub your ears but these and your toes were off limits. Ticklish girl. You might say I was taking advantage of the situation. This part of your body—your ears—are very dear. They never quite worked. I wasn't aware of your hearing problem until we began living together. I had to be near you twelve hours a day, seven days a week, before I could detect anything awry. A loud siren on TV didn't faze you. The screaming tea kettle went unnoticed. The high-pitched grinding noise in the air conditioner—the same. This didn't happen overnight. It took time before I saw a pattern. You had mastered the art of seeming to hear. Your uncanny way of hiding deafness behind a brilliant repertoire of expressive gestures masked the reality. I was fascinated by this trickery.

Do you remember the first time you were outed? We were in the kitchen nook in Arlington. Goldfinches were perched in the backyard maple. The cat stretched out across the sofa back. *Morning Edition* was talking on the radio. Over coffee I referenced an episode of *Seinfeld* ("Fusilli Jerry") we had just watched. I asked if Kramer's zaniness came from Larry David or Michael Richards. You looked up and gave me a glance of surprise, as if I had said, Let's get naked. You didn't hear me but pretended to follow along by providing what you guessed was the right gesture. Wonder. I was puzzled. I produced a bewildered look, which ricocheted off your face. Back and forth in an error loop we went. I said, "What did you just hear me say?" You blushed and then said shyly, "Sadly the cross cross-eyed bunny needs a name." "Wow!" I said. I wasn't being ironic but impressed by the sheer poetry of mishearing. You called this underhearing. Because you couldn't hear enough to produce a context for a spoken sentence you were at the mercy of your own inventiveness.

I usually mishear in ways that are creative, you said, but not flattering to me, as my slips sometimes lead to social blunders. That's something I can't forget. It was the error that vexed you most. It was unbecoming to take away the wrong meaning. Mishearing is inexact, no matter how ingenious your guesswork. Your loyalty to correctness—to being right—is inspiring. I've never felt that desire. It's a flaw in me that you were happy to live with. Thank you. I'm ever so slightly unethical. I'd rather have my fancy teased than be edified by you know what. And so for me your adaptive hearing was brilliant. So what if the peripheral temporal coding in your brain stem was off base? So what if you experienced interaural decorrelation? Deep down you were a poet.

Of course, this is easy for me to say because I can hear, mostly. But age has taken its toll on my higher-frequency response. I'm more susceptible to the degrading effects of reverberant energy, as experts say, than I was ten years ago. It's stressful, I now know, and I can't figure how you coped for so long. I'm sure at least 25 percent of everything I said probably wasn't worth listening to anyway—and that's charitable. At least that much. Many of us are in various states of mishearing, you said, but carry on anyway, as if partial deafness were a selective skill. I'm sure it was agonizing coping with hearing loss. You had developed your own version of Sturgeon's Law, that 90 percent of everything is crap.

No wonder we shied away from having children. You

know, it's funny that we don't have kids, I say one day. Do you think that was a mistake? I wonder. Not necessarily, you say, but our lives would be different. We're both silent for a moment. This conversation takes place in the living room. It's 2008 and our retirement accounts have just fallen off a cliff. I'm not sure what else has brought us here. I wasn't convinced you were up to the task, you add. What do you mean? I say defensively. Well, that you would share the workload evenly. I wince. I know you're not saying this to make me feel bad. Can you see yourself changing diapers? Waking at three in the morning? Pacifying a screaming newborn? Well, yes, I say. Every once in a while I wouldn't mind doing that, I say. Like mowing the lawn. I could do that. Case closed, you say with a smirk.

Neither of us sensed any kind of biological necessity when it came to children. We liked kids well enough but never felt as though the fate of the species was on the line. Actually, maybe we did and there you go. Yet parading around town with a toddler harnessed to our chest—can't see that. But don't let me put words in your mouth. Maybe you secretly wanted a child and were disappointed I didn't show more interest. I doubt it, though. Down deep we were both terrified of our gene pool. We didn't trust natural selection. It was probably perverse. Our little creature would have bad hearing, lousy eyesight, a big nose, and maybe six fingers. That we were sure of, six fingers.

Being childless did put us at a disadvantage. Conversations are more demanding if that's all you've got, two players. The family plan has its perks. Studies suggest that parents spend a large chunk of shared time chatting abut their kids. Maybe 50 percent. Nights out would be effortless if we could resort to family talk. There'd be problematic kids to discuss. Our imaginary darlings, Mary and Larry, are no doubt troubled teenagers. By the way, how did Larry do on that geology test? I ask. We're dining out and you're nibbling on roasted brussels sprouts. My question produces a frown on your lips. Science is not a strength, you say. Oh, that bad? I ask. He's lazy, like his father. He won't study. I don't think he has looked once at his book. I wince. As far as he's concerned, the Jurassic era began in 1993 and is still roaring ahead. I laugh. Motherhood has sharpened your wit. I blame it on his Xbox and then change the subject.

You know, I'm not exactly wild about Mary's new boyfriend, I say. What's his name, Jared? By now your pizza is here, amply overlaid with arugula and caramelized onions. Already on your second slice, I see. You seem really hungry tonight. Jared was last month, you correct me. Hunter followed soon after. This week it's Noah. Have you seen his Facebook page? You don't like Mary's new boyfriends either. Dare I look? I wouldn't if I were you, you say. Lots of anger issues. You're on slice number three.

I change the subject. I recently stumbled on this bizarre account of Noah in the *Dead Sea Scrolls*, I say. You perk up. How's that? you ask. At birth, Noah was this weird little baby with long white hair, a red body, and unnaturally blue eyes. The Noah in Genesis is pretty banal, you say. But not this kid, I say. He's so uncanny he scares the shit out of the midwife. Lamech, his dad, passes out completely. Noah probably wasn't his kid, you say. Lots of strange fathers back then. And when baby Noah first spoke, I resume, he quotes Wittgenstein. You laugh. Really, his head is full of cosmic thoughts and so forth. Hardly what one would expect, you suggest.

Mary is smart and restless, you say, returning to the topic, and she likes to piss me off. Serial dating is her weapon of choice. We're finishing our dessert. Mary scares me a little, I say. She's got your brains and my cunning. That's a dangerous mix, you say. I change the subject. Maybe Larry has a bum teacher, I suggest. I had Mr. Clements at his age. He drilled a lot of stuff into our little brains. I still remember "Charlie Oliver Still Drives My Purple Plymouth to Jersey City Through Quicksand"— the memory device he taught us. What's that for? you ask. That's for the periods, you know, eons and epochs and things. Who's Charlie? you ask. Cambrian, I think, but I forget the others, except for Triassic and Jurassic. And quicksand? Life, I say.

CHAPTER FOUR
TITAN (THE ELDER)

*Saturn has nine moons, the greatest of which is
Titan.*

—Kurt Vonnegut

Black walnuts are falling in the yard—I'm listening now as I write—bouncing off the porch with
some violence. My head feels like a cracked walnut. I look around. I see a coffee pot on the stove, out the
window a bird feeder. Across the street Wally is changing
the oil in his motorcycle. It all seems so natural. I don't
feel natural. I don't belong here. There's a twenty-four-
hour depression hotline but I'm not depressed. I just feel
like I'm on the wrong planet.

I have no one to talk to. I really feel like I don't belong
here. I invented Space Boy, as you know, to give form to
this inward change in position. Everything needs a name.
That's why we write. Obviously, I need to invent other
voices. I wouldn't call Space Boy chatty, but he does report back every now and then. You won't talk unless I cue
you up in memory. Far-flung me, Space Boy. He's all about
audacity. Displacement has its rewards.

Kierkegaard thinks of displacement as *no* placement, an aspect of exile. The exile lives in relation to himself as if he were constantly out, never at home. That's me in a nutshell. For Kierkegaard, a spiritual diaspora isn't such a bad thing. But I don't know. We have been pulled apart. Heidegger says this sensation is accompanied by dispersion, instability, and anxiety—that it defines us as human beings. Small consolation.

I'm learning things on the fly, no one teaches this, such as death is impenetrable dark space. Anything inside that space should be disappeared from the known universe. But death is also a border region, a zone of the incomprehensible that leaks information. Everything leaks. Radiators leak, my nose leaks, tires leak, faucets, hoses, the heart, the soul, secrets leak. This form we call life, I'm sure it leaks. Right now my voice is seeping across an ontological boundary that separates us. It's leaking into another dimension. Love is not irrecuperable. This thought has for me a primitive lyrical validity, as Kierkegaard might say. When death leaks, time dilates. There is a barely discernible dilation of time and in that dilation not the slightest trace of resignation. Why shouldn't death leak? Everything leaks.

This is what the mind does when it's a cracked walnut, a rapid onset of confusion and tremors, an unpredictable turbulence of signifiers. I should be flogged.

I am such a sight. I have no choice but to babble into emptiness. A lost wife can come alive in the mind, can't she? I often feel you nearby. Your dream visits are random but poignant. When you visit, you are sometimes so enigmatic. This is not the Claire I remember. You've changed, perhaps. In one dream, you tell me to let go of time. Let go of time, you say. It has wrapped itself around you like a snake. Let go and see its coils. I woke from a deep sleep and rubbed my eyes. What could that possibly mean? Time and death, what could be more inscrutable? You used to be so sensible, so down-to-earth. Maybe it's fun to whisper riddles in my ear.

Space Boy radioed to say he should bypass Pluto and visit Titan instead. I've heard Titan is inhabited by stunning women, he said dubiously. Quite beautiful. Nothing else like it until Betelgeuse. He read this in a book, I think, maybe Vonnegut.

If all goes well, Space Boy reports, I'll soon pass by the rings of Saturn. It took *Voyager 1* three years to make the trip, I radio back. I'm trying hard not to be skeptical but Space Boy's bravura is a bit much. I'm working the gravitational pull of dark matter to good effect, he boasts. Quite a speed bump. It would be very cool to park my spacecraft in proximity to Saturn, where I can get a glimpse of Titan. But can you really do that? I radio back. All those rings and ringlets, just a lot of rock, crystals, and ice, some smaller than a pebble. Plus the rings don't sit still—they whirl around the planet. Sounds awfully precarious, I warn. Who could resist such beauty? he says.

I worry neighbors will see me talking to myself, right here beside the big window. How embarrassing. It's overcast today. It thundered early this morning. The rains were heavy. Still, many trees are leaf-filled. I took comfort from this fact on my walk. The grand branches of the sycamores held onto their broad maple-like leaves, not giving in to wind and rain. As a family, the sycamore tree is over one hundred million years old. Living sycamores can reach the age of six hundred years. I once wrapped my arms around a much younger one. The ginkgo tree is older—Jurassic even. The ginkgoes are still green. The pretty fan-shaped leaves show little sign of yellowing yet. The ginkgo near the park is a male. It has no stinky seeds. Some ginkgoes have lived to be over three thousand years old.

You were all by yourself when you last saw the light of day, that Wednesday morning in late July. The sun was bright and shone through your east window. What exactly did you see? Was it the ceiling as you lay on your back? Was it the window, the chair, your toes? What was the last thing you heard? Did you feel the sparkle leave your eyes? Could you hear me screaming, could you hear your own growling? When the oak leaf falls or the ash blade, the descent seems accomplished, a job well done, a life full of color. The spectrum is fulfilled, from green to yellow. When a woman or a man dies unexpectedly it seems a catastrophe. But when is death not untimely? I turn red asking these questions because they seem so naive, so beside the point. But what is the point? I keep waiting for my phone to ring. Lingering is a delirium. I haven't moved from this spot for hours. I have to pee but I won't even go to the bathroom. Why am I so sure you will phone me? You're not here and I feel stupid and naked, stripped like a bare oak in early winter. Thus speaks the always-present "I," who is but a shadow of the always-absent you.

I finished your obit with a bit of help. Judith and Perry's kindness was big. Drove to the funeral home to visit your body one last time. You were in a long shelf-like container covered by a quilt, pale and cold as snow, and in your hands you held Victoria's small gathering of rosemary and lavender. Your face seemed weighed down, your lips thicker, and your eyes closed shut, as if surrendering to gravity. No more luminosity. I preferred the ambiguity of your not-technically-dead body in the IC unit, where I could kiss your warm forehead, each node on your shaved scalp, and rub your reactive fingers and toes. So here is the finality of the cold body, and it is so anticlimactic. Details: I have several locks of your hair. Mike the undertaker is planning to cremate you this evening and will keep your remains until I choose an urn. He recommended a biodegradable one.

You'd think it would be harder to separate the spirit from the body. I look at your face and can't imagine that body is now gone forever. It remains only in memory and in countless photos. I've been looking at these and find myself in love with you all over. I want to begin again, only this time with a baroque eagerness. Of course, this would be awful and you would have none of it. Love's gestures are always absurd, you would say.

A case in point. Late 1980s, Washington, DC. We've just begun dating but neither of us dare call it that. It's Friday afternoon at my apartment, a week of teaching over, and here we are sitting around an IKEA table. It's happy hour. I uncork a bottle of wine. A long week, I say. You sip your wine. Your silver earrings are dangling in a flirty way. The late-afternoon light makes them glitter. I can't take my eyes off your earrings. What are you looking for in a woman? you ask. I didn't expect that, like a bolt of lightning from the clear blue sky. I snap to. What am I looking for? I wonder. I'm clueless. But this is theater and I'm ready to play my part.

I can't tolerate boredom, I say, hoping to sound formidable. If this were a movie, I'd be smoking a cigarette and there'd be low-key lighting. As this is not a movie, what I say sounds lame. Plus it's a lie, as you know. According to the Boredom Proneness Test (which I just took), I don't get bored easy. I don't think, as a matter of fact, I've ever been bored in my life. Anyway, I check your face for a re-action. You are drinking your wine very slowly. I'm mes-merized by your dangling earrings. It dawns on me this is a chess move, your opening question, a very clever one. I'm only now realizing just how clever as my fib takes me deeper into stupid country.

I like complicated women, I say. What do you mean? you ask. Women, I say, who seem full of secrets. I have no idea where this is going. The only reason I say this is because I'm fresh off reading *Crime and Punishment.* I'm drinking and improvising. Folks do this much better in Plato. I'm eating a lot of potato chips too. What does that have to do with a relationship? you wonder. Always on topic. I realize I'm dangerously close to self-parody. The point is to sound a little Dostoyevskian. My initial reading of your type—a smart, no-nonsense intellectual—is that you may have a slight weakness for this sort. You know, to offset things. I'm a difficult guy, that's what I want to project, full of contradictions, but I'm getting lamer and lamer. Too much wine.

Your turn. You tell me about your bike-shop boyfriend. His name is Mike. He's got strong calves and biceps. He owns a shop in Bloomington, Indiana, where he sells pricey Cannondales and Treks. I'm immediately jealous. How close are you to this guy? I ask. You say—get ready—*He's a good fuck.* I'm stunned. Such smutty words from such an exquisite mind. I can't move. I feel calcified. Mike the biker is big, handsome, and robust (you show me his picture), which makes me feel small and shrill. Mike's not a talker, you say. Suddenly I don't want to talk.

Theatrically speaking, you win the game deftly. I try to be alluringly dark and impulsive but you are the one full of surprises. Many years later, I'll remind you of that evening. Do you remember, I say, once in my Capitol Hill apartment—we were drinking a cheap bottle of merlot—when you told me about Mike, your biker boyfriend from Bloomington? You don't say a word. Maybe you have forgotten or maybe you are inwardly cursing my remembering. You said the strangest thing that night (I say)—already your cheeks are a-blush—you said that Mike was, and I quote you, "a good fuck." That was a long time ago, you say, but your face looks like a bowl of cherries.

Naughty Claire disappeared shortly after her debut that afternoon but I've never forgotten her. I often wonder if she was an invented character or an alter ego. She scared me—that you could say that about a guy. I don't think you understood your impact. I was so imperious in my role as angry young man that it was hard for anyone, including you, to see the startled boy behind the Hamlet mask. That was precisely the thing to say to put me in my place. Clever girl. It was difficult to sustain my Hamlet gig after that. No more brooding in the corridor. No more antic disposition. Imagine if Ophelia told Hamlet that he had a small dick but that Rosencrantz (or was it Guildenstern) was a good fuck. Game over.

The naughty-Claire act was a bold trick. As a female intellectual with a promising career, you had to compete with self-absorbed male academics who often enjoyed the unearned benefit of a doubt. Maybe, you might have thought, I was one of these arrogant assholes. Back in the day, these guys were legion. They could be blowhards. They could be abusive. They could and did take advantage of younger women. One professor, you later told me, had a sofa in his office which he kept warm with female grad students. In his office—holy shit! I say. And he didn't get into trouble? He was pretty disgusting. Everyone knew the guy was screwing his students, you say, but it seemed normal at the time. Did you take any classes from him? Sure, but I never stopped by his office alone. English departments were dangerous neighborhoods back then, you add. There were jokes about medieval lays. So you survived to tell the tale? More or less, but I was lucky. Some weren't. It was easy to go off the rails once you crossed that line as a woman. What do you mean *more or less*? I ask. You let the question pass.

I wake in the morning after a vivid dream. For thirty seconds the dream holds its shape. What a peculiar dream, I say to myself, following the narrative in my mind. Unfamiliar people standing in line, high ceilings, morning sunlight. You are there too, right beside me. An appointment at ten a.m. But where have you gone? I turn around and you're not there. My heart sinks. I try calling but can't access the phone app on my cell. My cell is running a different operating system and fixed on an unknown app. For thirty seconds this dream holds its form and then like fog turns to mist. Is that how my life will pass: all the content in my mind, memories, dreams, thoughts, will turn to mist thirty seconds after death? No cell service. The dream exists in the moment. It is momentous. Where have you gone? What I don't know about this dream is what really matters.

CHAPTER FIVE
MARS (THE CONTRARIAN)

I think somebody watching us from Mars—they would think this planet has gone insane.

—Noam Chomsky

Bloomington, 1985. You're a hotshot grad student with a hip hairstyle at the University of Indiana. I have a photo. I try to piece together a story from this picture, even though I have so little info. I can't stop looking for you. No longer home in Cincinnati, you're in your element, surrounded by clever people and admiring professors, folks who recognize your smarts. Self-assured is what you are—poised too. I see also a trace of sexiness. What happened to the timid classicist stacking books four years earlier in the university library? She's gone. You're even flirting with the cameraman.

I am in South Carolina. This place is new to me and a terrific shock. The drive was harrowing. My U-Haul broke down twice in the Poconos. Charleston, such a weird town. It's my first teaching job and I feel so far out of my element I want to hide. Many of my colleagues are white Southerners. They're out to get me. That's my first impression. I haven't even unpacked my boxes and I'm scared of white Southerners. How did I wind up here? I don't even feel white anymore. That's my second impression. There's talk in the hallway, I learn later, that I'm gay because I'm unmarried. Wow, I say to my informant. Yes, there are informants in my new department, which thrives on intrigue and innuendo. Also, I learn, machinations are afoot. So soon? I say. I won't even mention the pesky bugs (chiggers, sand gnats, fleas, ticks, no-see-ums, fire ants, jumping spiders, black widows). And the cockroaches—they're not only huge but they fly—zillions of them. That's my third impression: so many biting insects.

What a traumatic arrival. I never told you the full story. I had survived the Cold War only to wind up here, in the Carolina Low Country. Such a spectacularly beautiful place, but insidious. I wasn't the only misfit in Charleston. There were others. Like POWs, we formed a close circle and fed off one another's paranoia, always on guard against the plots of our senior colleagues. Our crime: we're not from the South. Worse, we're godless smart alecks. Especially me.

Charleston may have changed since Hurricane Hugo, but before then the college was a backwater. On pain of censure, we are told to flunk any student who makes three or four grammatical errors in the course of a five-page narrative. Come again? we say. It's all right here in the *minimum standards sheet*, says the chair, who wears absurd electric-green golf pants. His name is Norm. He is tall with curly red hair. He smiles a lot but without conviction. Norm passes out the mimeographed sheet to each of us: Pam, Rob, Mike, and me. On it is a list of unpardonable sins, like dangling modifiers and such. Okay, Norm, we hypothesize, say you tell a story about an old-timer who makes moonshine with sharecroppers in the woods of South Carolina, maybe he's your uncle, and you tell it with flare and suspense, rendering the chase scenes with the AFT—*vroom, vroom*!—particularly vivid. And let's say the story contains two forceful sentence fragments, an effective comma splice, and one dubious dangling modifier. But the story is so good it's like Tom Wolfe all over again. It's an automatic fail, says Norm. What's so hard to understand about that?

Low Country students are good storytellers but they can't tell a run-on from a flat tire. We can't flunk these kids. It's unconscionable. This was the land time had forgot. The humidity is Jurassic. Even the insects seem larger than normal. At night shadowy creatures with twelve-foot wingspans fly overhead. There are manatees and sea cows in the Cooper River. Live oaks drip with Spanish moss on Montague Street. At first, it all seems like a Pat Conroy novel. The place is scarred by a troubled history and the locals are on edge. We could live with that. But once the good old boys take arms against junior faculty, we all scramble out of there. We had seen the harm done to J, a popular and productive teacher who was the casualty of a vicious tenure case. I was the first to leave because I am fast on foot. I was soon followed by others. *Exeunt omnes.*

When I think back, I often seem to be on the run. My dad will advise me to slow down. Stop and smell the roses, he'll say. Who has time for that? I'll say. Maybe I should have lingered longer, taken in the sea breezes. After Charleston, I moved to Washington where we met. Had I stopped to smell the roses, this doesn't happen.

Speaking of flowers, I have to tell you about the floral arrangements at your memorial service. One bouquet after the next, gaudy flowers with satin bows, Asiatic lilies, fuchsia carnations, pink roses, chrysanthemums, green hydrangea, larkspur, gerbera daisies. Mike the undertaker delivered them after your service. I could hardly find room for the flowers, which looked and smelled like an aromatic mortuary. In minutes they started drooping and shriveling. Cut flowers begin wilting at thirty-four degrees. It was much warmer than that. The lilies and roses were the first to go, turning flaccid, and then the gerbera slumped, the carnation petals curled up, and the red gladiolus just crumpled. The doom of the flowers was haunting. I braved the slimy glass vases, recut the ends of stems, tossed in vodka, and read Billy Collins poetry out loud—to no effect. The flowers perished *en masse*. It was sad. It took days to dispose of the once-pretty flowers.

I'm flipping through photos and find one of Ulysses the cat. We rename him Pooka because Ulysses really doesn't fit. He's a born stalker and a little spooky. Here's a photo of Pooka in Vermont. We are at Bread Loaf near Middlebury. You're teaching summer school and Pooka and I are along for the ride. We're staying in a high-ceilinged old room with the Green Mountains out the window. The wooden floorboards are wide slabs of pine. No screens, no air-conditioning. The cat has just come in through an open window with something in its mouth. He has caught a mole. We are both awake, listening to crunching sounds. Pooka is crushing the mole's tiny skull. It's a shrew mole. He'll leave the remains for us to handle in the morning. How many decapitated bodies have we buried so far? Little velvety figures often turn up by the bedposts: itty-bitty pools of blood where their heads should be. Mountain shrews. Such a blood-thirsty cat, I say. He likes animal brains, you say. Little ones. It's a delicacy. The cat looks at me suspiciously, wishing I were smaller.

Pooka likes being out of the city, so do we. Idyllic green everywhere you look. There's Vermont cheddar cheese and wine at five in the barn. That's my favorite hour. We arrive before others to avoid the socializing, and there it is, a giant slab of white cheddar. I pour two glasses of white wine. Here's to your health. Salut, you say. I think we brought our canoe along, which was really stupid, and our bikes. In the mornings, while you're teaching, I ride up the road toward Middlebury Gap. Surrounded by birch trees, I dodge the little red-spotted newts crossing Route 125. They're everywhere, the juveniles, red efts. By the time I return, another headless shrew awaits me. On weekends, we drive into town and eat mud pies on Otter Creek. Whenever we can, we head up Route 7 to Burlington and lie on a blanket at Waterfront Park beside Lake Champlain. We have to fight off the churlish Québécois for space. The Canadians are noisy and obnoxious, which surprises us. We think only Americans are abominable. Then it's over to the Metropole downtown for a glass of wine.

We've only been married two months but already I could never imagine life without you. The return drive up the mountain is difficult. We try not to run over red newts. So many salamanders plodding across the roads at night. In the morning we find a hundred flattened efts. Dried out in the sun they look like fried bacon. After we do a count, we mourn their loss. On Sunday, we follow the theater people to their swimming hole, a small mountain lake rimmed by huge blocks of granite. The water is deep, dark, and cold. I'm afraid to swim. Little signs are posted: *Beware of Leeches*. I hate leeches. This doesn't bother you. A water girl, you dive in and go through your strokes. You in your green bathing suit. Nice legs, I say. No they're not, you say. My calves are too big. No they're not, I say. Yes they are, you insist. I'm sitting on the rocks, safe from the slimy slithering shadowy things in the water. But I'm still searching in my shorts for leeches. I keep looking down at my crotch. I won't even dangle my toes in the lake. This makes you smile. I'm checking your body for leeches as your climb out of the water. I know they're around some- where. You have goose bumps on your thighs. Pretty legs. We've brought along tuna fish sandwiches, but I won't eat mine. Finally, someone in the water yells, Leech! I feel vindicated.

Tiny flashes of light in the nebula of memory. Pleiad Lake, your green bathing suit, leeches, my jitters, your laughter, granite rocks, tuna fish sandwiches neatly packed for lunch. You sparkle in my mind, light up my narrative. It's all I have left. How different the bewilder- ment I wake to each morning. I am in the shadows. You are my light. I feel silly writing that. I'm not a poet and yet I am sometimes bewitched by language. It's the summer solstice and out my window I hear festive voices, carous- ing twenty-year-olds at play in the streets. There's a block party. If only I could join them. Death is on my mind. How could it be otherwise? The quieter you become, I've read, the more you hear.

The natural cycle may seem uniform and predictable but it's not. It's moody, chaotic, and violent. Things turn on and off in nature with little forewarning. Stunningly volatile. I've been watching. Everything moves, nothing remains still. Men and women, like candles in the dark, are kindled and then snuffed out. So says Heraclitus. Today is the first day of fall, in theory, but the heat wave lingers on in these parts. Almost ninety degrees for the third day in a row. Some of the trees are beginning to turn. I saw a maple go up in flames near Hickory Hill Park. Small-leaf trees are losing hair by the minute. Birch, elm, locust, walnut, beech. One black walnut let loose a snowfall of yellow leaves in the wind, a surplus of form and color, bursting into beauty and then dispersed in a cloud of particles. Walnuts plunging, leaves swirling, dogs barking, schoolkids screaming—life's stirring racket—never so feisty as when in flux. And yet you expect to be sad in the fall, Hemingway wrote. Part of you dies each year when the leaves fall and the branches are left bare against the wind.

Literary types are infatuated with sadness, as if it were seductive. Poignant beauty and all. A student once asked me why we read depressing stories in English classes. I said (insincerely) because humans are mostly miserable, mostly. The student said he wasn't miserable. I said it's early in the game. Motivational speakers advise against sadness, as if it were an exceptionally bad form of trans fat. They talk of six steps to living in the moment. When you become mindful, they say, you realize that you are not your thoughts. Not a great tip for a writer. For me the simplest diversion is tracking you down in memory. The comedy of our life together twinkles in my mind. Love is funny, in flashback. Venus, the prankster.

Our first encounter. I'm wearing a colorful tie, 100 percent silk. It's an Italian tie, I think, though the label says, *Made in Korea.* Anyway, it's colorful, if not flamboyant, with splashes of red, yellow, blue, black, and green. I'm not a tie guy, but moving to Washington has changed that. Everyone wears ties here, even in the English department at George Washington University. It's the ethos of the village, a necessary formality. I don't go in for blue blazers or shiny loafers from Neiman Marcus, but I've taken a fancy to gaudy ties.

That's a new development. I'm evolving, I think. That's not all: I am about to become the department rogue. I'm making fun of my betters. Just yesterday I told the chair, who has a Beatles haircut, that his John Lennon look was too cool for words but that the aviator glasses had to go. That's right, he had on tinted aviator glasses—remember? He's a Melville guy, and most of the Americanists at George Washington are kind of weird. What's worse, I'm reveling in my rascal-like behavior. Every word that comes out of my mouth is derisive. How baffling. Everyone is very nice here, don't get me wrong. I'm sure it's me. My prior job has tainted my mind. Some serious creepiness in Charleston. And now I'm taking it out on the good folks of GW. It's not fair but life never is.

Oddly enough, my colleagues tolerate my bad behavior: scowling in the hallway, mumbling to myself, arguing with senior colleagues, provoking others. I'm doing everything a junior faculty member shouldn't. My irreverence is a little shocking. What's happening to me? I wonder. I've become irritable and intolerant and feel increasingly out of place among my own kind. Here comes Bob Ganz down the hall, another Americanist. He's an affable guy, he's whistling in fact, but the moment he spots me he ducks into Jon Quitslund's office. It's a desperate vanishing act, as though he's just seen a flesh-eating zombie. I smile. I enjoy the menacing act. If only they knew.

Connie, the administrative boss and de facto chair, relishes my roguishness and eggs me on. She tells me what colleagues are saying behind my back, which makes me even more ill-tempered. For her, it's a nice change from the usual. I'm entertaining. We drink beer together on weekends and poke fun at others. We even plan capers, like hacking files from the chair's office. I should be embarrassed recalling this, but I don't know, I kind of miss it, breaking bad. A little deviltry wouldn't hurt the industry today, moribund as it seems. Behind my badness, I think, was class resentment. Many of our colleagues have Ivy League degrees, and some are partnered to wealthy and powerful politicos. They command large homes in the more exclusive parts of Cleveland Park. I myself, poor slob, live in a basement apartment in a part of town where Ted Koppel of *Nightline* appears every now and then to tape a show on urban conflict. Ted's very friendly. My neighborhood less so. Washington, a divided city, Ted says on TV in that wry and measured way of his.

That's how it goes for a year. I'm lonely and alienated, polishing up my Hamlet routine (*nay madam*), when you, Claire, show up. Just in the nick of time. Who's the malcontent stalking the corridors? you ask Connie. Don't mind him, she says, he's pissed off at everybody. I pretend not to see you walking out of Connie's office because, well, I'm really into this Hamlet thing. I've even memorized his major soliloquies. *What's Hecuba to him or he to Hecuba?* It lowers my blood pressure, which is counterintuitive. Now that you're here, I keep my office door open and sneak a look as you round the corner. I like the way you walk—more sway than you'd think. You often catch me peeking but I pretend to be deep in thought. You're not fooled.

Amazingly, you fall for the department rogue. Connie has put in a good word for me, explains how my raffish spirit has livened things up. You've seen my type before, nothing you can't handle, but that tie! You're thinking of the navy-blue one with daffy pink elephants. My god, why does he wear those strange ties? you ask Connie. He's worn them all year, Connie says. It's kind of weird. I think he was going for a hipster look. You laugh. Later, you'll tell me I looked like Soupy Sales. Such a goofy tie, you say. That's when I knew you weren't a conceited jerk. No one, you go on, wears a tie like that. I have, like, the coolest ties in Washington, I protest. You smile back. It takes me awhile to recover my mojo.

Why did you fall for me? I was atypical, I'm guessing, but highly spirited. Later, you'll tell me I seemed troubled and unpredictable, and that's why you found me attractive in the first place. I was a paradox. I had dashing hair back then and a complicated form of arrogance. Not really arrogance, but not really not. I wasn't a careerist, didn't fetishize my résumé. Above all, I was bitterly sarcastic. You liked that best, my sarcasm. But my sarcasm was clearly out of whack, and this may have scared you a little. Frankly, it scared me. I never knew what I'd say next. Thank goodness the classroom was a Hamlet-free zone. The kids were fine. It was the good-natured adults who triggered the angry, brooding devil in me. The details are boring but you remember. Like Connie, you found me amusing, but you were puzzled why I didn't just play along. Obviously, this angry-young-man thing, you said, is unsustainable. Everyone plays along. It's just a game, you remind me. I was puzzled too. I sometimes felt like Edward Scissorhands.

An atmospheric early autumn morning. It's a leafy world today and squirrels are yapping and so are the magpies and crows. The nut-laden trees are flourishing: black walnuts, hickories, pecans. An abundant nut crop is good for the local ecosystem. I can hear squirrels gnawing on the shells of walnuts. Starlings are jabbering high up in the maples, drowning out the helicopter overhead. The sound of October. Someone is mulching fallen maple leaves on Reno Street. On Center Street AM radio is blaring Top 40 music while a potbellied painter squeezes caulk around the kitchen window. Our patio stones, by the way, are a mess this year, thanks to the walnuts. The tree excretes an allopathic chemical to drive out competition. Juglone is the evil element exuded by all parts of the walnut tree, including the fruit's green husk, which is as toxic as an herbicide and is in fact sometimes used as a weed killer. It inhibits plant respiration. But I digress.

I'm still sleeping on my side of the bed. If I don't encroach on your space, maybe you'll come back. Your gardening clothes are neatly folded on the laundry basket in the bathroom, just as you left them. Every morning I visit your study and recharge your phone. I make sure your laptop is running smoothly and open the slats on your blinds. It looks like your calendar is outdated—I'll get a new one. Quo vadis? I check your ink cartridges, sharpen you pencils. Apparently this often happens to widowers who can't let go of their wives. I heard of one man who kept his first wife's clothing on a mannequin by the front door for over a year.

Suzanne Witte from the hospital e-mailed me today with a report on your body parts, what the extracting surgeons took and where they went. As we are nearing Halloween, the timing is impeccable. *Good morning, Jeff,* Suzanne writes. *I want to fill you in regarding Claire's donation.* Such a harmless word for such a grisly business, as if we were talking about the Pew Charitable Trust. Your liver, Suzanne says (without irony), went to a fifty-year-old male—no names, of course—who now feels well enough to play golf again. Your right kidney went to a fifty-five-year-old woman, a nurse, who is married and has three children and as many grandchildren. After spending the past four years on dialysis, she is on the mend. Your left kidney went to a sixty-eight-year-old man who is married with one child and is a retired mechanic. He too was on dialysis for four years and is now besides himself with joy to be free of the machine. Your lungs are going for research. In the biopsy, they did spot a nodule on your lung, but it was scar tissue from an old infection. Otherwise, your body parts are in splendid shape. Had your brain not exploded—here's the painful news—you would have lived to at least ninety, probably longer, like your centenarian Uncle Steve. Imagine that. Despite my grumbling, I know you are happy to hear that parts of you have been recycled on behalf of good working people.

There was, however, one curious complication I should mention. During exhaustive interrogation by the donation coordinator, I was asked several questions of a highly personal manner. I was asked if I took drugs or had relations with prostitutes. They wished to make sure you weren't married to a hazardous-waste site. This to verify the purity of your tissues. I chuckled no to heroin and no to hookers. Have you ever had sexual relations with any-one from Africa? I was asked. What do you mean? This was getting weird. Then I was asked if I ever had an ani-mal bone graft. Well, yes, as it turns out, several years ago when I had a dental implant. The surgeon used bovine biomass for the graft. I got red-flagged for that, which meant they couldn't donate your corneas or your tissue. Essentially because you kissed someone with cow bone in his mouth, someone with the teeniest chance of develop-ing bovine spongiform encephalopathy. They were afraid that, along with my French kisses, I had given you mad cow disease.

The day you collapsed keeps replaying in my head, looping over and over. An ordinary Wednesday in late summer. Mild, sunny, busy day. The plumber would be by any minute now. He would tell us how urgent the water leak was, whether or not we could travel east. You asked me why I never chopped fruit in the morning for break-fast. I said it was unforgivable of me to be so lazy, that I was myself puzzled by my unhelpfulness. You said you were surprised by my gracious reply. Those were your last words as you climbed the stairs for your morning yoga. Your last words. You were surprised. It was just an ordinary Wednesday morning in late summer. The sun was shining, the black-eyed Susans were in bloom. You can sense life unfolding all around and it's such a myste-rious feeling, but deep inside my belly is the aching reality of loss. It's hardening like a rock, like Martian glass. I carry this polished stone wherever I go, and I know what it means. There are no answers. Obsidian is the form of not knowing. We were to drive east, to Cincinnati first to visit your mom. Then on to Buffalo to see mine. The widow tour, we called this. Two women who lost their husbands, who were lonely. I had a queasy feeling because of the water leak. It was probably a ground leak in the main line, and we feared the worst. The tearing up of the front lawn at thousands of dollars. The real leak was in your brain upstairs—how ironic. Carl Jung would call this synchronicity, as though the house and you were bleeding in sync.

As I write, the wind is roaring out my window. The wind rises and falls and troubles the ear, swells and surges. It's a sound that makes small animals seek cover. Out of nowhere comes the wind, with hey, ho, the wind and the rain. When I close my eyes, the house rattles. I feel small, like a crumpled old man lost on the heath. I have only words to speak to you by. That's all that's left. How do I tell you I love you in a way that does not seem trite? Your olive-green khakis and yellow-checked shirt, what you would wear later that Wednesday, are still folded on the laundry hamper in the bathroom. The smell of your body lingers here. Your shirt is wet from tears. Love doesn't know itself until the hour of separation. I forgot who said this. I just keep hearing voices. The emptiness is filled with voices.

I received a pamphlet today from the organ donor network which offered guidance in writing your organ recipients. They suggest that sharing information about you with these people will help with the grieving process, as they put it. Communicating with recipients may not be easy, however. *Sometimes the hardest part is writing those first few words*, the pamphlet says.

Let me give it a try. *Dear right kidney recipient (whoever you are), let me say how glad I am that a part of my wife now lives on inside of you. My wife, you may be interested to know, was a woman with a strong mind and an invincible spirit whose force of character was so great it pervaded even the smallest nook and cranny of her being. Do not be surprised then, dear right kidney recipient, if in the middle of the night that spirit wakes and decides to run the show. Your show. You'll know your days are numbered when your thoughts suddenly become crystal clear and your sense of duty increases tenfold. My advice to you, when that happens, is run. As fast as you can.* That wasn't so hard—I could in fact do this all day. The pamphlet recommends using "simple language." Check. It also recommends referring to the donor's passions or interests. Check. Lastly, the pamphlet suggests explaining the circumstances behind the organ donation. That would mean writing about Creon. I've said enough about him. I notice with alarm that my letter must be approved not only by the donor network but by the transplant center. Fat chance.

A mild mid-October day. The alley is a mess. More black walnuts. Yard work was something we did as a couple. How strange to be standing here by myself—with two brooms. I have one broom for docile leaves, another for stubborn. Obviously I don't need a pair of brooms, but I can't help myself. They are a prop for the idea of twoness. The twoness of nature is something so profound it can't really be put in words. All I know is that once we achieved twoness, life was never the same. As I sweep under the viburnum, I'm slashed by an overhanging branch. The viburnum thinks I'm the one who butchered the large black walnut tree across the alley, and not the utility company. I need to wear a bike helmet around this bush. All of the walnuts are gone. Last year, you circled the yard with the blue bucket, collecting the final fall. You in your straw hat and khakis. So hawk-eyed a gardener, you didn't miss one. There were hundreds to gather in various stages of decay. I've gathered them in that bucket too, for continuity's sake—an oily mess—but I failed to spot a dozen or so. I'm not good with my eyes. Soon I'll have to hang the storm windows, weed the side bed, and find new plantings for the southeast corner of the house. You were scrupulous about yard work, so I wanted to give you a full report.

I have been feeling a bit shaky. I didn't want to let on because I know this will concern you. I don't think it's a medical thing. I mostly feel this way around the edge of things, like stairways and steps. It's as if my umwelt has changed without me knowing it. The small subset of signals I've been trained to detect has shifted in subtle ways. The truth is I haven't much confidence left. Past midnight, alone in a chair. No lights and such silence. The earth might be abandoned.

I rewind the tape in my head a few months back. It's late June in Dublin, a month before you died. We're walking along the Grand Canal toward Lower Baggot Street. It's early evening. Rush-hour traffic has slowed and most pedestrians are home. It's cloudy but doesn't look like rain. We're in sweaters and jeans. The canal looks haunted, the tassel weed and eelgrass swaying with the current, long, bright, ribbon-like leaves. A fresh breeze blows as a bottle of stout stands up in the canal, and beyond that a submerged orange traffic cone. Along the canal on benches are young lovers, Russian, Muslim, Polish, and Chinese. Cyclists are returning home with baguettes and sacks of fish and chips. Canal boats are docked along the bank for hire. We watch for little dogs on after-dinner walks. We spot a white Westie crossing Wilton Terrace and you poke my arm and say, Isn't that the actor? I look up and see, yes, an actor. It's Littlefinger of *Game of Thrones* on foot with his terrier. Previously, Tommy Carcetti of *The Wire*, the combative politician. We stand still and gawk at Littlefinger, the Irish actor Aidan Gillen out with his jolly Westie, while he sits on a park bench just below lock forty-three. Mr. Gillen pulls out his mobile and takes a phone call. The Westie looks at his reflection in the canal. You and I gaze and ogle, too shy to approach any closer. I give an enthusiastic wave of my hand. Littlefinger gives a weary one back. We return to our apartment with a carton of Tesco Tomato & Basil Soup (your favorite) and reminisce about *The Wire*.

Its violence is unwatchable, you said of *Game of Thrones*. I said, Yes, for sure. You watched all of five minutes on my recommendation, and then left the TV room. I later promised to avoid the show when Eddard Stark lost his head but I watched in secret. We crossed paths once more with Aidan Gillen in Dublin and chatted amiably with him and his Westie. A bit shy and soft-spoken, he seemed too good-natured for his notorious roles on TV. What does he do on that TV show you watch? you asked later. He's a skilled manipulator and master of brothels, Lord Petyr Baelish, and not be trifled with, I say a bit too enthusiastically. You laugh. Quite the fan, you say.

We are still on Baggot Street and I'm reminiscing for some reason. Remember that day in Washington, I say, when we walked by the Desert Storm parade on the Mall? Just after the first Gulf War? The floats, the military bands, the tanks and missiles. Yes, sure, you say. Why? Those two antiwar protesters, I say, they were just kids, walled in by an angry flag-waving mob. The crowd was teeming and unfriendly, and the teenagers were trapped in the middle like Dorothy by the witch and her Winkie guards. We were close to the fray. You were so upset by the mob's hostility, I go on, you waltzed into the center of the circle and shook hands with the protesters for solidarity's sake. There were three hundred flag-waving, nasty xenophobes. I couldn't believe it. I was waiting for serious consequences but nothing happened. I don't remember doing that, you say. I do, I say. Remarkable, really. Did you join me? you ask. No way, too timid. I'm just an ordinary guy. But you, such nerve, I say. You roll your eyes.

I can't do that, roll my eyes, not like you. Makes me dizzy. Monkeys can't either. People have been rolling eyes since before Shakespeare, but the gesture had a different meaning then—sexual desire. Fancy that. Eye rolling today is big with teenage girls, accompanied by the tossing back of the head. You were married to such an absurd guy the eye roll was a necessity, not as a sign of contempt so much as benign acknowledgment of the fact.

Anyway, Mars is a planet with a violent past. Space Boy said he could barely see it in his rearview mirror. All that dust. He chose to zoom past the red planet. A shame really, as it has such an interesting past. Evidence of fierce volcanic activity is ample, and so are signs of massive impacts early in the planet's history. Quite a thing to witness, I imagine, were one present then, around-the-clock explosions and debris raining down from the sky. You wouldn't know if this were a world starting up or winding down. Add to that solar winds, charged particles traveling a million miles per hour, which stripped the planet's surface down to its rocks and then peeled away most of its atmosphere.

The sun was younger and more ferocious back in the day. Global storms have and continue to rage over its surface. When *Mariner 9* arrived to take pictures in 1972, Mars was engulfed in a massive cloud of particles that obscured the entire planet. The satellite never got to click a picture. The storms are so bad they can be seen from here with a telescope, some fifty million miles away. No surprise that Mars is the rockiest planet in the solar system. For me Mars was a flyby, Space Boy reported. Not dropping in on that mess. Understood, I radioed back. Life is difficult enough.

Mars, the red planet, was named by the Romans after their god of war—obviously. Who would know better that business? Given the planet's past and present violence, though, it seems a lucky choice. To the naked eye, Mars was the red planet, and the Romans—being the Romans— saw red and thought *fire* and *blood*. This nuttiness doesn't end there. According to Roman myth, Mars rode on a chariot pulled by two horses named Phobos and Deimos (*fear* and *panic*). And thus were the red planet's moons so named, after horses. A moon named after a horse. That's how the rocks in the sky got their names. What could be sillier? If I could, I would roll my eyes. Imagine I am. By the way, did you ever wonder why the folks on *Star Trek* never took photos? Certainly not for lack of gadgets.

My last photos of you were taken on opposite ends of Ireland, where the setting was so remote as to seem not of this world. We drove from Dublin to Galway and stopped at the usual places, the Cliffs of Moher and the Burren, and the following day took a ferry to the Aran Islands. And so here you are, right now, on the Isle of Inishmore. We are on a walking tour with the study-abroad kids, led by the impeccable Cyril Ó Flaithearta. The weather has been typically volatile for these parts. Cold and raining one moment, hot and sunny the next. Always blustery, though. You grab onto your straw hat lest it blow into the Atlantic. Down the stony road we go, Cyril out in front, you and me in the rear, keeping an eye on the strays. There are a few waifs in this group. Some of these kids shouldn't be on their own so far from home, you say. No kidding, I say. Cyril is hustling so we might make it to the other end of the island, to the cliffs of Dún Aonghasa that beetle o'er the sea. But that's unlikely given the leisurely pace of this bunch. A keen walker, you have the stamina of a medieval pilgrim and are the only one among us who can keep up step for step with hardy Cyril.

I myself am still reeling from the forty-five-minute ferry boat ride from Rossaveel to the islands, half of which I spent in the bathroom doubled over. You look like a drowned fish, you say, and as green as the sea. I'm like the waifs—how embarrassing—and keep pushing myself to keep up with the pilgrimage. This little journey perks you up, medievalist that you are. A stone cairn ahead grabs your attention. It's a roadside cenotaph, you point out. This one says, *Oh Lord Have Mercy on the Soul of Duane O'Brien*, and dates back to the mid-nineteenth century. I trace the inscription with my finger. There are more dead than living here, you say matter-of-factly. The island is thirty-one square kilometers, you add, with a population of barely eight hundred people. Maybe why Inishmore seems inhabited only by rocks and stones and the dead. What a strange place, I say.

There may be no holy blissful martyr on this trail, but many shrines lie ahead. It's half a day's walk across Inishmore. The island is otherworldly, with its Glacio-Karst landscape. Slabs of limestone everywhere, what are called *clints*, you say. Such a stony place we've never seen before. All of this building material but so few structures. Imagine clearing garden space here, you say. Everywhere the eye looks, rectangular shale and limestone, bare rock. It's like the beginning or culmination of something, you suggest—hard to know which.

It starts raining and you pull out an umbrella from your cloth bag, but it's so blustery the umbrella is turned inside out. We huddle together near the cairn until the mist and rain pass. Later we returned to Galway and walked down to Ballyloughane beach to get away from the kids. We could see the Burren Mountains to the south. The tide was out as we walked along the footpath. Estuary coastal water: seaweeds and crabs and a multitude of sand hoppers. It was almost dusk. Not far out, we watched a man and two horses enter the shallows. One horse was reluctant to go farther into the sea, but the man insisted with a light lash. Three dogs let loose by their owners ran circles around the horses, and one got kicked in the butt for being a nuisance. The air was chilly and damp. Farther out, gray skies gave way to blue.

We turned back up the bike path lined with wildflowers, yellow ragwort, and foxgloves. Irishmen are flyfishing for trout in the River Corrib. In three weeks you will be gone. How are we to know this? I have a photo of you walking beside the wildflowers in your cheap sneakers and black quilt jacket. Your blond locks are wooly with sea air. You sway to the rhythm of the wind. You have never been happier. Ireland is like a second home. Its gray skies and coolish climate are so agreeable you want to return next summer, walk along the stony road of Inish-more, circle the well of the four beauties, look up at the seabirds. Yes, I say. For sure. I could do without the child care, but sure, if that's what you want.

Neither of us knows that you have been marked by death. Does anyone know? It will come without any warning, not at night but in broad daylight. Blood is flowing through your brain at a rate of 750 milliliters per second, 15 percent of your cardiac output, as you walk along the wildflowers on Ballyloughane Road. And there is already a bulge in the wall of a cerebral vessel. This is the terrible secret your body is keeping from you. Such a betrayal. The bulge is getting bigger. It's like a little balloon swelling with blood. You should feel dizzy, you should feel a migraine coming on, but you have never felt better. Treachery. The blonde with sea air in the photo should live to be ninety—at least. Why aren't your pupils dilated? Why aren't you having trouble speaking? Why isn't your brain screaming out, like Cassandra, Stop everything! It's less than half an inch in diameter, fix it now, an inborn abnormality in my artery wall. Lend me ten thousand eyes and I will fill them with tears.

CHAPTER SIX
PHOBOS
(BRINGER OF TERROR)

*Thus Ares spoke and ordered Phobos and Deimos
to harness his horses, while he himself put on his
gleaming armor.*

—Homer

*I*n Greek mythology, Phobos is the god of panic and
was said to accompany Ares into battle. He appears in several tragedies and even on the shields
of Achilles in Homer and Heracles in Hesiod. Along with
the Gorgon, he belongs to the genre of dreadful heads. To
gaze on the face of Medusa (a Gorgon) was catastrophic.
Those who did were petrified by terror, literally turned
to stone. Phobos also aspired to great heights of horror, if
we can trust the ancients, but such was not his fate. Phobos lost his prestige by the eighteenth century when he
was psychologized—reduced to a *phobia*. The modern encyclopedia of phobias includes several bizarre examples,
such as *papaphobia*, fear of the pope. Ironically, Phobos,

Mars' potato-shaped moon, has good cause itself to fear as it gradually spirals inward toward the planet. (*Basiphobia*, fear of falling.) Eventually, Phobos will break apart to form a Saturn-like ring or will simply crash, kaboom, into the red planet.

I expect you home in fifteen minutes. I warm up my coffee in the kitchen and wait for your arrival. I have to remind myself that won't happen. All was not perfectly well in Dublin. You were jumpy, remember, shadowed by a strange sense of dread. Even in cheerful Ireland, which is (by the way) happier than the UK, Germany, and France, according to the UN. Anyway, you were anxious. In our small Dublin apartment it was hard for a stumble-bum like me not to kick a table leg or drop a plate. Little accidents startled you, even provoked small screams, as though our building had been seized by ISIS. But it was only my clumsiness. Oops, there goes my coffee cup. You shriek. Why so tense? I ask. You make me nervous, you're so accident prone, you say. That's true, I say, but still. It seems deeper than that, your uneasiness. The Milo syndrome, I wonder, haunted by a dead dog? No, you are worried about me, you say, that I will find a way to do injury to myself in my carelessness, that I might do damage to my brain. I think you were afraid for my brain. You didn't want to see me on life support, like Leo in *Twin Peaks*.

Dread was new. When we first met, you were known for your composure. Everyone counted on you for balance and poise. Just being near you calmed me down. I first sensed the change two summers ago traveling to the Northwest, when, for once, we didn't take work along. You drank beer with me in Portland, even liked it. We took long walks on the beach. We played our dice game. We flew there partly to see your niece Lauren but also to drive along the ocean and over mountains, to be immersed in epic geography. It had been years since I lived there. I wanted to see the ocean with you, and so we wandered out of Portland and over to the Pacific Highway.

Route 101 winds down from the Columbia River in Astoria all the way to California, but even the mere 184 miles we drove to Florence took almost three days. The twisting highway, much of it high above the sea, took us close to the edge. There was little between you and the ocean hundreds of feet below. On my side, an impenetrable wall of old-growth forest, hemlock, Douglas fir, and cedar. We stopped frequently, if only to halt the vertigo. The monoliths at Cannon Beach, Thor's Well, Cape Perpetua. There, Devil's Churn throws the white spray of the mad sea hundreds of feet into the air. When the right tide comes in, the sea surges upward from the bowl carved out of volcanic rock that rims the shore and then drains back down the giant hole. It's like the opening to the underworld in Homer, and if you look long enough at the mesmerizing uprush you can hear the voices of Sirens just above the clamoring sea.

It's easy enough to write these pretty words now, two thousand miles away from the ocean. When we stood fifty feet from Thor's Well together, looking down at the crazy black hole in the sea, we just gazed in wonder, wiping the salt spray from our glasses. We were silent. It was a form of dread and beauty. How many thousands of years did this take? you asked. One feels outside of time here, where seawater settles in translucent pools of memory, safe from the corrosion of words. I can't imagine we'll never walk along the beach again. I can't. It breaks my spirit. There are no words for this.

On to Eugene, where I had once lived as a grad student. We stopped at the Sundance Market on 24th Street on our way back to our flat. I forgot to turn on the car's headlights when we left the market and moments later was pulled over by the police. It was a dark night. I should have sensed something but I wasn't thinking straight. Most cars run their headlights all day. I can't remember the last time I flipped the light switch. A bad lapse as I was well oiled when the officer came around and knocked on your window. You were terrified. I thought you might pass out or give me up. Officer, arrest that man. He's drunk and out of his mind. He scared the living daylights out of me yesterday along the coastal highway, trying to pass the tractor trailer on a hairpin turn! I was alarmed too and expected the worse. I'd spend the night in jail (maybe two) and lose my license. What would you do? We didn't even know our way back to our Airbnb. It was pitch-black out. There'd be a breathalyzer test, of course, and my blood alcohol level would come back at 0.080—technically drunk. In Oregon, a DUI charge is severe: the first offense is forty-eight hours in jail, a two-thousand-dollar fine, and a one-year suspended license.

The last time I was pulled over by a cop, the guy almost locked me up for not using my left turn signal at a busy intersection. Just imagine what I was in for now, having really broken the law. These dire calculations were going through your mind more quickly than mine. I could see your brain twitching as you processed the likely outcome. We still had hundreds of miles to drive, and here I was in my old college town about to be tossed in the slammer. Have you been drinking? the officer asked. Just a glass of wine with dinner, officer, we both said. Maybe two. Like anyone else terrified in the presence of the law, we were servile and obsequious. I had an absurd smile on my face. I kept nodding yes to imaginary questions. The officer looked into my eyes keenly, searching for sobriety, and I nearly peed my pants. He got out his ticket book. Then by the grace of god, or some guardian spirit, the good-natured officer gave us a short lecture on the necessity of headlights and the challenges of nighttime driving. Only a warning. No jail time, no ticket. Yes, officer, absolutely. Never again. Don't worry.

Thank goodness I didn't slur my words. You were still in a state of terror and didn't say a word—not even a *phew*. It was a night full of unexpected close calls. We were glad to find our way back to the Airbnb, but you were so upset with me you wouldn't sleep with me that night. We were 2,500 miles from home, only sixty miles from the Pacific Ocean, closer to a real edge than ever before, and you were so frightened it was unsettling. You were aware of something I wasn't, an extremity beyond the mind or the vast sea. Deep in your intuitive heart, you detected an edge whose danger sign flashed some dire forewarning. What it said I'll never know, but something more than a traffic ticket was at work.

The next day, you had recovered your spirits. We had yogurt and honey for breakfast—yogurt was your soul food—and said goodbye to Eugene. We were about to drive up the McKenzie River into the mountains on a tree-lined highway, through Douglas firs so dense it was like traveling through a tunnel. We passed guys in hip waders angling for salmon and fly-fishers after rainbow trout.

We passed lilies and ferns and bear grass and lupine and mountain ash. Waterfalls and covered bridges, cyclists in bright Lycra outfits. The road through the McKenzie Pass is a winding one—and steep—as we drove up the foothills of the Deschutes National Forest toward Mount Washington. We both gazed out the car window at the charred remains of ponderosa pine and white fir, thousands of ruined trees above Blue Lake, from the Bear Butte fire twelve years ago, when flames burned over ninety thousand acres of forest. We had entered the volcanic zone. The Belknap Crater was on our left and the snowcapped Sisters out your window, dormant volcanoes. Towering above was Mount Washington. On either side, hundreds of miles of black lava fields and the fiery kingdom of Mordor, broken only by straggling mountain hemlock and the chalky ghosts of whitebark pine. As if there had been a great war between good and evil, the jagged peaks broke the sky.

As the Camry climbed above the tree line through the McKenzie Pass, you became agitated and shaky, acrophobic maybe. Slow down, you said, and keep your eyes on the road. Me and my wandering eyes—I couldn't take them off the lava fields and mountains lakes. I turned and saw how tensely you were holding onto the dash for security.

Here in the mountain pass I see terror on your face. Some kind of subliminal fear has slipped behind your eyes. Sixty-one percent of forty- to fifty-nine-year-olds are afraid of heights, something that worsens with age. Maybe that's it. These winding mountain roads are catching up with you, wearing down your ordinary sense of calm. You'll be fine once we reach Bend on the other side of the Cascade Range. But up here, among the volcanoes and lava beds and charred trees, you are a wreck. I can understand how a spectacular image of natural destruction might be unnerving, but you're not looking out your window. Your eyes are on the road, following the yellow lines. If possible, you would lock my head in a vice so I too saw nothing but the center line on Route 242. With all of your strength you are willing us out of the mountains. Your fear is contagious. I begin to grip the steering wheel much more tightly with both hands. I look in the rearview mirror. I notice the Honda CR-V behind me is much too close. Back off, fella. We are near Sisters and in the middle of a spectacular cedar forest. But I'm afraid to look out the car window. The canopy overhead is so thick that little sunshine filters through. It's only two but the sun has set. The paranoia is spreading. Thank god it's only twenty-five miles to Bend.

It's windy but radiant today. Leaves swept up by thirty-two-mile-per-hour gusts sail by, swirling in mad circles like something possessed. One mass of spinning leaves rose up above the street and whizzed toward me, slapping at my face like cardboard poltergeists. Had I been a field of wheat I would now be a crop circle. The wind roared all night long, like a terrible portent, gusting with a certain violence. This is outdoors. Indoors it's different. Sometimes the inertia is simply tremendous. I can't seem to move any limbs, as though I'm trapped in a vortex of self-canceling energies. Even my thoughts slow down.

Calmer now. I linger near Hickory Hill. Most of the trees are bereft of leaves, but they seem relieved. Unburdened. Now they can sleep until the cycle starts again. The shaggy-barked hickory trees stare blankly at the sky.

On my left, a black-and-white magpie perches in a young red oak. A male cardinal darts into the park. To my right, a pileated woodpecker hops from limb to limb, drumming on dead spots in between piping calls, wok, wuk, wok, wuk. The ash has no leaves. As the magpie flies to the next tree, a single red oak leaf drops to the ground, twisting in the wind one last time. An alder on Davenport is nearly stripped, its remaining leaves waving in the mid-November breeze. The ecstasy of leaves in the final light, no longer driven to absorb sunshine, free now to merely reflect it. The disappearance of green is a sign of change. Few things are as spectacular as this, the slow drama of nature's death.

♃

CHAPTER SEVEN
JUPITER (THE COMBINER)

~~~

Fly me to the moon and let me play among the stars. Let me know what spring is like on Jupiter and Mars.

—Kaye Ballard

*T*he distance between planets is insane, and the darkness out here is mind-boggling. That's what Space Boy just radioed in. Better off we are, I radio back, on solid ground with blue sky overhead and birds chirping. There's no turning back, however. This I understand now, but I can't resist razzing Space Boy a bit. I hear the drive to Pluto, I say, is at least forty astronomical units, ninety-three million miles times forty. You'll need to excite a lot of dark matter to arrive there in time.

Space Boy doesn't miss a beat. There's an optimizer here, he radios back, just to my right that runs calculations nonstop on how much, when, and where (there's no better word for it) to *tickle* dark matter. That's Space Boy's metaphor for manipulating flux gravitons. Tickling dark matter—what an idea. Who would have guessed? So much for dilithium crystals and tylium ore, I radio back. Luckily, there's a lot of dark matter out here, he says. The kind of atomic matter we grow up with, dirt, water, rocks, and toothpaste, comprises only 4.9 percent of the universe. Dark matter, on the other hand, 26.8 percent. Beyond that—the missing 68.3 percent—is anyone's guess. What a universe! I radio back, truly amazed. She's out here somewhere, Space Boy says with zest.

It's not easy to be in two places at once, but that's what woe is all about, hauling one's aching body around the cosmos while chopping onions. Says Space Boy: I still haven't got the hang of the dark-matter tickler—it's really fussy—but things are far from hopeless out here.

Friends are concerned I'm getting skinny. Commiseration. They'll furrow their brow, make sympathetic sounds, and ask about my weight. M. said, You've lost a lot of weight, haven't you? She's worried I'm dwindling. No, I said, I've actually put a few pounds on. Yes, I've gained weight—I'm not fat—only four pounds but enough to dispel any illusion of weight loss. You might think I'm falling down on the job of grieving, but no, that's not the case. I can weep and be chubby at the same time. Oddly enough, it was M. who didn't look well. She seemed quite shaky, as a matter of fact. Her whole body was atremble. Not good, I'm sure, but what do I know? Meanwhile, I had a warm bag of french fries in my hands, which I was dying to eat, but had to stifle my teenage desire, especially now that you are not here to do that for me.

The burning bush out front is turning. I count twelve red leaves. In another week or so it will explode into a ball of fire. If I hear a voice, however, I'll turn and run the other way, unless that voice is yours. Then I'll stay and brave the weird metaphysics. Half the sumac on Brown Street has gone orange, and a tribe of towering maples on Davenport has begun its flaming out. The chloroplasts are retreating, exposing the carotenoids in leaf cells, the yellow, orange, and brown pigments. Chemically speaking. Soon after reaching peak color every leaf in town will cascade to the ground in a poetic flutter. There, they'll shrivel up desiccated, which is the way of all things. The color green will have vanished, and with it yellow, brown, red, and purple. The black walnut trees are the first to go, the oaks the last. And in over half the world, nature will seem dead and wolves will howl.

I've begun harvesting all the colors (soon to be lost) in my optic memory. The showy white and violet of the gaudy hibiscus, the heart-shaped purple and pink of morning glories—to shore myself up against the dark and achromatic world of winter. Alone in a discolored universe.

I'm looking at a photo I took of you in southern France. It's 2011 and we are at the Abbey of Gellone in the village of Saint-Guilhem-le-Désert. I'm on a teaching gig. An eleventh-century Benedictine church with cloister and garden, the abbey had the curious fate, you tell me, of being abandoned and sold off piece by piece to various museums, including the Cloisters in New York City. Medieval columns and pilasters are scattered across Europe and America, you say.

You are sitting in the restored cloister resting against a square column. Midday Mediterranean sunshine falls on your back, its light reflecting from a nearby column on your face. You seem aglow. You are wearing a navy-blue net sweater over your black top. Your hair is cut stylishly and blends in with the medieval limestone. I'm struck by the look of serenity on your face. Your lips are slightly parted in an evocative way—you seldom allow yourself to be caught off guard in a photo—but right now you seem unaware of the camera. Ordinarily, you strike a sporty pose in travel photos, smart and energetic—poised for the folks back home. But here you seem to have given yourself over to the abbey, as if it had called to you and you had answered. What did it say to you?

I shouldn't read so much into a photo, but how can I resist? These images are all that remains of you. How long before my memories flutter away. Back then, time was on our side, a quarter of a century yet on the clock. But here I am now looking at your face, fixed in a single moment, your swirling hair caught in midair as you turn your head toward the camera, and I am futureless. I can't type the word without feeling empty. It no longer exists. How many other words are gone? As I write, our eyes lock— your shy blue eyes. The square limestone column leans your way. I think the abbey has fallen under a spell. In the photo you're about to speak, a word that was said following the click of the shutter but now lost. We are always losing things, socks, hair, sight, hearing, dreams, lovers. In this photo you will always be about to speak, just as your hair is about to fall back into place.

Today I bought a pumpkin for four bucks and hoped to buy an orange potted mum for the porch, but the mum was expensive. I'm not paying thirty dollars for a three-letter plant! You never seemed fond of mums. They were too gaudy. As you know, I have a soft spot for kitsch—my teenage desire. Speaking of which, I also bought stamps at the post office this afternoon, not the Madonna and Child series or Advances in Aviation but *Star Trek* stamps. There's a stamp with the Vulcan hand salute, one with the transporter, another with the Starfleet insignia. By the way, my mom said she saw another object out her window the other night hovering over the neighbor's backyard. Her sightings began just before Milo died. Like you, she sensed something. The Cassandra syndrome.

It was cold and bleak today, a peek at what's to come. Doomsday sky and cool damp air with gusty winds. Like a switch, the low front set off a wave of change in the arboreal world. Elm trees that were indecisively green yesterday are paranoid yellow today, as if they had seen a ghost.

I have a bad headache, you say. Suddenly it's Sunday in October and you are curled up in a fetal position. What's wrong? I say. You don't speak. Your head is throbbing. Any moment you will bolt for the bathroom to vomit. I lie down beside you and stroke your back like a pet. Can I get you anything? You don't speak. It's a bad one. Second migraine this month. Have you taken any Tylenol? I ask. You shake your head. I'll bring a Tylenol and some ginger ale, I say. The room is dark but I can see your eyes watering. Your forehead is creased. The first migraine was in graduate school, you say. Then it became chronic. It followed you here to Washington. You're in agony, three days rolled up in a ball. It scares me to see you paralyzed like this.

Your migraines seem to come out of nowhere, I say. It's the change in temperature, you say, drier cooler air, maybe the ragweed. I don't know. It's painful to speak. Would an ice pack help? I say. I'm stupid and helpless. You won't see a doctor. What's the point? you say. You're having vertigo. Help me up to the bathroom, you say, white as the sheets. I drag you across the hall and position you in front of the toilet. You gag and heave for ten minutes. I drag you back to bed. Momentarily, you feel better. Thirty-six million people suffer from migraines, you say, and no one knows why. I've never had one, I say, feeling guilty. Tension headaches, but nothing as glamorous as a migraine. You don't know what you're missing, you say. Migraine auras, though, I've experienced these—a fuzzy cloud of blues and greens—but without the head pain. A faint smile.

I rub your shoulders and talk about the time Willy Lahiff dropped a bolder on my head. Luckily, it was mostly caked mud, a clump of dirt and stones, so the blood streaming down my face was from shallow wounds, but my mom almost passed out. Why did Willy Lahiff drop a ball of dirt on your head? you ask. I think I did something bad to Willy. I had it coming. Such a devil, you say. Afraid so, I say. Do you have any appetite? Maybe tomato soup and crackers? Your head is spinning again so no tomato soup and crackers. Shortly after our move to Iowa, the migraines stopped for a while but then returned.

Do you remember our first date? We are in Georgetown on Wisconsin Avenue near M Street seated at a table for two. Tonight it's crowded, but there's one seating in the middle of the room. I am wearing a herringbone jacket. You, in a long skirt, a solid crop blazer, and a dazzling silk scarf. Because this is a date, you are wearing lipstick. We're both dressed like grad students for job interviews—you more smartly, though. Herringbone is not a good look for me, but I won't know this for some time. Neither of us has the courage to look the other in the eye. That would seem romantic which is not acceptable behavior here. It's a job interview, after all.

We talk about many things. Bette Davis. George Bush. Janet Jackson. The Berlin Wall is about to come down. NASA launches a space probe to Jupiter. Whatever happened to the moon? you say. Russia has just pulled out of Afghanistan. A week ago, the TASS agency reported that three-eyed aliens landed in the city of Voronezh. Tall tales from the tundra. Walmart is about to open its first store in the Northeast. Walmart, what's that? In between Gado-gado, Nasi goreng, and lamb and chicken curry, we talk about movies, *Batman* and *Roger and Me*. You're drinking red wine, me beer. The food is great. We love Indonesian, but it's time to leave. Who pays? We have a mile to walk in the brisk October night to Foggy Bottom.

There's no moonlight but it's a good date. We like each other. Do we hold hands? Down M Street to Pennsylvania Avenue, across Rock Creek, around Washington Circle, over to 23rd Street. Descend into the underworld of the Metro. Just eight weeks ago you were in Indiana finishing your PhD. When a woman resides a long time in the vacant Midwest, you say, she feels the desire for a city.

We both live in underground apartments with little natural light, a lot of mildew, and the random rodent—it's all we can afford—and pretend our digs aren't expensive cellars. It's the perfect location for two underdogs. At night, the spotted camel crickets will come out like creatures in a creepy film, leaping six feet in the air and looking nothing like a cricket. But tonight, on this first date, there are no moonbeams or camel crickets, just you and me and the cat. The place is unfurnished so we sit on the floor and talk. All those words. I'm thinking of only one thing as I speak, however, about the first kiss. It's the end of the evening and I've never been good with this. Something tells me you're no better. It's a classically awkward moment for normal people, but quadruply so for two young nerds dressed for job interviews. How to get through the last ten minutes without agonizing embarrassment—well, that's not easy.

My palms are wet and I'm feeling hot. A wave of shyness comes over me—and you too—this is not good. I'm losing the power of speech. I get up to say goodbye. You walk to the door. I love the way you walk, so light on your feet, like a ballerina. I want to say something witty but I can't even form a sentence. It's like cerebral palsy. My gait is unsteady, my hand is shaking, I have no respiratory control. Precisely at this moment you bend forward and pucker your lips—and so do I. Maybe this won't be bad after all, I think. The butterflies flap their wings and I put my hands on your waist for better leverage. Two more inches of dead space to cross between our moistening lips. And then the terrible click, clack of eyeglasses. Our monster frames have collided, in fact have interlocked like a Norfolk latch. You try to pull away but take my face with you. I tug my way but your face follows me. We are fastened together, and we still can't kiss. My nose is in the way. This is embarrassing. You are blushing, as am I, but neither of us can see this because the two pair of eyeglasses have become one, creating a pattern of optical interference that leaves us both groping in the dark like blind cave crickets. At wits' end we produce word sounds that have no meaning, excruciating sounds, while making every effort to unlock our eyeglasses. If this were a job interview, I wouldn't expect a callback.

It was a lovely evening, until the ritual kiss when our giant eyes got in the way. A tiny fiasco but a telling one. Why didn't we simply remove our glasses? A suspicious couple we were. In your eyes, I seemed rakish (I was). You needed to keep things in clear focus and not be taken in by my devilish ways, and I don't blame you. And me, I was afraid my large nose would seem even more conspicuous without the glasses. I had a mask on, and I wasn't about to remove it quite yet.

On Sundays, we began the day at the Kalorama Café in Adams Morgan. This was our dating routine. Start with a hardy breakfast. We took the Metro to Dupont Circle and walked north for a mile to Kalorama Road. We then stood in line for ninety minutes, observing the funky Latino kids skateboard down 18th Street. The black kids were across the street at the Marie Reed Rec Center in four-on-four basketball. It was a long wait for a table but what the hell, we thought. I liked the whole wheat pancakes, you the eggs Benedict. We shared an order of hash browns. Then it was up and over to Idle Time Bookstore near Columbia Road. Browse for an hour and then back to Dupont for more grazing at Kramerbooks. We dawdled, meandered, and joked, two ramblers falling in love, sharing a conspiracy of avoidance. By then it was six p.m. and time for dinner. We'd take the Metro to Clarendon for Vietnamese—remember Nam Viet—where you always ate the lemongrass tofu with mixed vegetables? Me and my bottle of Singha and the sticky rice. I'd grab the *City Paper*, we'd scan the movies, and then it was off to Georgetown for a film—this was fun. But then came Monday and the oppressive pile of ungraded papers.

A hot summer-like day has thrown many trees into

confusion. A steady, stiff wind sends leaves to the ground in bunches. Everywhere, the yellow and orange leaves afloat in the breezy air. I found two six-inch mums at the farmers' market yesterday and arranged them in our big pots on the porch. It took half an hour to jerry-rig the garden pots—the only way to elevate the mums was with paint buckets—but in the end two lurid yellow mums were stationed on either side of the front door, like fallen stars. The blossoms are so bright I have sun spots on my eyes. They say the blooms on forced mums won't last long— what does?—but I'm hoping for two weeks.

I returned home from Grinnell along US-6. A number of farmers were still at work on last-minute runs in soybean fields, racing to beat the predicted weekend rain. I drove along the unlit highway under a Hunter's Moon, larger than most, mesmerized by the swarm of John Deeres on secret missions. Out in the vast darkness of the soybean fields, the combines looked like fleets of invading spaceships, their high-intensity beacons lighting up the dusty fields with weird intent. Alone in the car at night, there's nothing to keep my imagination in check. On Friday morning the furnace wouldn't go on, and it was plenty chilly. I finally pruned the flowering quince, by the way, which had overwhelmed the front steps. Took forever to bag the debris. My lower back is moaning.

These are the quotidian facts. Much of our existence is devoted to such unmemorable moments, not that you're curious to know any of this, but I'm telling you to remind you that between life and death much is forgotten. All of this I now refuse to leave behind, even the most tiresome detail. The secret to sorrow is remaining vigilant. Had I not been so careless, I would have chronicled every blink of your eye.

Our romance wasn't extraordinary, but there were some funny quirks. Remember our strange coupling ritual? We were about to make our first big purchase as a couple. It was Friday and *Twin Peaks* was set to debut on Sunday night, but neither of us had a TV. New territory for both. Most first-time shoppers buy a coffee maker or a blender. Besides a bottle of wine, we had never bought anything together. We bought a big-screen TV, and it wasn't cheap. A thirty-five-inch RCA at Fred Myers in Maryland. We had to take the Beltway and were in the car forever. It took hours to find the TVs, and when we did there were so many. Hundreds of televisions, little ones, big ones, even bigger ones. We felt like third-world immigrants dazed by the opulence of America. Our hands were shaking, we both fumbled for our wallets. Big and heavy, the whopping machine was not your kind of purchase—you who preferred the scale of a bento box.

But this collaborative act wasn't about aesthetics or about economics. It was about making a pledge to one another in the bizarre language of consumerism neither of us understood but which we spoke with surprising excitement. We knew what this meant. Our English basement apartments weren't large enough for such a TV. We would have to move in together, somewhere big enough for you, me, and the RCA. How terrifying. You knew you had crossed a line. There was no going back now. An adorable blue-eyed blonde with a laser-sharp mind had just become entangled with a dark-haired hothead who gave the evil eye to unsuspecting colleagues. If you were ambivalent you did a good job of hiding it. But there it was, the RCA, the Log Lady, and the beginning of a life together.

The RCA wound up in my apartment, though I can't remember why. It was twenty-six years ago. Some of the details escape me. But there it was on my kitchen table when the pilot of *Twin Peaks* aired, surrounded by granola and coffee bags. That Sunday night we switched on the RCA and sat back on the sofa. We saw the tumbling slow-motion waterfall on the Snoqualmie River during the neon-green opening credit roll. *Welcome to Twin Peaks. Population 51,201.* A snowcapped mountain rose up in the background. The foghorn is blowing behind the dark sounds of the synthesizer when Pete calls the sheriff after discovering a body bag with Laura Palmer washed up on a riverbank. "She's dead. Wrapped in plastic." Poor Laura. We both looked at each other with bright eyes when Sheriff Truman crams a giant bear claw into his mouth, just as Agent Cooper walks in with important updates on the murder. Caught in an awkward moment, the sheriff struggles to chew and swallow the pastry but to no avail. It's huge. Everyone has a donut in their mouth—Lucy and Andy—which they gobble up with childish abandon. Damn fine donuts. Cooper runs down their upcoming tasks while the sheriff continues to toil with his bear claw, the camera holding on the hard-working jaw of Michael Ontkean for what seemed like hours.

We looked at each other and exchanged smiles. There was a twinkle in your eyes. For once, we seemed to be in the right place at the right time, an alternative reality. The show was everything Washington, DC (then), wasn't. Such an unusual arrival tale, forming a lasting attachment over a weird TV show. We were outsiders in Washington's conservative, close-knit culture—fugitives really. Washington had been so effectively corporatized it was no place for the whimsical. In *Twin Peaks* we found a hideaway where we could recover our lost selves. This is what sealed, as Shakespeare would say, our fate.

"One day," said the Log Lady, "the sadness will end." The Log Lady, Catherine Coulson, died last September. She was seventy-one. From cancer. And so she will not appear in Season 3 of *Twin Peaks*. We might have celebrated our twenty-fourth anniversary with the watching of episode one of the new series, and lamented together the passing of the Log Lady. Catherine Coulson kept her log, having bonded with her piece of ponderosa pine. The log is thought to be worth a quarter of a million dollars. "There is a sadness in this world, for we are ignorant of many things. Sadness, in our ignorance, is very real. The tears are real. Then the day when sadness comes, we ask: will this sadness which makes me cry, will this sadness that makes my heart cry out—will it ever end? The answer, of course, is yes. One day the sadness will end." So said the Log Lady—may she find peace.

The city's silver maples have turned into Chinese lanterns, aglow in soft yellow and orange light. Layers of fallen leaves carpet the sidewalks in burgundy, purple, and browns, a vivid explosion of earthy hues and tones. So animated is the air with color and light I feel like a small figure in a giant painting. It's the final outburst of radiant form before the dark and cold arrive in their generalized gloom, until the shoots of grasses, goldenrods, and other wildflowers rise out of the soil in spring. I'm clinging (in my prose) to the moment between lightness and dark. In my heart I am clinging to you; I am here beside you in the intricate space between the imaginary and the real.

I have a milkweed pod on my desk. Held the right

way, the pod is the size of a bird without a head, five inches long, a bird with folded wings. My seedpod is dried out and has begun to open up like an oyster shell. (It's a metaphor machine.) The brown angiosperm seeds inside seem eager to germinate, each a white silky fluff. The silk "parachutes" catch the wind and float far and wide over valley and mountain slopes, riding wind currents for days at a time. I can see Baron Munchausen soaring through space on a milkweed pod. Milkweed fluff was used in life jackets as a flotation device during World War II, by the way, collected by American schoolchildren. It's quite buoyant. Some have stuffed pillows with milkweed fluff. In the veins of the milkweed plant flow the milky white sap used by Native Americans to remove warts. Somehow I know you're listening.

Scheduled an appointment with the retirement guy. More forms to fill out. There's this fund and that to roll over. I'm like the Borg, absorbing all of your assets. Matters have become complicated with your ING account, I should warn you, which is listed solely in your name with no beneficiary clause. I've had to lawyer up. The machinations necessary to retrieve this account are strange and daunting. There's the creation of an estate, the appointment of an executor (me), letters testamentary (so that I can represent the "estate"), and so forth. And then there's a legal public proceeding, probate court, where anyone on the planet (in legal terms creditors of the deceased) has four months to make a claim against your assets. All of these (your assets) will be listed and valued as part of the public record. So if you're shy this won't be pleasant. Do you have any creditors out there, invisible entities circling your corpse? Take the University Hospital. It keeps a close eye on the probate proceedings of the recently deceased, staking claims for unresolved hospital bills, just in case. And then there are probate fees I will pay, the lawyer's and the state's, a fixed percentage of your assets. This is all new to me and probably comical but also insane in a way only a novelist could enjoy. Call me K. Death is complicated. So many hidden variables—how not to feel implicated?

The meeting lasted well over an hour. The whole thing was pretty unnerving. Not the money part, thanks to your extreme frugality. It was the innuendos that spooked me. I took careful notes this time because this stuff goes in one ear and out the other. The TIAA guy had on his blue shirt, black tie (beware of men in black ties), and gray trousers. Today he had on his Mark Hamill look. Imagine a middle-age Luke Skywalker working for Geico. He's a really nice guy, make no mistake about it. I think he enjoys these meetings. I got together with my team and we looked closely at your situation, he said, where your moneys are, your expected retirement date, your Social Security profile. How will this really look? That's the question we ask, not just today but five, twenty, thirty years down the road. How do you create a thoughtful plan around your assets based on your goals? So here we have an overview of our agenda. You remember the four main areas of financial well-being? Not really, I said. Okay, there's retirement income. The goal here is how to replace your salary with something you could feel good about down the road.

He pointed to another category on the whiteboard, asset allocation, which he called my *sleepability*. Sleepability? I asked. We don't want you suffering from insomnia because of money concerns. Okay. Sounds good. Now your asset allocation—the combination of stocks, bonds, guarantees, fixed income, and real estate—we have to figure out how aggressive or conservative you want to be with these. Given the volatility of the market going forward, we need to make sure you are as diversified as possible. And then you need to determine your risk factor. Moderately conservative is what you told me earlier. That rings a bell, I said. Right now, with your assets, you are a little bit riskier than that.

That made me anxious. I already feel at risk. I don't need to aggravate the diceyness of my situation. What can we do about that? I said timidly. But you also have the CD money, the money-market cash, etc., and these accounts are totally conservative. I think you're in a good spot. You're not too aggressive where you could lose 20 percent, if the market plunges, but it's still working for you, depending on ups and downs. And, of course, the number of years you have left to live, whether it's five or thirty. Jeez, that sounds dark. I try not to look that far into the future, I said, but I saw by the look on his face I was already there. So, he resumed, we want to make sure there's sufficient moneys for any and all outcomes. How then do we *silo* your money. Since we're in Iowa I like to use that term. For some reason I couldn't think of grain storage but only missile silos. The TIAA guy drew four silos of varying height. The little silo was earmarked for emergency funds. You always want to have a certain amount of cash, he said, for the what-ifs. Say your roof blows off, your car explodes, or you lose a leg—who knows. You mean my whole leg? I said. Just a figure of expression, he said.

My TIAA advisor was beginning to sound a little like

an Allstate commercial with the Mayhem guy. He was using hyperboles but they seemed awfully real to me. I honestly felt the roof of our house could blow off at any moment. Some people like to have more cash on hand, he said, for their own sleepability.

He named the last little tower the "never" silo. This was the storage bin for money I would never spend because I would be dead. The never silo was my legacy, money for my beneficiaries. Also, a hedge against catastrophic health problems. So we need to think about incapacity planning, he said. Unfortunately, this is just part of life. My palms were sweating by this point. The never silo was so ontologically spooky I felt light-headed. The TIAA guy asked if I needed coffee or water. I need to lie down, I said. I didn't expect this meeting to be existentially disturbing. Remember, the RMD comes into effect automatically at age seventy and a half. So at a certain point in time, you will have to pay taxes on these accounts. They can't be deferred indefinitely. But this is exactly what I want from money, I tell him. I want to defer my death indefinitely.

One day, we decide to teach the same class. We're feeling nostalgic. We live in Washington, a city of lawyers and lobbyists. Too many Republicans, I say. I want to gag, you say. It's so depressing. We miss the 1960s. So we collaborate on a syllabus about counterculture America. Drugs, music, war, dissent, conflict, angst. The whole works. This will be fun, I say. We're in my kitchen drinking wine. My kitchen is so small you can't cross your legs. You move the jade plant out of your way. We need Tom Wolfe, you say, the *Kool-Aid* book. Okay, I say. Good. How about Joan Didion's *Slouching*? For sure, you say. What else? Well, how about Carlos Castaneda? I say. Really? you say. Castaneda and Huxley. Okay, you say. How about Ken Kesey? you ask. The *Cuckoo Nest*? Yes. By all means, I say. We're halfway through the wine already, so I tell you my Ken Kesey story.

I'm working at this classy restaurant in Eugene, Oregon, and downstairs in the pastry room is Jack Kerouac's daughter. You're kidding, you say. No. Her name is Jan and she's an assistant pastry chef. A very attractive woman. You are enjoying the merlot. I fetch corn chips. I even asked her out, believe it or not, I say, reaching into the cupboard. But she looked right through me, like I was a window pane. Didn't say a word. Out of your league, maybe, you say. Absolutely. More wine? Yes. But it's possible she had a drug problem.

Well, one afternoon Ken Kesey drives up. Wait, what's Ken Kesey doing there? He lives across the tracks, I say, in Springfield, a blue-collar town. Everyone there works for the lumber giant, Weyerhaeuser. I lived there too for a while. The whole place smells like cardboard on LSD. What does he look like in person? you ask. Short and stocky, balding curly hair. Looks like a fighter who hangs out in Irish pubs. Another glass of wine? Sure. Anyway, Kesey drives up in a convertible, charges through the back door, descends the rickety stairs, grabs Jan Kerouac by the hand, and races back upstairs and out the door. Off to Albuquerque. Vroom goes his convertible. I think it was a T-Bird. We never see Jack's daughter again. The pastry girl vanishes. Why Albuquerque? you ask. Some kind of event on the Beat generation, I think. So we both agree to add *On the Road* to the list. By the end of the bottle, there's over forty books on our syllabus.

Indian summer continues well into November. Balmy

and seductive. The white oak's leaves are turning dark red like wine. Autumn's slow fade, its long goodbye. A squirrel gnawing on a walnut pauses for a moment to look at me. He's perched on a limb. We are eye to eye. But as I'm standing perfectly still, he is puzzled. What am I? He can't tell. He takes the walnut from his mouth, darting his head to the right and left. He really needs to know. What am I? he wonders. Just to be safe, he scurries up the spindly limbs of the maple, returns the walnut to his mouth, and begins re-gnawing. He keeps his big eyes on me, though. Not to be trusted, he thinks. Small bits of walnut shell fall from the squirrel's mouth onto the carpet of maple leaves. It's the sound of dry rain. Partly covered by leaves is an empty bottle of Corona Extra at the base of the tree. A fossil trace of primate culture. The nearby ginkgo is the last to turn colors, from flamboyant green to drunken yellow. This one is a girl and has begun to drop her fleshy nuts. If you can get past its repulsive smell, the ginkgo nut is a thing of beauty. It tastes like a plum, I'm told, though more complicated. In a hundred years, which is a flash of light, will any of this be here?

These are things we would not have paused by to see on our walk. They matter now more than ever. Later today I stopped on my way up the stairs in midflight and sat down. You flashed before my eyes. Again, the horrible gasping for air, the fading light of your eyes, your body stretched out for sleep. My coffee spilled, little brown splatters staining the bright maple treads. I sprawled on the landing like a midnight drunk, rehearsing my own heart attack or stroke. You didn't see it coming. I see mine only too well.

CHAPTER EIGHT
EUROPA
(MASTER OF SUBZERO)

All these worlds are yours. Except Europa.
Attempt no landing there.

—Arthur C. Clarke

An icy moon of Jupiter, Europa is a bit smaller than our earth's moon and thought to have a global ocean of water in contact with a rocky seafloor. The surface is unimaginably frosty and besieged by dangerous radiation. Galileo laid his eyes on Jupiter and its four largest moons in 1610 with a nifty homemade telescope. Today, the Galilean moons of Jupiter, being so large, can be viewed with a pair of binoculars. Last night, I viewed Europa with my naked eye. Very icy. Galileo initially named Europa and her kin (Io, Callisto, and Ganymede) the "Medici Stars" in the spirit of Trump Tower, but that didn't hold. Someone else (Simon Marius) gave Jupiter's moons their more colorful names, three of them women under the thrall of Zeus—or in this case the gravitational pull of Jupiter.

Fifty-three of Jupiter's sixty-nine moons have been named and some by the same logic, either girls and boys pursued by Zeus or women in peculiar relationships. There's Leda, as one might expect, Jupiter's thirteenth moon (and setting of the 1956 film *Fire Maidens from Outer Space*), who was raped by Zeus in the guise of a swan. There's Iocaste, Jupiter's twenty-fourth moon, better known as the mother-slash-wife of Oedipus. My favorite is Pasiphae, Jupiter's eighth moon, the wife of Minos of Crete who made love to an extraordinary bull with the help of Daedalus. Sixteen of Jupiter's moons still await names. Good luck. I'm guessing the database has run dry. Why not name the remaining moons after women in Russian fiction? Tatyana from *Eugene Onegin*, Sonya from *Crime and Punishment*, Natalya in *War and Peace*, Irina in *Three Sisters*, Olga from "The Darling." And so on.

All of this I say to amuse you. I know you don't miss winter or housecleaning or doing the taxes—but it's possible you miss my boyish sense of humor.

I just returned home from a long drive and it finally sank in I was coming back to an empty house. It was a delayed reaction. I had kept this from myself for months, that no one was home. But now the simple fact struck like a blow. You and Milo would not be there. No one. Such a hollow feeling, returning to a deserted home, groping for the light switch in the pitch-black, falling heavily onto the sofa, not even removing my backpack, sinking down and not wanting to move. That line from Frost keeps replaying in my head: *what to make of a diminished thing*. I feel it mostly at night, so full of shadows. Of course I'm back on my feet in an instant. The automatic light timer has switched two lamps on and I've snapped to, but not without recognizing the siren call of descent. I still have miles to go.

On an early evening walk, darkness everywhere. The moon is gone away and the humidity is inky black. The stars are pinpricks in a sky so vast I want to faint. As I walk I hear a strange sound, a droning of sorts, but it's not coming from the school on my right or from the apartment building across the street. It's coming from me. The murmur is in me. A humming inside. It's the feeling of a noise somewhere in my chest, a subliminal signal from a faraway place.

The holiday break was difficult. Choppy flight to Buffalo and then the long drive across Upstate New York to Connecticut. All under bleak skies. From Syracuse to the Berkshires snow accumulation. Almost a foot in some parts. Hard to keep alert at times. My mom doesn't drive on the highway, so you can imagine the ordeal. Past Utica and Frankfort and Herkimer I drive. With winter on its way, the picturesque Mohawk Valley is stripped bare. The downswing of New York's canal towns. Such sadness in the air. What does one do in Herkimer on a Friday night? Miniature golf? There's the Belly Up Pub on Albany Street, if you like loud noise, which I don't. I drive on, following the curves of the river. On my right the lyrically named Canajohare, once capital of the mighty Mohawk nation, now a city of 3,500 and an ever-declining tax base. The melancholy brick of the industrial past, a-crumble.

Years ago, my family would drive along the Erie Canal. I'd look into the valley where the towns rose up and see canoes and redcoats. Central New York was Leatherstocking country in the tourist trade. The eye inevitably wanders in these parts, drifts across the Mohawk

River and over the locks and up into the streets of once-flourishing river towns. I'm driving along Amsterdam. It's to my right. Just past canal lock number eleven are the screaming white bones of the 850,000-square-foot Beech-Nut factory, the baby food makers, founded in 1891. A few buildings remain intact, but much of the plant has been demolished. Random piles of white bricks lie all over, like little tumuli. The factory's big red letters have vanished. When you saw that sign—*BEECH-NUT*—you knew it was only fifty miles to the Hudson River. All of Upstate New York seems to be crumbling.

Obviously, I'm not keeping my eyes on the road. I swerve over the yellow line into the left lane. I'm jolted out of my reverie, but it's not the veering. You're not there reading the *New Yorker*. Instead, my mom is asleep in the passenger seat, and she's snoring. Her head is rolled back, her mouth open, innocent of the moribund signs all around. I have to tell you this, and it will make you smile: Pat is going on eighty-seven and still no gray hair. Maybe one or two. How can that be? I feel guilty for being envious, but you already know that. I don't understand how people hold on to their hair.

Few leaves left. The dark comes early, too early in the late afternoon and heavy. I can feel its cold fingers on my shoulder and elbows. I say your name but I know you are not in this place. Sometimes I hear you breathe late at night.

It snowed today. Winter is here. Were things different, you would be dashing outdoors with a broom to clear the porch steps—but I can't rise out of my chair. Arvo Pärt is on the radio and I can't get up. A few leaves linger on trees and shrubs. The grass is green but soon it will fade too, and the snow will fall softly upon every tomb in the lonely churchyard. I counted thirty-eight shining red leaves on the burning bush in the front yard. Like ornaments, the remaining little leaves. Should I fetch a Christmas tree? I don't know if I can do this. I see ruin wherever my eye goes. The collapsed barns around the city, their red paint worn away by wind and rain, structures reduced to a mound of wooden bones. My mind is sunless, my skull cracked. Sadness leaks out like the fumes of a smoldering fire. The unsmiling faces of older men and women, the downcast eyes, the frowns, sagging spirits. I watch from my chair as another pointed red leaf falls from the burning bush and drops to the ground. Below the bush, blood. Arvo Pärt once wrote that the instant and eternity are struggling within us.

A dream last night. On a speedy bullet train traveling through a spectacular landscape filled with dazzling waterfalls. The train was improbably elevated above numerous cascades and moving on a track whose rails were covered by ice. The fantastic landscape was a mix of water flows and ice, primeval. Mesas, canyons, escarpments, ice fields, and cataracts. I was on a moon of Jupiter, Europa. Bizarre, beautiful, and terrifying. What am I doing here? The train is very modern and the agents in control— Europeans—are very competent. I'm in good hands, although I don't know who these people are. The train seems to be moving in a westerly direction. I'm looking out the window: the tracks are covered with ice the way a tree branch is glazed after a freeze. How can the train possibly move this fast over ice-covered rails? I wonder. Others are on board as well, but I'm too absorbed by the spectacle out my window to pay attention. Where are we going?

In dreams, says Anne Carson, we get a glimpse of something incognito, something hiding. A peek perhaps at another world.

Heavy jacket on, even though it's a mild winter day. No resistance to the cold. Everything is frigid, even the ice cream aisle in the grocery store. A mile into my walk I can't remember where I am. How did I get here? I look around. The white pine, the naked ash, the holiday ornaments, the bird feeders. Where am I? Then the familiar herd of deer on Davenport Street. No huntsmen and plenty of pine trees. The people up Pleasant Street leave small piles of corn. I thought they were large dogs. And then a real dog, a happy black and brown spaniel with big floppy ears. He doesn't want to go home. He's pulling on his leash, a goofy happy dog. Hi doggy, I say like a child. The solace of animals. There's a light wind that wraps around me near Hickory Hill. It blows against my beanie with its lonely whoosh. I feel its aloneness and give myself over to the wind. The mild current takes me along. There's empathy in this. Me and the wind and no you. I know you're here but I can't see a thing. Just the wind.

It's funny how sometimes you look back at me in photos, expectantly, as if already here in this moment waiting for me—but not always. Here's a photo of you in the backyard with a cat on your lap. It's a chilly day in April but you've found a sunny nook on the porch. Your eyes sweep over the garden. There's a woodpecker in the walnut tree and daffodils and hyacinths are breaking through the ground. You like to keep an eye on your world, watchful.

Especially on pets. I hear you call from the living room. I scamper downstairs. What's wrong? I ask. Binky just peed on the sofa, you say. The big white sofa? Oh no, I say. I see a big stain and the smell is awful. Binky is a stray so we shouldn't be too surprised. Still, you're concerned. Me too. We may never get rid of that smell, I warn. You're more worried about the cat. Binky doesn't have the cleanest bill of health—he's had a rocky life. We get out the Nature's Miracle but his pee is pungent. It's ruined, I say of the sofa. I really like this sofa. Three days later, Binky will pee again in the same spot, and off to the vet we go. I have the exact date of these events: the first mishap on March 12, 2001; the second, March 15. I even know the weather— damp and chilly with overcast skies.

Is my memory that good? Hardly the case. You wrote this down in your garden journal. I've begun reading this volume because, well, I seem to be doing the same thing, more or less. I'm logging observations, taking field notes. What does the world look like through sad eyes? That's my project. Yours is called *A Gardener's Journal: A Ten-Year Chronicle of Your Garden* but is free of sorrow. It's a big green book, over five hundred pages long. I've seen this lying around for years, but I always guessed it was an encyclopedia of sorts, not a journal, a compendium of plant lore. The diary pages are where you're most busy and there are lots of nongardening entries, like those about Binky's pee episodes. You kept at this for the better part of eight years, recording over 360 notes each year.

Let's see, here's an entry from January of 2001: *A large variety of birds at feeder at 8:30 a.m.: downy and red-bellied woodpeckers on walnut (the downy peckers are at the suet), junco, nuthatches, sparrows, doves, starlings, chickadees, a house finch, cardinals. Some sort of warbler. Another damp, chilly day. New short haircut—good in back but shaggy and, annoyingly, in my face up front.* Rarely were you happy with new hairdos. You have sharp eyes, though. You record what you see, not what you think. You keep your thoughts to yourself. They interfere with accuracy. I can't do that. I look out the same window but see only sparrows and chipmunks (to this day) because my head is full of noise. Here's two years later: *Sunnier and warmer, looks to be a lovely day. We drove up to Coralville Dam for a walk, by which time skies were gray. Space shuttle* Columbia *crashed in TX; if I were Bush I'd take it as a portent.* A rare editorial moment. We struggled with the younger Bush. It was hard not to despair. Back then, neither of us have a clue what lies ahead but at least you've been spared this absurd future.

In March of 2003: *Sunny and warmer, though still a bit chilly. Saw* Talk to Her *at Bijou, then went to Fitzpatrick's for drinks with friends.* I remember that night well. Over beers, we chatted about melancholy—Almodóvar's film is seductively sad—and the weird premise of *Talk to Her*, two guys waiting by the bedsides of women who have suffered severe brain damage. You said Europeans do sadness better than Americans. Hannah, who was German, said Americans hadn't suffered enough. I said the protagonists, Benigno and Marco, were compelling, though weird. The women are not expected to recover but they speak to them as if they were fully responsive, with surreal devotion. Almodóvar, said Denise (who taught Spanish literature), is someone who is beloved by women. Speaking of films, here's another entry: *Snow last night, about 2 inches, wet and heavy, most of it melting on walks and roads. Awful dinner party for self-absorbed documentary filmmaker and wife. Yuck.* I remember that night too. Yuck.

Several entries document your struggle with migraines. They have followed you to Iowa and are just as awful as they were in Washington. February 16, 2003: *Cloudy for most of the day. Came down with a headache, alas. Spent the day in bed with a bad migraine.* Three weeks later: *Back at ten p.m. last night from LA after an agonizing day spent sick with migraine—vomiting, chills, headache—all while flying and trying to navigate O'Hare. I wanted to die. It was good to be home and able to crawl into bed. Saw a goldfinch at the feeder this morning.* I dare not advise you see a doctor because migraines, you insist, are untreatable. What's the point? Plus, you don't like doctors. You figure if Joan Didion can survive hers, you can get through yours. For the most part, the migraines faded away during your last ten years. It's hard now, though, not to see them as warning signs—but that seems so simpleminded. Death makes everyone stupid.

MidAmerican Energy will not leave us alone. More elevator-bucket trucks, these equipped with new utility poles and giant corkscrews. They are all over town, these bucket trucks. It feels like a takeover. Two weeks ago orange-hat crews landed in our alley and planted a new utility pole on the corner of the lot, near the garage. They hacked away the red twig dogwood, hostas, and a gooseneck loosestrife, all which were flourishing thanks to your handy work. It was like cattle mutilation out west. Clean incisions and no sign of blood. The utility people cast them to the side like roadkill. Running new lines with significantly higher voltage, I was told by the foreman, whose parents were college professors in Upstate New York. How did you wind up here? I asked. One thing led to another, he said. The story of life, its true form: one thing leads to another. Such random creatures we are. I looked up at the new power line and wondered when it would fall on my head, when the hot wires would snap in a gust of savage wind and coil around my neck like a deadly snake.

Since you left, things are topsy-turvy. You were at heart a skeptic so that shouldn't surprise you. You expected awful things to happen—and you were right. So naturally you were baffled by my blind trust in an ability to navigate an unpredictable universe. There's a cup of coffee in my hand filled to the brim and even swishing over the spillway as I walk, and you say, How could you possibly not expect to spill that coffee? And I say, With a steady hand. But proof to the contrary is everywhere, you say, the floors, for instance, polka-dotted with your coffee drips. And true enough, there they are, hundreds of driblets from the kitchen up to my study, proof of an unsteady hand, evidence of an unstable universe. Without that blind trust, I should add, I would not be talking to you. The difference between you and me.

The cold creeps through my mind and stirs a memory. It's the winter of 2014. We are driving home from Cincinnati on I-74. We first encounter snow in Indianapolis, quite a bit. We slow down. At this rate, I say, it will take all day to drive to Iowa. By the time we cross the Illinois border, the sun is gone. Totally. It's really dark and that only makes the blizzard stranger. Is this a snowfall or a snowslide? you say. Milo is in the backseat and knows something's wrong. You lift the dog onto your lap. He has really big eyes and looks worried. I'm getting nervous myself, and that makes you even more nervous because I'm the snow guy from Buffalo. I know hazardous driving but

have a look on my face like I've just swallowed Drano.
What's wrong? you ask. I can't see much out the
windshield, I say. Be careful, you say. Ghostly cars are
stopping, pulling over, but who knows where the shoulder is. Between the empty cornfield on my right and the
highway's left shoulder is an expanse of sheer white. It's
bewildering. Maybe we should pull over, you suggest.
Where? Maybe a rest stop, you say. Okay, but I really can't
see out the window. The familiar green highway signs
have disappeared. Use your low beams, you advise. Sure,
I say, switching the high beams off.

I've driven in snow squalls in Upstate New York,
but there's something different here. This is not a forty-
five-minute blizzard and it's only eight degrees above zero
and falling. Should we be stranded, say skid off the road
into a snowdrift, I don't think we'll survive. No one would
reach us in time. It only takes ten minutes to get frostbite.
Numb nose, cheeks, ears, chins, fingers. In another ten
minutes the mind begins to go, loses focus. Once our body
temperatures drop below eighty-five degrees, the heart
slows critically, respiratory and nervous systems switch
off, other organs crash. With so little body mass Milo
would be the first to go; you next; then me. Funny, isn't it?

Milo is shivering. I'm really scared. We need to get
off the highway, you say. Agreed, I say. In the left lane—I
think it's the left lane—a tractor trailer barrels by. Can
you believe that guy! I say. The snow swirls in a rumble of
madness. We crawl all the way to Urbana, hands shaking,
eyes twitching. Milo seems shrunken. Up ahead, I see a
ramp but can't read the road sign. The milepost is buried
under snow. Let's take this, I say. Where are we? you ask.
I'm not sure. I think we should get off before the snow

gets any deeper, I say. My voice is high-pitched because I'm really nervous. As it is, I go on, there's at least four feet of snow piled up on this ramp. Even with snow tires— thank the gods we bought snow tires—it's an uncertain exit. You give me a double take—*uncertain exit*? I blush. It will be tricky, I say.

That's grossly understated. We leave the highway and creep along at five miles per hour down the curvy ramp. No sign of plows. The radio, in fact, reports I-74 has just closed down. Boy, I say, this is some storm. I've had enough snow for a lifetime, you say. On the ramp, the powdery stuff reaches just below the car windows. I'm trying to guess where the road is. The blizzard hasn't let up. Five hours and counting. It's like another world out there, you say. Milo looks up imploringly, waiting for reassurance. We're too scared. An abandoned car, its headlights beaming SOS through the snow, helps me get our bearings. Where did the people go? I wonder. I hope someplace warm, you say. The sight of a forsaken car is unnerving. Do you think there's ice underneath the snow? you say. Probably, I say.

We're rounding the halfway point of the ramp. The new tires are digging in, I say. I think we might make it. Up ahead we see the ghostly outlines of homes and streetlights. You perk up and so does Milo.

It's uncanny how dogs understand things, you say. It's a well-known fact, I say, that dogs are psychic. You give me one of your looks. No, really—canine precognition. That's why Milo hides in the basement before a bad storm. Whatever, you say. We are so glad to be alive. We're in Champaign, I think, I say. I don't care where we are, you say, as long as we're not on I-74. The temperature has dropped to negative four. It's subzero out there, I say. Let's find a place to hole up, you say. Okay, I say. Unfortunately, all the hotels are booked and few are pet friendly. We drive around for another hour and then take the last room in a La Quinta on Center Drive. I think it's Center Drive. By then, the temperature has sunk to eleven below zero. We celebrate our survival with an orgy of junk food: Doritos, M&Ms, microwave popcorn, Snickers, Cheez Whiz, Ritz Crackers, and grape Fanta, all three of us on the sprawling king-size bed. Milo can't believe how good Doritos are. On TV, the weather people are blathering on about the polar vortex. That was some vortex, you say. That sure was, I say.

CHAPTER NINE
VENUS (THE JOKER)

Venus favors the bold.

—Ovid

Went for a walk all bundled up like a child. Crunch, crunch over powdery snow. Several white oaks have not lost their leaves. All brown and crumpled, curling inward, but clinging to their branches. No one knows why trees retain dead leaves, marcescent foliage. My, what a word, *marcescent*. Makes me feel authoritative. But what I really feel is the cold. It's creeping under my gloves and up my fingers and down my socks between my toes. Like permafrost. The wind chill right now is negative thirty. How do the trees bear up? Somehow they have to keep their cells from freezing. They can produce sugars to decrease the freezing point of water. Proteins too. If the temperature plunges to negative forty for any length of time, though, freezing and cell death are certain.

Crunch, crunch over powdery snow I go. There's a deer fifty feet away. It's a whitetail doe. We both stop. I'm so bundled up she isn't sure exactly what kind of thing I am. She's wondering if I am human or nonhuman. I stay perfectly still in my puffy jacket, my olive-green snowmobile pants, and my giant microfleece ski hood. I myself don't know what I am. The doe is perplexed, does not scamper away until she resolves the mystery. I remain still, confusing her more. Neither fish nor fowl. She cocks her head like a curious puppy. What are you? she says. I'm in the middle of the road standing still, like a man from space who has crash-landed. I would not have thought that deer are inquisitive. For almost ten minutes we stare at one another, the doe and the spaceman, but then she slips away, bored at last. Blue jays and cardinals whoosh by. To my left are the fake animals, a lone wolf, several foxes, a herd of dear, lawn art. The foxes are mostly buried by snow.

This morning in class, my brain played a trick on me. I'm talking about Coleridge's poem where a sailor shoots an albatross out of the sky with a bow and arrow. I called the protagonist, the man with the long gray beard and glittering eye, the "ancient *marinator.*" Not once but twice. My poor brain. Must be the cold. Few students these days read Coleridge's poem, so my gaffe fell on deaf ears. But imagine the one dutiful soul who googled *ancient marinator.* What's that? she wonders. An alternative rock band? A sous-chef at a seafood restaurant? Linguists call this a *disfluency disorder* and consider it on a par with stuttering. I'm telling you this because it will embellish your morning coffee. Also for the sheer symmetry. You with your bad ears and me with my weird phonemes. A perfect couple.

It's easy to take for granted how extremely involved accurate speech production is in the brain, but complexity is no excuse for sounding like a stranger. Adding an extra syllable is said to be a rare articulation disorder, which doesn't make me feel any less stupid. I once said *astut-a* instead of *astute*—on TV no less—sounding like *SNL*'s Father Guido Sarducci. I should add that my disfluency gaffes have been on the rise lately (I called the *Odyssey* the *Odyssiad*) and I'm wondering if it's not a side effect of being alone. It's not that I'm elongating vowels, like some kid tweeting *helloooo!!!*—but that I'm creating malapropisms (*is it kisstomary to cuss the bride?*) in the manner of William Archibald Spooner, who had a keen intellect but was also (memo to self) absentminded. In the case of Spooner, his tongue could barely keep up with his brain, producing sounds entirely at odds with his intentions. The more agitated he became, the more bizarre his word botching. I wonder if he lost a wife.

My problem could also be a case of dysprosody. People diagnosed with the disease can comprehend language and vocalize what they intend to say; however, they can't control the way the words come out of their mouths, as if struck by lightning. Now, the scary thing is that dysprosody is usually attributed to neurological damage of some kind, such as a brain tumor or stroke. You can see where this is going, so let's change the subject.

Your brain was a marvelous machine. It hummed capably at all hours. I could hear happy birds chirping in the warm sunlight of your thoughts. The clarity of your mind astonished everyone, especially me. Not just clear-headed but scarily resolute. If there is a scale to measure everyday cognition—there is—I want to stay far away. My head is like a parallel world where David Lynch fiddles around on some unmakeable film. May the gods help me now that you're elsewhere.

You've probably forgotten the weekend we moved from Capitol Hill to Virginia—but I haven't. We were merging households. It was only a matter of time before we moved in together, once we owned the RCA, and that happened sooner than later. Escaping from our urban cellars was motivation enough. Where would we go? Arlington was cheaper to rent in than the Maryland suburbs, so there we went. A giant Colonial house in the suburbs on 23rd Road off of Glebe Highway, on one side next door to William Rehnquist and on the other to Tom Shales, film reviewer for the *Washington Post*. The change in scene was mind-boggling. There we were, one moment living in isolation in cramped basement apartments on Capitol Hill, besieged by creepy things like cockroaches and silverfish— the next in a manor house beside the chief justice of the Supreme Court. Our rental wasn't your common two-room apartment but a four-bedroom home with dining and recreation rooms and a sunny nook. The front- and backyards were enormous, and so were the giant firs and cedars. On Capitol Hill nature wasn't, with its three-story row houses and small front gardens enclosed by black wrought-iron fences neatly laid out block after block. I felt I had come out from under. There was the Potomac down the hill, gorges, startling hills, and trees everywhere. It's just like *Twin Peaks*, you said. Freaky, I replied.

It was a big spread. It would take days to mow the lawn, but I couldn't wait. You were amazed by my suburban longing. I hadn't mowed a lawn in twenty years, but that's all I could think of now. And you got your hands dirty in the garden, plucking ivy and planting irises and tulips and hydrangeas. That's when you began wearing your straw hat for sun protection. Your large-brim hat and always a trowel in your left hand—you circled the grounds (what an idea) like a park ranger, on guard against poison ivy, grubs, and groundsel. Our landlord had planted zoysia grass, because it's supposed to be a status symbol, but zoysia is as thick as cogon grass and as tough as ivory. Common suburban lawn mowers will crap out, as did ours several times. I had to push and push a machine that easily got bogged down in the densely packed blades of grass. It was like mowing a sand dune. You smiled at my efforts, seeing how my wish had come true. Troglodytes no more.

These are cheering memories. What isn't so sunny is remembering how agonizing it was to move two households from the city. Relocating your things was uncomplicated and filled us with confidence. My apartment was a black hole. It defied theories of space-time how I crowded thousands of books into an English basement apartment that wasn't big enough for a thirty-five-inch TV. There was some serious voodoo at work here. It wasn't until midnight that we lugged the last box of stuff up the U-Haul's ramp. At that point we still had to dispose of my hideous hand-me-down floral sofa.

Let's handle this tomorrow, I said, equivocating. By this point, the smell of cardboard was so disgusting I couldn't will myself back into the truck. We still had the white sectional sofa bought in Maryland to fetch and then drop off the U-Haul in Virginia by noon. I was dog-tired but you were tenacious, always have been, in your jeans and sneakers and navy-blue sweatshirt. You wouldn't stop.

You gave me that don't-be-a-fool look and off we went, after midnight, in search of a Goodwill drop-off site. I was foul-smelling from a day's worth of lifting and lugging. You and Connie (our school buddy) sat next to me in the cab of the truck—we all stank—and soldiered on as the U-Haul roared through the lower gears. My mom had given me her favorite piece of furniture ten years ago, and it showed few signs of wear. I felt beholden to it, and you to me, and that's what I call love. All night we drove in search of sanctuary for the floral sofa. At wits' end, we dumped it in the rear lot of a used-furniture store, hoping someone would get the message. It was now four thirty in the morning, and as I looked behind I felt a wave of guilt, as if abandoning a troubled pet on a stranger's porch. We had made the move, and it wasn't easy, but here we were in the Virginia suburbs. Neither of us had coupled before. But we were such a good fit we just let things play out. Down deep we knew that nothing could divide us. Maybe death but death wasn't real.

Your room is exactly as you left it, by the way. Each morning I sit on your ottoman, look around, and lace up my shoes. I stare at the empty desk chair where you sat composing e-mails, your back up straight. I also keep the photos of you here in this room. My favorite photo (right now) dates back five years ago. You are posing with a rake out front in a green ribbed sweater, a dark-brown scarf tied around your neck. It's a sunny day late in October. You have a smirk on your face because I'm wielding a camera rather than a rake. Late-afternoon light, a soft glow that breaks my heart. "No photograph can truly recall the beloved's smile," says Madeleine L'Engle. That's not true. Your photos reveal a warm smile I never saw when clicking the camera—a smile that crosses the cryptic expanse between us.

Where have you gone?

Space, the final frontier. It's inspiring to think that the edge of space is just sixty-two miles away. That's where the atmosphere thins to nothing, replaced by a stream of violently charged particles. The Kármán line. To set sail above the trade winds, the Himalayas, the Gobi Desert, to leave the sadness of the earth behind—what could be more inviting? I know my thoughts drift. My mind is frazzled but what of it? You're still listening. It's natural to be frazzled. When Milo died, you became visibly frazzled. You said, I'm worn to a frazzle. And so we went away to Ireland and you felt better, which turned out to be a horrific illusion.

For the mind to wander, well, it's natural. Sometimes the mind moves freely from one notion to another, but other times it returns to the same idea. I always come back to you. I'm loyal. Neurologists now think that wandering is the default state of the mind. Wandering minds, they say, have a greater capacity for working memory. It's how I look for you. I wander up and down the trail of memory. It's the way of all things, even big cosmic-size things like stars. I sometimes get the feeling the universe is wandering too. If I can't feel in sync with life on this planet, maybe there's an elsewhere.

Space Boy is in sync with something I can only guess at, that dark flow that's moving things in an unimaginable direction. He says he's leaking gravity from moving so fast. I say slow down, this is way over my head. He says the weird correlations of the quantum world are totally cool. I say that explains nothing. He says it's all about entanglement. I say what?

This brings me to the word *planet*, which comes from the Greek word for *wanderer* and it grew out of a misconception. Ancient astronomers assumed the earth was a fixed object around which other bodies, like Mars and Jupiter, moseyed. Today we have a pretty good idea that wandering is the most predictable action of an unpredictable universe. Cosmic drift, however complicated, is one thing all bodies share, big and little. No matter how regular our solar orbit, we ourselves are straying off course (as I write) at a speed of five hundred thousand miles per hour, along with the other big rocks in our system. Whole galaxy clusters, and their millions of stars, are traveling through space at an even faster speed: two million miles per hour.

But where is everyone going? All galaxies are drifting, cosmologists say poetically, beyond the boundary of what we can see. It's not random drift. There's a patch of the sky past the edge of the observable universe in the direction of the Centaurus and Hydra constellations. We're all going there, pushed along (this is my favorite part) by the "dark flow," not typical red-shift expansion but something quite different, a stunning example of nonrandom cosmic drift. No one, so they say, expected this. Ironically, that's where Space Boy is headed himself, to the Boomerang Nebula in Centaurus.

Message from Space Boy, who has just whizzed by Neptune. He really knows how to fly that thing. Says he saw someone walking around a rocky pile of nitrogen on the surface. Why didn't you beam down? I radio back. People don't do that in real life, he says. We don't quarrel—no point in that. Besides, I rather like the multiplicity of me, given the task at hand.

I'm not surprised that a part of me is not here. Maybe we are dealing with displacement not only on an existential level, as when suffering loss, but also in weirder ways. In a dream I see you on a bench. This isn't the past but now, you say. You are here with me now, you say. Wow, I say in the dream. The bench is made from a large piece of maple. The grain is terrific, I think to myself. I'm running my hand along its surface. I look around at the trees and sky. We're in a park. You have on a full-length, loose-fitting dress, salmon colored. We hug. You seem different. You are in your twenties, younger than I ever knew. I tell you how much I miss you. We hold each other. This is Planet Claire, you tell me. There is no death here. It's true, I say, I can't feel time. Where did it go? It's not here, you say.

I'm wide awake now. We're in Pennsylvania on a highway. It's overcast and you and me are in motion. Nana? I say, not sure I hear right. Nana, you say. Her name is Ruth, my dad's mom. We call her Nana. Okay, do I call her that too, instead of Ruth? Yes, you say. Just sounds funny. You know, I say, I think *nana* is derived from *nonna*, Italian for *grandma*. My mom called the old ladies in her neighborhood Nonna this and Nonna that. That's ironic, you say, because Nana doesn't like Italians, I should warn you. How badly does she dislike Italians? I ask. Keenly, you say.

We're driving southward on the back roads of Pennsylvania through tiny towns like Falls Creek, Luthersburg, and Tyrone in the Allegheny Mountains. We're on our way to Altoona, your ancestral home. I'm about to meet your grandmother. What if your nana doesn't like me? I ask. Well, you say, time to pack your bags. When did your grandfather die? I can't remember, you say, a while ago. So Nana is now with Charlie? Charlie, yes. Who is this guy? You'll like him. Very working-class type. Factory guy all his life. A broken man. How'd they meet? Don't ask so many questions, you say. Wait till we get there. Okay. Is your dad close to Ruth? Not really. Why not? Hard to say. What's Altoona like? It's a train town where they repair locomotives for Penn Central. Great roundhouses, you say. What's that? They service engines and cars. We'll go there. Sounds good, I say. Did your whole family work for the railroad? On my dad's side, you say. On my mom's, coal miners.

Nana and Charlie live in a small two-story home on the downward slope of a large hill. A white Cadillac Seville sits in the driveway. We park along the street. Everywhere we look the tops of trees have been lopped off, as though to satisfy some bizarre rule of taste. The trees have been midgetized, I say, to the same scale up and down the street. That's weird. You haven't seen anything yet, you say. It's a place of strange desires. All the houses look alike, as do their backyards. There are no fences so you can spot identical lawn chairs, barbecue grills, and patio furniture as far as the eye can see. Welcome to Nana and Charlie's world, you say.

Nana and Charlie greet us at the door and show us to our upstairs room. Nana is an attractive woman in her early eighties. Dyed-blond hair, bright blue eyes, and even brighter red lipstick. She's wearing a yellow blouse and white slacks. Nana is happy to see you. She's in the kitchen making egg salad sandwiches. The house is blanketed in beige wall-to-wall carpeting. Soft on the feet, I say. Your nana, Claire B., says Charlie, had this installed last February. You could feel the cold with your feet. Not anymore. Charlie is wearing tan trousers and a white T-shirt. He looks like Bing Crosby if Bing Crosby had been born in Detroit, moved to Baltimore, and then settled in Buffalo. It's the middle of summer and he has slippers on his large feet. I can't get over how cushy the carpet feels, I say. Don't get any ideas, you say.

Nana and Charlie are smokers with unreformed eating habits. They love processed foods, white bread, donuts, potato chips. Still, they're not overweight. Your nana is petite and Charlie, though with chronic back problems, is tall and lean. He's handsome in a kind of 1940s way, though tragic-looking. Your grandmother, by the way, will outlive you by at least twenty years, cigarettes and all. After dinner (Domino's pizza), Charlie and Nana take us to their favorite haunt, Denny's. Denny's is pretty lively for a Tuesday night. The senior crowd is out in force. I haven't a clue what to order—nor you. The last time I was at Denny's was prom night. Charlie recommends the apple pie with cinnamon ice cream. The chocolate lava cake looks nasty good but we both say sure to the apple pie.

So here we are at a booth in Denny's. It's 1994 and we're in the middle of Pennsylvania wolfing down pie and ice cream with two elderly types who couldn't be more different. I'm having mighty-fine-pie thoughts and so are you. We are loving our pies, especially me. How'd you both meet? I ask Charlie and Nana. Your nana, Claire B., says Charlie, is a pretty fussy woman. Charlie explains that he first dated Ruth's sister Naomi and only later got up the nerve to ask Ruth out. I don't know why he wasted his time on my sister, Nana says, but that's Charlie for you. Charlie smiles ruefully. I swallow another forkful. I don't remember apple pie ever tasting this good.

Was it love at first sight? you ask. When dating? Charlie and Nana stop eating, sit up straight, both seized by a look of surprise, perplexed by your question. Love at first sight? repeats Nana. She looks at Charlie who looks at me. They are mystified. And then laughter. Nana and Charlie are laughing out of control. Because they're smokers, they are laughing and coughing at the same time. Even cackling. Charlie's lungs seem to be collapsing, he's laughing so hard. Nana's eye shadow is running down her cheeks, the mascara all gooey. We look at each other, not sure whether to be concerned or confused, but then burst into laughter too. Love at first sight! What an idea! Everyone is laughing. It's like a Beckett play. You're choking on the pie and I've dislodged my glasses, which only makes Nana and Charlie explode into more uncontrollable laughter. It's a communal fit. We feel like potheads. All of Denny's is staring at our booth. The waitstaff seem alarmed. We look at each other in total glee. We suspect that in some inscrutable way the meaning of life has just been laid bare. It's a mute understanding, and we don't bother to look for words.

We spend the rest of the evening giggling. Then we climb into Charlie's Cadillac and drive back Highway 220 to the street with the stunted trees. There's reminiscing and gossip. It's a big family but you're obviously the favorite granddaughter. You and Nana, whose eyes twinkle, catch up on family matters, while I play with two brass balls, turning them over in my hands. They're heavy. Charlie just gave me these two-inch spheroids after a tour of his workshop. I love basement workshops. It was dark and cobwebby but lots of tools. You might need these, Charlie said, if Claire B. is anything like her grandma. Need what? I said. Brass balls, Charlie said with delight.

Last night I dreamt of you again. We were in a bedroom, perhaps a guest room, and you and I are kissing. I said the word *beaujeanello* at a certain frequency, tempo, and resonance that entirely turned you on, unlocking your inner desire and allure. You become so seductive and so irresistible I am dizzy with gazing and kissing.

The made-up expression—beaujeanello—was like a password that opened up a part of you neither of us ever witnessed. You wore a sexy black dress.

Speaking of acoustics, I found a Word file on your laptop named *A Year in Decibels*. Plans were under way to write about your hearing difficulties. I'm very taken with your writing, as you know. The entries contain acute observations about sound in the manner of an aphorism collection. Here's an entry dated July 22, 2011: *Just 2mm in length, the tiny river-dwelling animal known as the water boatman produces a noise that can reach 99 decibels. Someone walking along the bank can actually hear these tiny creatures singing at the bottom of the river. For its size, the water boatman is the loudest animal on earth.* I feel as if I'm prying into a secret corner of your mind when I quote you, but why lose such a poignant thought, an aquatic insect singing *La Bohème* at the bottom of a slow-moving stream. *The water boatman has very fine dark brown striation marking its wings*, you write. *Its hind legs are long and hairy and shaped like oars. Thus its name. Unlike other aquatic bugs, such as the backswimmer, the water boatman is nonpredatory. It feeds on algae, not other insects. The water boatman sings its song by rubbing its penis against its abdomen, using stridulation like the cricket. Its song is a display of courtship and reaches an ear-splitting 99.2 decibels, equivalent to taking in a booming orchestra from the front row. When the boatman cries*, you write, *he weeps in the key of D minor, the saddest of all keys.*

We were in Santa Fe when you logged that entry. There are no boatmen in the high desert, just rattlers and horned lizards. We arrived in Santa Fe in early June and holed up at St. John's College where you directed the Bread Loaf

School of English. We had no choice but to stay in an insipid dorm room, but we made the best of it. We'd unload the truck and rearrange the apartment, moving particleboard beds and desks and dressers from one room to another. Three hours later, it was cozy. Behind us was Atalaya Mountain and the Sangre de Cristo range, and below that was the giant Arroyo de los Chamisos. Twice a day we hiked up the Atalaya trail and down the arroyo. You in your shades and straw hat, me with a camera. That's why your transcendent smile yet smiles for me. Nothing made us more real than hiking together under the New Mexican sun, deep in Piñon country, surrounded by scraggly ponderosa pine, stink bugs, and green lizards, alert for jackalopes and diamondbacks.

The silence above the arroyo was uncanny, and the aroma of sweetgrass and sage was hallucinogenic. Yet somehow, you stopped to write about the water boatman in your notebook. It was our final summer in Santa Fe. That year we rented an adobe house on the north side of town, the place with spiders. Big ones on the prowl. We placed plastic cups in each corner for spider expulsion. At least twice a day, pine cone spiders, jumping spiders, grass spiders. Snakes don't alarm you the way they do me; spiders strike terror in your heart. You would issue your spider scream, and I would run for the plastic cup and begin the extraction. The wolf spider, though, startled both of us because of its enormous fangs and violin-like markings.

That summer was drier than a sand dune. The winds kicked up huge clouds of red dirt and yellow dust. Fires broke out everywhere. In the eastern foothills of the Jemez Mountains, a tree fell on a power line and kindled the worst wildfire in New Mexico history. In two weeks' time, more than 156,000 acres were ablaze, threatening the Los Alamos labs. We looked north from Atalaya Mountain and saw a big plume of smoke. The hot dust burned our cheeks. The lab was evacuated on the eve of July 4. We took sizzling drives with the dog, tracking wildfires and eating tacos. I drove to Roswell, and you traveled to the pueblos. These were our tall tales. The deafening sun and the red earth, the ancient mesas, the dry riverbeds, booming cicadas, the raccoons and coyotes. We lived among them all, the trees and the stones and the Zuni bears, through the parables of moonlight and the forever morning, down the slopes of the windswept mountain.

So much busy work. I'm sitting in a "wealth management" meeting with the TIAA guy—again—who is drawing all kinds of triangles with little boxes of money on a frosted-glass eraser board. He keeps adding acronyms to his doodles, RMDs, IRAs, QDROs, and esoteric numbers, 403(b) plans, 457(b) plans. He's a typical Midwestern type. White shirt and tie, straight sandy-brown hair with a touch of mousse. I'm a bit unnerved by his bland face. He's a nice guy, for sure, but he's so smooth-faced there's something unreal about him. His back is to me right now as he scribbles on the board rollover options. I ask him about the RMD. Required minimum distribution, he says. What's that? I ask. At age seventy and a half, you will need to begin withdrawing from your retirement account, so that the government can tax your moneys.

He seems to enjoy standing up before his whiteboard, blue marker in hand. The little professor. I try to imagine the training session where he learned his spiel. I ask him whether I should become more or less aggressive in investing my retirement funds in stocks and equities. It's up to you, he says. More aggressive, I say. I'm getting into the spirit of the game. I mention this because these are the little tasks that you, not I, enjoyed performing. Managing our wealth. You had a thing for money—not me. You liked the feeling of security an array of accounts produced. But the accounts you opened are little ones, with tiny dividends, no more than 1 percent. I'm going after 5 percent. I will tell you right now that I'm getting to like this.

Later, I had to ransack my downstairs file cabinet, looking for our marriage certificate, which is nowhere to be found. Had to write to Arlington Courthouse for a replacement. While looking in your closet, stumbled across your memorabilia—from before we met—including letters dating back to 1976. I will have to go through this *pre-me* archive to find out more. Young Claire in her midtwenties. Had to sit down on your ottoman. Vertigo.

Getting married is hardly romantic—it's mostly rehab. Remember how linoleum once covered the hardwood floor in the kitchen, lovely maple? A layer of linoleum and a blanket of tar. It took a while but we eventually peeled away the floor covering and revealed a dark, thick coating of adhesive. I got down on all fours and gave it a good scraping. It wouldn't budge. I got the heat gun but still no luck. Oh my goodness, I said. That's really awful stuff. And you said, Yep, pretty bad. These adhesives grow stronger the longer they're down, and this has been down for fifty years. Off to the library you went, returning with a pile of books. And so we started boiling large pots of water at night, that's what the book said, poured hot water on the tar, added shredded newspaper, waited fifteen minutes, and then scraped until our hands cramped up.

On a mission, you wouldn't let up. Three hours every

night on hands and knees. The tar was stubborn, bonding with the wood on a molecular level. Take care not to dig the scraper into the wood, you said. Work in small sections at a time. I grunted and growled. I had no idea homeownership could be so punishing. I cursed the man who glued the linoleum to the floor. I was too exhausted even for a beer. Baseball on TV called to me. I thought it better not to leave my post, though. The moral imperative was here in the kitchen, and you were in command. In the end the rescued maple floor was beautiful. I smiled proudly, as if the project had been my idea. Truth is I couldn't see that far ahead, from the tawdry linoleum to the radiant maple. You could. You always did. It was a real talent, the vision thing.

You were something of an alchemist, someone with a keen eye for things of unexpected value, things overlooked by others. You had a magic touch. I remember the armoire you had inherited from relatives just before we married. It was the ugliest thing I'd ever seen. Really ugly. A dark, ungainly piece of furniture, all gloomy with age and grime. Somewhere under the blackened stains was oak but I couldn't see it. You're not moving this to Iowa? I ask. It's hideous and big. Where will we put it? It's not that big, you say. It will fit in the dining room. I don't know about that, I say. It has a postwar look that is creepy, as if its previous owners had met a terrible end or had entombed dead cats inside. I was hoping to escape it. But you won't abandon your armoire. It will look fine refinished. It just needs a little love, you say. Hmm, I say.

A year later and here it is in the corner of the dining room, a radiant piece of furniture. An eye-catcher. What a stunning armoire, visitors say. Is it a reproduction or has it been refinished? It's exquisite. I usually hide in the kitchen when this happens. The process was involved and laborious. Lots of chemicals, knives, paint scrapers, sandpaper, rags, rubber gloves, masks, varnishes, stains, alembic, retort, more chemicals. Your blond hair in a bun under a baseball hat, your oversized khakis, white T-shirt—but no flowing robes. The armoire's innards were carefully disassembled and laid on sawhorses, drawers, doors, shelves. The hardware in a Rubbermaid container. I was mesmerized by your work habits, so clever and orderly. As I watched great gobs of darkened goo amass on folded sheets of newspaper, I began to worry I had been entirely wrong about the armoire. Every afternoon for seven days you labored over this large bit of furniture, applying various stripping agents and patiently scraping away the detritus. Gradually, the armoire lost its darkness. And then there it was—a tract of golden oak. Uh-oh, I said to myself, as I watched you work. That doesn't look good. Radiant oak! In order to save face I offered to help, but you weren't tempted. Stay away from my armoire, you said.

About the armoire I was stupid, but I was right about the dog. There seemed to be something missing in our lives—we didn't know that until we got a dog. At first you were skeptical. Dogs require too much care. They're like babies, you say. I am stubborn. I want a dog. Why a dog all of a sudden? you ask. It's not like you grew up on a farm surrounded by adorable animals. I want a dog, I repeat. You wonder if something might be wrong with me. I'm robotic. I want a dog. I'm feeling needy. I want a dog.

A suburb of Cedar Rapids, Marion is a lonely drive up Highway 151. It's known for its antique shops and is home to Jadzia Dax of *Deep Space Nine* (Teresa Ferrell). Her parents used to run a sandwich shop on Main Street, a kind of *Star Trek* museum. Ms. Ferrell, by the way, is married to Leonard Nimoy's son Adam. So we found our way to the Cedar Valley Humane Society, which advertised two small dogs, Cavachons with adorable eyes. What exactly is a Cavachon? I ask as we enter the building. A Cavalier King Charles spaniel mixed with a bichon frise, you say. Predictably, you've done the research. Smart and friendly dogs, and they don't shed, you say. Plus, they're not yappers. Not too small, not too big. Just right. Okay, I say.

We meet Milo, then named Tink, and his brother Harvey. The two dogs are in A-block, prisoners with visitation rights. Seven-month-old Tink looks worried, doesn't trust anyone, gives us a wary look as he leaves his cage. Harvey is younger and wants to party. The older guy looks a little sad, I say, don't you think? Probably sensitive, you say. Didn't like getting abandoned by its first owner. We take the dogs for a walk. Already you're hooked.

Twelve parties have already signed up for Tink and Harvey. It seems like a long shot, especially as we have no previous history of dog care. So we write an essay. It's your idea. Brilliant, I say, yes, let's write an essay. Why we love dogs. Out comes your blue ballpoint pen. I supply adjectives and adverbs. *While we never owned a dog before*, you write, *our continued and steadfast care* (I add) *of three cats* (we inflated the number) *has awakened us to the intimate and necessary role pets play in the fragile lives of their owners.* Why *fragile*? you ask. Because we're humans and humans are so improbable it's kind of sad, I say. But the rescue people want to feel confident about us, you say, that we're solvent and stable, good citizens with empathy and means. How about *long anchored in a community of caring professionals*? Much better, you say. Two days later, Cedar Valley calls to say Tink—soon to be Milo—is waiting. That was in September of 2004.

I hear water running in the bathtub upstairs. It's Sunday afternoon six years later. I know what that means. Milo hears it too. He gives me a nervous look. Sorry, pal, I say. It's that time of the month. You give a holler. The tub is ready. Milo is stoic, resigns himself to his fate. He stands still in six inches of warm sudsy water. Grin and bear it, he thinks, but he's not liking this. We're both on our knees. You're working his front end, me the back end. No soap in his ears, you say. Okay. And watch his eyes. Okay. Be sure to wash his butt carefully. Yuck. Scrubadub. Milo looks like a wet rag, only one-third his normal size. I trundle him up in several large towels and roll him around the floor like pizza dough. He climbs out of a mountain of cotton and shakes off bathwater like a vibrator. There's fire in his eyes. When released from agony, he goes insane, dashing around and downstairs so fast I'm dizzy. The bichon blitz, you call this, ten laps around the dining room. He throws himself on the sofa and digs his back into the cushions as if boring down to pure rank earthy soil. He's releasing stress, you say. Got a lot of it, I guess. Wish I could do that.

A bleak day. Everything vanishes beneath the gun-barrel-gray sky. On Reno Street, a dead gray squirrel is nestled at the base of an oak. Not dead long, I think. His paws are bright pink and his dim eyes half open. No light. He looks fat enough to have survived the mild winter. A fall? Hit and run? A predator? Thick fallow grass makes a cozy bed and the gnarly oak a perfect headboard. I snap a photo, though I don't why. Waldo has become an archetype. It's the dying time of year and maybe I've been summoned here as a witness. My thoughts run morbid. Thanks to the photo, I see later how the squirrel and the oak are a prefect color match. Pieces of bark cover the squirrel, and desiccated leaves, as if the oak were tending to the dead.

There is no good death, but this is better than evisceration by hawk. But what do I know? I returned later for a better photo (shamelessly) but the squirrel was gone. Perhaps his corpse was snatched by something hungry, or a kind homeowner laid him to rest. Perhaps he woke from a deep sleep—but I don't think so. You know death when you see it, how something once frenetic with movement is now motionless. The black whiskers, the curved paw, the woody brown fur, the elegant tail. All so still. Not a twitch. There are no lessons in death, unless it is this. Alive no more.

I carry you and Milo wherever I go. Dead things in my heart, as though it's a mausoleum. I'm taking the squirrel with me, at least for a while, to mark this bleak moment in time, the dead center. I walk briskly on toward the park into the wind. The gray tree bark and the gray sky are all one. But for their swaying limbs, the trees would vanish. There is no meaning in death, but everything that means owes something to it. These silly thoughts rise from my brain like smoke. Today the ground is frozen and the walking surer. Last week my feet slid out from under me up on the ridge and I toppled over in the mud. I had to laugh. Suddenly, you are here beside me in memory, the dog behind us, sniffling around tree trunks for pee marks. You have your black quilted jacket on and your blond hair is fluttering in the wind. We're holding hands because it's cold. You whisper something in my ear but I can't make it out. The wind through the trees, so loud. Where do we go from here? I say, but you're gone. I stop and look around. There's no one here today. No dogs, no joggers. Just the naked trees swaying in the wind. The creaking wood.

Valentine's Day. I bought your card a year ago. *I only have eyes for you*, it says. There are ten cartoon eyes of varying sizes on a yellow background. They're like cyclops eyes—not paired up—Polyphemus-like. In Ovid's *Metamorphoses*, Polyphemus sends a Valentine card to Galatea, who is not interested. For goodness sakes, who falls in love with a cyclops? she says. Galatea has a crush on a high school quarterback, Acis, who has blond hair, a square jaw, and two eyes—some kid from Thessalonica. The cyclops could break Acis in half and eat him like a Mars bar if he wanted. But Polyphemus mopes mostly, a pining giant. Later, though, he throws a boulder at the kid, squashing him. Everyone flees. Rock-throwing cyclopes are scary.

Anyway, we would have gone out to dinner tonight, revisited the past, made plans for the summer, drunk red wine, talked most of the night. I might have asked you about past boyfriends, even though you aren't the memoirist I am. You are in the moment, looking vaguely ahead. We would have discussed your mom's depression, my mom's health, whether or not to visit Lauren and Casey in Portland.

Did I jinx you, I wonder, by buying your Valentine card early? It's not like me to plan ahead. I do remember the first Valentine gift I bought you and it was a doozy. It was midway through our first year of dating in Washington. I got you a large-handled camp ax with a red blade from a hardware store on Pennsylvania Avenue. As a tool enthusiast, I was delighted with the ax. It was for the oak bundle you fed your fireplace. The wood needed splitting. I meant well. Anyway, it was a stupid idea. I was thinking only of your chubby oak logs that wouldn't burn right, but you thought, smart-ass that I am, I was communicating in code. You were getting the ax. You later said you didn't expect to hear from me again and I said, What?

Our last Valentine's Day together we dine out. We even dress up, not to the nines but maybe to the sevens. You look good, I say, and you did. You look nice, you say. Thanks, I say. I even put cologne on, and you lipstick. You take my arm and we walk to a restaurant just around the corner. This was a husband-and-wife ritual, you and me arm in arm on Saturday night. When it was cold, you'd shiver and press closer. What are you in the mood for? you ask. Fish, I say. How about you? Maybe pizza. We are people of modest desires. We'll have a glass of wine—me, maybe two—and share dessert. We feel lucky we can do this. Academic salaries are modest. If we had two kids, it would be a different story.

Today, tree-removal people surrounded an old elm on Governor and Bloomington streets. Nearly half of the elm's antique limbs had been sawed off. They lay stacked up by the side of the tree, giant logs. Seeing so much of a tree's vertical parts lying horizontal on the ground is disturbing. An Iowa City official was on-site to explain that the old tree was the second-largest American elm in all of Iowa. It was so famous arborists from Iowa State drove here to take photos. Recently, it had split down the middle from old age and rot. It was structurally hazardous and had to come down. There are signs everywhere. It's frightening. Who knows what death means, but it can't stop expressing itself.

CHAPTER TEN
THE MOON
(STRANGE ATTRACTOR)

The moon is a friend for the lonesome to talk to.
—Carl Sandburg

I f I were a coyote I'd be howling at the moon, even though coyotes really don't do that. But moonlight does induce howling deep in the forest when the flowers close up at night. The light of the moon triggers odd behavior, like sleepwalking and fits of violence. The Londoner Charles Hyde committed a series of abominable crimes under a full moon, as did the infamous Son of Sam. Hippocrates attributed night terrors to a moon goddess in the habit of visiting dreamers in their sleep. The moon's gravity is thought to tug on large bodies with terrific force. I would certainly be howling at this very moment, under moonlight no less, if I weren't talking to myself. There's no one else. I keep looking around the house for someone, anyone, to talk with.

I'm worried about what an extended silence will do to my brain. It's not like I have any margin for error. I'm beginning to feel like a cyclops, a solitary boob. You probably didn't know this but when two people "click," they experience something like a Vulcan mind meld. The two brains link up. Their neurological responses, including higher brain areas, begin to mirror one another. Once there's a neural match-up, the listener and the speaker heighten mutual understanding by anticipating what the other says and means, which in turns strengthens the neural match-up, and so on. There's a feedback loop, and this is really what love is, a feedback loop. That doesn't bode well for me—or for melancholy types in general. The human brain in isolation is sad and gooey. Simply to exist calls for interaction. All alone, I could turn into a troubled rhesus monkey, given to staring blankly and rocking in place for long periods, circling the living room repeatedly, and even marring myself. I cling tightly to my blanket. My faith in existence is of no more substance than a moonbeam.

Plus I sometimes whimper. Coyotes do that too, yip and whimper. Grief reaches down into the animal side of nature, releasing pent-up sounds. I feel something warm and fluid welling up inside, followed by boiling-hot tears and a series of choked-off wailing sounds. Not really sobs but whimpers. I surprised myself the first time I made these sounds. My lips did indeed quiver, in fact my whole body jerked, which made me feel childish and undignified. As if something crawled out of my chest and into my throat. It was a bit like a howl but it wasn't a howl. It was deeper than a howl. A screaming comes out of my heart. It's embarrassing so I try to save most of my weeping for

home. Whimpering in public is humiliating. At least I'm
not falling ridiculously to the floor, but I am whimpering.
Why do humans cry? Some say to purge the body of
toxins caused by stress. Puppies whine to rouse help. It's
even possible that tears contain a natural painkiller, I've
read. Men cry an estimated ten times a year. As far as I go,
a thousand tears would be a very conservative guess. The
Homeric sound of that is appealing, as if my grief were of
epic proportion. Achilles and Odysseus, by the way, cried
their eyes out. Achilles lost a dear friend, Odysseus was
simply lost. But you, a classics major, know that. As Edgar
Allan Poe writes, *deep in earth my love is lying and I must
weep alone.*

They say angels come nearest those who cry. I sometimes listen closely for the flapping of wings, but all I here
is my juvenile whimpering. Tears form, tears fall. Never
did anyone look so sad. Friends avoid your name in my
company for fear I might cry. It would be awkward for
them, which is true. Bob Newhart said he laughed to keep
from crying. Apparently, there is no natural limit to tears.
They are produced by the lacrimal gland, a secretory duct
that drains into a canal along the lower eye. With weeping, the canal floods easily and down your cheeks the
tears cascade. Beckett writes that the tears of the world
are a constant quantity. Every time someone stops weeping another weeper somewhere else begins anew. Maybe
I need a testosterone shot, which inhibits crying. But
then, of course, I'd lose out on the catharsis. People with
Sjögren's syndrome have great difficulty producing tears.
That doesn't sound good.

I was surprised by your decision to chair the English
department at Iowa. You didn't seem the type. For one,

you didn't have a big mouth, and for two, you didn't relish attention. But then there you were directing Bread Loaf for several summers. Your first stint was in Alaska. I made fun of you in the beginning. My native perversity. You were a natural, though. I see you now at a lectern welcoming students to Juneau. "Hello everyone, I'm Claire Sponsler, the on-site director of Bread Loaf, Juneau, and I'd like to welcome you to the edge of the universe." That got a laugh, especially from the preppy types who were spooked by the isolation. It's early summer but only fifty-four degrees outside. It's misty and raining. Out the window to your left the Sitka spruces look cold. In the near distance, the Chilkat Mountains loom over the channel. Milo is summering in Cincinnati with your mom and dad. He's chasing squirrels and getting fat. This is not a pet-friendly place. If the bears don't eat him, the hunters will. You really take to Juneau. You love its strangeness, the wandering misfits, the hardy women, Tlingit culture. There are few if any cars, just boats and float planes. On weekends we walk down to Auke Bay and watch the fisherman slice up salmon and halibut. The halibut are huge, bigger than Hemingway. Overhead eagles flock. Of all the bald eagles in the world, you say, about 50 percent live in Alaska. Wow, I say. We look up in amazement. A pair swoop down, skimming the water. One grabs a herring. Wow, we both say.

My goodness but this chair thing is demanding. You're in your study and it's ten thirty. Milo is curled up on your lap. I have to leave for school but drop in to say bye and cheer you up. Each morning you respond to e-mails. I don't know how you do it. You'll start at nine and go until noon. There's an e-mail from a colleague who needs time off for medical reasons. This will set off a chain of twenty-six more e-mails involving a half a dozen different people. There's a complaint from someone who is not making enough money. A warning from the dean's office that so-and-so's classes are underenrolled. You'll have to break the news to so-and-so about the cancellation and then find a makeup class. Someone has spilled coffee on his laptop and lost most of his files. He needs a thousand dollars for hard-disk recovery. I shake my head.

You answer every e-mail, no matter how half-baked, thoughtfully and tactfully. I'm of little help. Why don't you tell so-and-so to chill out, I offer, but you only roll your eyes. I have to watch what I say, you warn, as there's a paper trail in every case. You wouldn't last five minutes on the job, you say to me. No kidding, I say. In the morning over coffee, you'll rant about the greed and vanity of certain parties—of he- or she-who-must-not-be named, you'll say. I'll feign indifference only to get you talking more. I'm embarrassed to admit, but learning things I would never have guessed about he- or she-who-must-not-be-named is really tantalizing. Why are you doing this? I'll ask every now and then. Someone has to stick up for the women in the department, you say. Otherwise, the guys will take everything.

Undeniably, you are really good at this. You may look shy and retiring but you are fierce. And driven. Not by ambition or anything like that but simply by the need to get things right. That includes me. You want to get me right too. Not straight or virtuous but more complete and productive. Attentive too. It takes me four years to realize this, and when I do I wish you all the luck in the world. Good luck, I say, because I'm a lawless son of a bitch with an incurably wayward mind. You smile. I've seen worse, you say. Little do I know how stubborn you are. By now you know I'm a softie inside, a pushover in fact. So much for the bad boy of Foggy Bottom.

What worries me about your managerial stint at school is that you can't hear a thing, not even now as I sneak up behind you. The floor creaks like a haunted house and my sneakers are squeaking. Milo turns and gives me a wary eye. He knows how devilish I am. Noisy as a Kakapo I am, but you hear nothing. I'm looming behind you as you type another e-mail reply. The sender wants you to visit Maryland for a keynote speech. That's great, I say, breaking the silence, and could be fun. You can drop by DC. My voice startles you and Milo leaps down from your lap. He likes peace and quiet. What are you doing here? you ask. Nosy Parker, I say. I begin kneading your shoulders. This is a nice gig, I say again. You don't agree. I don't like these events, you say. They're awkward and embarrassing. I can't hear anyone. How can I answer questions or hold a conversation? You read lips, don't you? It's hard with strangers, you say. Golly, I didn't know the hearing thing was that bad, I say, truly surprised. You go anyway, and it's not that terrible, you later tell me. But there's a toll on your brain, I can't help but think. All that chronic stress. Your hearing is lousy and yet you are inclined, given your tremendous civic spirit, to take on leadership roles. This is not a good equation.

One day in March you will show me an article from the *New York Times* about a saint's festival in Brooklyn. You're researching a book about medieval rituals in Europe that wind up in America. The festival occurs every July in Brooklyn. It's an Italian-American thing, right up your alley, you tell me. Who's the saint? It says here he supposedly freed his fellow townspeople from slavery. Why are you interested? I ask. The festival came to Brooklyn from Nola, a small town outside Naples. It goes way back to the 1500s. Perfect fit for my book. Anyway, you continue, you need a film project, right? Yes, I do. Well, what do you think? Sure.

So come July we fly to New York. We've been married four years, and this will be the first test of our marriage. I'm not the problem—it's my film gear. There's so much of it. This is twenty years ago when cameras were as big as Fiats. You sure you need all of this? you ask me. Lights, batteries, stands, tripod, camera, microphones, cables, more batteries, chargers, tapes, more tapes. Of course, I say.

The taxi drops us off at Our Lady of Mount Carmel Parish on Havemeyer and North 8th Street in Williamsburg. It's Monday morning, July 15, 1996. We wait inside the lobby for Monsignor David Cassato. We're both already exhausted from hauling the film stuff. It's hot.

The monsignor joins us after a short wait. He is charming. Early forties. Fit. He has thick, dark, well-manicured hair, a Burt Reynolds mustache, and an untroubled smile. He's in a purple-trimmed black cassock with a sash. Take away the cassock and you're looking at a talented high school principal with political ambitions. He says there's another film crew here to document the festival. The monsignor likes media attention. Although the "feast," as he calls it, has been celebrated for decades, it has only recently captured the national eye, thanks to the *New York Times*, he says. So when I ask to film an interview with him, he's hot to trot.

It takes half an hour to set things up, and while I'm connecting this to that you are sweet-talking the monsignor. I overhear you ask him how the parish came to host the festival. It hasn't always been church-supported, you add, but now that it's affiliated with the parish it seems to have gained some stability. You have short hair for this trip, a boy's cut. You look like a teenager and very cute in your jeans, white T-shirt, and black vest. I glance up to see a look of surprise on Monsignor Cassato's face. His eyes light up.

I'm wondering where to put the five-hundred-watt light as the monsignor begins a spirited reply to your question. Oh no, I'm thinking, I need to capture this. Wait, wait, I say, wait for the camera you guys! The monsignor stops in midsentence because he too doesn't want to waste a word. He feels especially bright and articulate this morning. I see a hint of makeup on his cheeks. We quickly reposition his eminence, you clip the lavalier microphone to his cassock, I set the white balance, adjust the iris, and check microphone levels. I give you a thumbs-up signal and away we go.

Have you seen much change in the feast over the past few decades? you ask the monsignor. I got to tell you the truth, he says. It's changed but it hasn't changed radically. But the neighborhood is stable. It's a very strong, stable neighborhood. We've heard, you say, that a lot of Italians are leaving the area as other ethnic groups move in. Is this a problem? you ask. Well, I also feel, whether I'd be right or wrong on this—I'm not a sociologist on the issue— but I feel that this neighborhood has remained stable partly because of the feast and the parish. The monsignor is happy with this answer but before he can reach for his coffee you ask another question. I noticed that many spectators are not from Brooklyn, you say. They're from all over the country, Florida, California, Arizona. What are they looking for?

I never told you this but I'm so glad you are asking the questions and I'm just the camera guy. The monsignor pauses for a moment, gathers his thoughts, and then talks to the camera. You might use the word *anachronistic*, he says. And now he has begun moving his hands. What magnificent hair, I'm thinking to myself as I follow his head in the viewfinder. I don't know if I could agree with that, though, he continues, because I think today people by and large are searching and going back to their roots. Speaking of hair! You are nodding politely but I can detect a degree of wariness in your eyes when I glance up. You know firsthand how well Italian men like to pitch a story.

This goes on for another twenty minutes, but finally the monsignor has to run. He looks at his watch and offers his hand. He's a great interview—photogenic, good sound-bites, terrific gestures. We follow this up with more interviews, speaking with guys who run the show and who seem a bit like mobsters. I don't tell you this but I'm suddenly feeling ethnically indeterminate—the machismo of these guys!—and that's making me a little woozy. These clannish societies, you say.

I haven't done my homework so I'm still trying to wrap my mind around this event while lugging my camera around. At the heart of the festival is the *Giglio*, an attention-getting structure. The word means *lily* in Italian, but the structure is anything but a delicate flower. The massive five-story, four-ton steeple is made of papier-mâché saints, angels, and florets, and includes a platform large enough to hold a singer and a twelve-person brass-and-drum band. The tower is topped by a statue of Saint Paulinus. The whole thing is kind of preposterous.

The poor guys who lift this are all different sizes and ages, many who don't seem what I would call fit. You will point out several in their late sixties with big bellies and red, contorted faces. Point the camera over there, you say, where that old guy is toiling. I like the word *toiling*. The labor that goes into this is the whole point, you tell me. Through the viewfinder I'm seeing a lot of that. With my zoom, I can see their grimaces and buckling shoulders. Everyone is suffering, young and old. Their faces belong in a Bruegel painting. But still they come out in the blazing heat of mid-July to lift this absurdly large tower. I pan the camera to where I can see the life-size Saint Paulinus in full bishopric regalia, bobbling and swaying on top of the Giglio. He seems well rested.

We're on the roof of the parish where we have a commanding view of the festival. In the distance, Manhattan looms up tall and majestic. Reaching the rooftop was a chore. Talk about toiling. We have to haul the film gear here, a hundred and fifty pounds of ungainly electronics. That means climbing thirty feet up the fixed-access ladder from the subroof to the rooftop—twice. I'm now feeling pretty guilty and keep saying, Let me do this, let me do that. But you're not one to shrug off hard work. You grab the leather battery belt and the cumbersome recharger and up the ladder you go.

It's eleven thirty and the sun is sizzling hot. You keep lathering up with Aveeno sunblock. What a view up here. I'm setting the camera up close to the edge of the roof, right above the heart of the festival. You pass me the water bottle and an unfriendly look, which says, No good man makes his wife do what you just made me do. I feel terrible—but also giddy. Up here, we can see everything. I feel like Gary Powers. Once you take in the view, you smile too.

We have an hour before things begin, so we gaze at the street vendors. There's a sausage guy with long white hair in two braids and a Don Quixote white mustache. He's loading his skewer with fresh links. Delicate feathers trail down from the side of his hair. My camera pans from the sausage man to the dark-haired sausage lady flipping links over an open grill. Her face is hidden by swirling smoke. Hot peppers hang down from the canopy. I've never seen so much sausage in my life.

I'm on the rooftop with a zoom lens. No guy should be allowed to do this. I begin to feel like Jimmy Stewart in Hitchcock's *Rear Window,* spying on the private lives of urban villagers. The voyeurism bothers you more than it does me. What are you looking at? you ask. Interesting faces, I reply. I don't say a word about spying on the dark-haired Italian girls in the booths, but you know what I'm doing. Back on the street, an Asian family is frying strips of chicken. A small parade commences at the front of the church. The monsignor in his purple vestment and several stocky Italian-American males with that patented mafioso look. They glance warily around. Firecrackers are going off.

You point my lens toward the corner of North 8th Street. There, I see a middle-aged man limping with a cane wearing blue shorts and a white hat. "Pa, *como sta*, Pa?" he greets his father. They hug and continue on, the son's arm around his father's shoulder. The son has blue eyes and gray-blond hair, and a bit of a beer belly. He is probably much younger than he looks. The father is diminutive and bald and has a crooked nose.

The smoke rises up toward us. You rub your eyes and then point again to the crowd below where a nun in a traditional habit wanders through the large crowd requesting donations. Zoom in on the nun, you say. Shrewdly, she stops by a couple in the midst of eating fried sausages buried in onions and peppers. A guy in a green hat passes his sausage to his companion and reaches into his pocket for a couple of bucks. Later, the companion scowls at the nun. Did you get that? you ask. Yep, got the dirty look.

Funny how you could see everything without a camera lens, I thought later. I was lost without my zoom. Your hearing may have been poor, but your visual acuity was off the charts.

Copy, we have sync, I say. Another message from Space Boy. I don't know if this is a leak or what, he says, but a tiny rush of blue zodiacal dust is streaming my way from the Advanced Matter Accumulator, running in a straight line down the forward hull into a half-drunk cup of coffee near the Warp Plasma Conduit. Space Boy sounds stressed. Hope it's not seepage or blue rust or something even weirder, I radio back. I have no idea how to repair a space leak, Space Boy says. What if it's a leak, say a gash in the hull, and blue zodiacal dust is seeping through a stab wound? I'm not sure I follow, I radio back, a bit alarmed. What's with Space Boy? I wonder. It's not like him to go off the handle. That's my job. Maybe we're looking at a sentient life form, he continues in this bizarre way, maybe I'm not alone after all. Poor kid. Must be weird out there flying solo.

I ordered an urn at long last, a vase-shaped cherry-wood urn, for your ashes. This took forever. So much resistance to finality. From Stardust Memorials in Traverse, Michigan. A thriving business. They're staffed with twenty employees and a dog, all women, except for the golden retriever. The urn is simple but lovely. It's on the dining room table and startles me on the way to the kitchen. Among other things, Stardust advertises urn accessories, bags, nameplates, pendants, appliqués, stands. They have urns by size and theme. Every hour over six thousand people die. We are a fatal species.

Friday night and we have a dinner date. You're upstairs trying on different outfits. How's this? you ask. Gray pinstriped wool slacks with white blouse, charcoal sweater, and light-blue corduroy jacket. It's a good look for you, I say. Stylish and casual. You look great, I add. You beg to differ, however, approaching the mirror and complaining of being hag-like. You're nuts, I say. I look like an old woman, you say. Like a Gorgon. At first I don't know if you're being ironic about your appearance or dissatisfied with your wardrobe. I'm a fussy guy—how could you not be a beauty? Not fussy enough, you say. I think you really mean it. You disrobe and quickly climb into a different outfit. Jeans, dark sweater, smart green jacket, silk scarf. Frankly, you look great, but I keep it to myself. You're in a funk. I want to say you are very attractive but I know you won't believe me. Nothing I can do to convince you. I usually feel like a gnarly old coot myself but have little trouble deluding myself. I'm aging gracefully, I think to myself, and have managed to harness my eccentricities in clever ways. That's untrue but I pretend otherwise. That's a difference between you and me. You suffer no illusions—

but I worry you are too self-critical. Brains and beauty, I say, often go together. You're obviously suffering from the halo effect, you say.

It's been awhile since I last saw the little blue smudge (the earth) in my rearview mirror, Space Boy tells me. He has begun sending more messages lately. Must be the isolation. Interstellar space is big and empty, he complains. Well, not really empty, being chock-full of debris, but kind of empty in an existential way as there is no one at home out here. What did you expect? I reply. Space never ends, he radios me. It's endless. He's griping a lot and qualifying his sentences. He's beginning to sound more like me, which makes me nervous, and then I remember he is me.

The extremities of interstellar space are testing the nerve of Space Boy. I think I know what he's going through, even out there where the stars whirl around the center of the galaxy. Everything is reeling, really. The universe is reeling. And me too, I'm really reeling. I'm right here on planet earth but I feel so far away from home. Space Boy evidently feels this too, homelessness, only it's more visceral. Where he is no birds are chirping. No dogs or cats. No cows. Nothing of home but a stink bug.

Says Space Boy: She made those strange sounds—do you remember—the unforgettable gasping, a sound neither of us heard before? Yes, I say, of course—how could I forget? I remember only too well. I shot out of my chair, my coffee went flying, I rumbled up the stairs. It was the sound of death and no light in her eyes. That's when you flew away, dashed into space beyond Saturn, past Pluto, left me behind pulling my hair out. A large chunk of me was hurled into space, a very significant fraction of my allocation of being, flung into space without ceremony. How could I ever forget?

You weren't the only one suffering, Space Boy says. What do you mean? I radio back. Escape velocity was pure trauma. Try it sometime, he says. I'm listening, I say. My entire body cringing under the force of gravity. One G, then two Gs. I felt four times my normal weight, over six hundred pounds. The G-force crushed my head back into my chair. I couldn't move my arms. Three Gs. A terrific drop in blood pressure, a rise in cerebral hypoxia. Ruptured capillaries, small bruises on the back of the neck. Four Gs. Blood flow ceased to the retinal receptors.

Space Boy enjoys telling this tale, which is a new twist in our relationship. He fancies himself a storyteller. I don't know if this is good or bad. I couldn't see a thing, he says. My stomach was in my throat—I can't see the globules of vomit floating by my face, tissues swelling in my head. Five Gs. And then the convulsions, a seizure-like episode of jerks and spasms, like a funky chicken. What a way to go, he says. He radios me frequently now with excerpts from his journal, such as the above. He says he is writing a memoir. Nonsense, I say. Why not? he replies.

☿

CHAPTER ELEVEN
MERCURY (THE ENVOY)

〜

Mercury was raised in the solar system's toughest neighborhood.

—Ryan Mandelbaum

*I*f I close my eyes, I begin to drift. Toward what—who can say? There's no vertigo, no sense of having lost my bearings, just an agreeable sense of wandering off, like a hot-air balloon adrift over yellow corn stubble, green cover crop, and bales of hay, over barns and silos and rolling landscape. I'm going somewhere and I will not know how I got there. Death demands a kind of letting go. Did you feel that too?

What was gathered blows away. Astronomy 101.

We finally buy a canoe, a nice one near Sperryville in the Shenandoah Valley. It's our wedding gift. Black with oak trim, though a bit heavy. We had great fun paddling near Blake Falls Reservoir the last time we summered in the Adirondacks with a borrowed canoe, so why not do this more often? We are charmed by the idea of floating together in the dark on a lake under stars.

You know, it's not easy on the back, you say, as we hoist the canoe on top of the car. What happens when we get older? Jeez, you're right, I say. It takes the two of us to elevate the canoe on top of the Honda, plus a lot of huffing and puffing. You're sure it's going to stay in place once we're on the highway? you ask. You're looking at the peculiar array of tie-down yokes, bungee chords, and lashing straps, an uneven network of lines that doesn't inspire confidence. Hope so, I say.

We're on our way to Lower Saranac Lake in the eastern part of the Adirondacks, just west of Lake Placid. We are in motion. We've only been in Iowa two years but we're craving water. We drop off the cat in Cincinnati with your folks, say hi to my mom and dad in Buffalo, and then drive up I-90 to Albany and over I-87 into Russel Banks country. Lower Saranac Lake has islands. Look at this, I say. We stop for egg salad sandwiches in Keene. I get out a map. See, islands in Lower Saranac, I say. What do you want with an island? you ask. Well, maybe we can camp there. How would we get there? you ask. In the canoe, of course. So in addition to our camping gear, you say, we'll be loading the canoe with food, water, and fuel? It's a pretty big canoe, I say, undaunted.

We book the last site on Pirate Island at the Lower Saranac camp office and load the canoe for a short paddle to the middle of the lake. Two large bags of food, four gallons of water, and a sixteen-pound bag of Kingsford charcoal. Lots of camping gear. And lots of clothes. Plus books. Four nights' worth of cargo. The canoe slumps into the lake. Yikes, I say. Sure this is safe? you ask. If we're careful, I say. And keep in mind, I add, the return trip will be a cinch. Should I get in the front? you ask. Yes, the bow seat, I say—me in the sternum. You laugh. You can't see what I see: the waterline is close to the gunwale back here. Oh boy, I'm thinking. Maybe we should lose a gallon or two of water. Not a good idea, you say. Well, it's a short half-mile to the island, I say. Paddle like steady Eddy and we'll be fine.

We're not fine. It's really windy with strong gusts. These create a tremendous drag on the canoe; plus, Saranac Lake is teeming with motorboats. What a racket! I'm looking around for kayaks and canoes—none to be seen, only bowriders, cabin cruisers, and jet skis—even a float-plane! What have I got us into? I say to myself. Where's Pirate Island? you ask, because I think we're going backward. Are you paddling? I shout. What do you think I'm doing? you yell back. You don't see the floatplane because you're focused on your job, supposedly paddling. But something is wrong because we're going leeward (I think that's the right term). Pirate Island now seems far off in the distance. I start to panic. We're going downwind and you're actually paddling like a madwoman, I see that now, and me too. I'm paddling like a nutcase. But we're heading downwind where all the Chris-crafts and Bayliners are creating lots of serious wave action. Law-abiding citizen, you have the ridiculously orange life jacket on. I can't find mine. I think it's overboard. You're going to have to paddle harder! I yell. You choose not to answer. You've heard enough from the guy in the sternum. Some fear chemical kicks in, doubling my paddle stroke. Your motor is grinding too. Pirate Island comes back into view.

Astonishingly, we land safely. Some naiad must have

come to our rescue, you say. Someone intervened, I say, because we were headed for deep doo-doo. Let me count our losses, I say: one gallon of water, a John Le Carré novel, and my Radiohead T-shirt. Not too bad. Plus the hot dog rolls are soggy. We're both sprawled on the large rock that frames Pirate Island like survivors of a ship-wreck. How are your biceps? I ask. Killing me, you say. Mine are numb, I say. That was really stupid, you say. Agreed, I say. How deep is this lake? you ask. Maybe fifty feet. We're insane, you say. Agreed, I say. Promise never again. Never again.

Mercury is extremely dry, very hot, and almost com-pletely airless. The planet is hardly any larger than our moon and just as bleak with a heavily cratered surface. But it's our solar system's innermost planet, closest of all to the sun, in dreadful proximity to a flaming star—and so quite the enigma. The sun's rays are seven times more powerful on Mercury than earth, and because one day there takes fifty-nine earth days, that's a lot of heat from sunrise to sunset, with temperatures reaching eight hundred degrees Fahrenheit. Without any atmosphere to abrade incoming rocks, the planet absorbs the full impact of falling meteors and asteroids.

The ancient Sumerians were the first to record de-tailed observations of Mercury five thousand years ago. Its name then: Ubu-idm-gud-ud. The Babylonians called it Nabou, he who woke the sun each morning. The Egyptians called Mercury Thoth, a god associated with knowledge and regarded as the inventor of speech and letter writing. The Chinese called it Shui Xing. The Greek Hermes, the god of thieves and messengers. *Mariner 10* visited Mercury in 1974, detecting traces of an ancient magnetic field, something only earth, among all other luminaries, enjoys. *Mariner 10* also photographed a lot of craters. Nearly four hundred of these craters have been named over the years, all after artists, writers, and composers. Fancy that, celebrity impact craters. So there's one named after Pablo Neruda, in case you are wondering, as well as Dostoyevsky.

Anyway, Kurt Vonnegut writes that the planet Mercury *sings like a crystal goblet*. I read that as a kid in *The Sirens of Titan* (when the Dell paperback had the lurid cover) and for some reason that stuck. Mercury sings all the time, he wrote. The extreme variance in temperature—really, really hot during the day and unimaginably cold at night—makes the planet sing a song that is beloved of Mercury's cave-dwelling life forms, diamond-shaped creatures that thrive on vibrations. Also charming is the implausible physics. The novel's dubious protagonist, Winston Niles Rumfoord, runs into a *chronosynclastic infundibulum* in the vicinity of Mars that turns him into a quantum wave function, he and his large dog Kazak. Both man and beast exist at multiple points and lines in space-time, stretching from Mercury to Betelgeuse. Until they materialize at one point they remain extended among an infinite array of possibilities. Winston and his mastiff will appear on earth in Newport, Rhode Island, every fifty-nine days for one hour. They will also appear on Mars, Mercury, Betelgeuse, and Titan. Both are trapped, essentially, in a wormhole, though Winston doesn't seem to mind much, especially as he is unstuck in time.

Implausible physics—the secret to space travel.

It's nine thirty a.m. and we can't get out of bed. We're in Cincinnati with your mom and dad. A summer visit.

Why don't you take Milo downstairs and I'll feed him? you say. Milo is snuggled at our feet. He doesn't want to get up either. Okay, I say, but I don't move. Your dad is undertaking his morning exercises in the bedroom across the hall. Thump, thump, stretch. Your mom is spooning breakfast cereal while toiling over a crossword puzzle in the kitchen. So lazy I'm worthless, I say. You laugh. Breakie, breakie, you say in a singsong voice. Milo's ears perk up. I rise and scoop the dog up. Be careful, you say. The stairway is steep and slippery. Down go I and the dog. I hear my aging joints creak. Wary, Milo looks around for the cunning cat, the notoriously menacing cat. The coast is clear, Jean tells Milo, who actually understands. He walks nonchalantly to the cat bowl, finishes off Jack the Ripper's eats, and looks up at me. Is that it? he says. Is that all there is? No, that's not it, I say. Patience, pal.

There you are in the sunny kitchen with a morning smile. Jean is stumped on a crossword puzzle clue. Colds that last a long time, she says, seven letters. I'm at a loss. Not my area of expertise, I say lamely. Ice ages, you say, cracking the riddle effortlessly. Ah! Jean says. Jean and I both look at each other in wonder. What planet are you from? I ask. Your mom says they don't make brains like yours anymore. Fluid intelligence, I say. Your daughter has an innate aptitude for problem solving. Milo is not interested in this conversation and looks up impatiently. Talking heads make him nervous, especially when hungry.

You feed the dog, I head out the door for a *New York Times*. The local paper trends rightward so we give the *Cincinnati Inquirer* a wide birth. Madeira is a quiet place but it's hopping on Saturday morning. The rich folks drive down from Indian Hills in luxury cars to shop at Kroger's and coffee-up at local cafés. I fetch the last *Times* at Star-bucks and a pound of French roast. Over coffee we talk about the day ahead. I'd love to sit around and do nothing, but I don't tell you that, not that you would mind. Well, I say, do your folks need any work done around the house? It looks like the ornamental grasses are running amok, you say. Where? You point at a large embankment of healthy green things out the window. Really, I say, that's gotta go? Invasive, you say. Taking over the whole yard. You know, I say, they look pretty well rooted. I'm already regretting not sitting around doing nothing. It'll be hot and humid in another hour, and extracting sinewy grasses under the sizzling sun means real work. But I resign myself. Half an hour into the job I'm regretting the regretting because I really like working side by side with you. I feel uplifted, even though I'm sweating like pig iron.

March is the bleakest time of the year, the month with the highest number of Internet searches for *depression, anxiety, pain, stress,* and *fatigue.* People are more miser-able in this month than at any other time of year, even February. Trees and shrubs too. On my walk today, I took a photo of a small magnolia tree that had blossomed, up Church Street near Reno. The snowy magnolia is among your favorites, especially its fragrance. Its flowers were weakly unscented and seemed troubled. The temperature has been in the low forties for the past two weeks, and we've seen no sunshine. *Sans soleil.* The planet feels like a cave. The magnolia blooms are dispirited and droopy, al-ready wilting in the cold, not a good sign. Bad timing. Its flowers need sunlight to mature and show signs of petal burn, as if seared by a cigarette. The daffodils in our yard, knocked over by wind and rain, look even more wretched.

They join other double-crossed flowers, the forsythia, and snowdrops. The sycamore trees have stopped releasing seedpods. The pods began dropping two weeks ago but have since been recalled, owing to bleakness. I brought home one lonely seedpod intact. It's on a shelf in my study, next to the milkweed pod and a shock of your blond hair. The seedpod is so cold it shivers. The milkweed pod is in a Ziploc bag and has exploded over winter. Thousands of pretty silky fibers awaiting dispersal. I really can't tell the difference between those fibers and yours.

If I believed in a god, I might feel rage, as Job did, but I only feel bewildered. Emptiness is not a heaviness that can be thrown off with a bit of violence. C.S. Lewis says that bereavement is a universal and integral part of our experience of love. One of its many phases. Love is not love until separation comes between lovers like an earthquake, until we have been blindsided by loss. Strangely, that makes sense, though I can't say why. Funny how suffering turns the sufferer into a petty philosopher. This is what I get for reading C.S. Lewis. You would never tolerate such blather over morning coffee. The grand eye roll is what I'd get. Oh, how I miss your eye rolls.

I remember a picture taken of you last summer at the Cliffs of Moher in Ireland. We are in County Clare—how right—and you are standing at the stone wall. Behind you, miles of moss-covered cliffs hammered by the crashing sea. Your hair is shimmering. You grip the dark stone barrier with both hands. The wind is gusting madly through your hair. You are enchanted by Ireland. Windswept, you seem at home in this haunting place by the sea. No scorching heat or radiant sunshine. Birds swirl just to your right above Hag's Head.

They say there once was a clever fisherman who saw the mermaid of Moher. He sat down on a rock beside her while she combed her golden hair. He spoke expansively with her and while doing so noticed, lying on another rock, her magic cloak. Now it happened the mermaid needed her cloak in order to return to the sea. But the fisherman—thief that he was—grabbed it and ran off to his house, where he hid the magic charm. The fisherman knew this strange creature would be marooned without her cloak, and so the mermaid had no choice now but to follow the fisherman home. As he would not return her cloak, the mermaid of Moher agreed to marry the man and together they had a son and daughter. But one day some years later, while her husband was out fishing, the mermaid found her cloak. The fisherman came home to find her gone. She had returned to the sea and he and his children never saw her again.

You most always smile at me in these photos, and that's why I am still alive despite the sorrow—your smile rescues me each day. It keeps me mercurial. The Irish advise tourists not to visit the Cliffs of Moher in a "low state of mind." Troubled minds do not fare well here, I've read, and the suicide toll is high. There is a memorial—a tombstone of sorts—dedicated to those who either jumped off or slipped over the edge. Parting is not goodbye, sings Billie Holliday, we'll be together again.

Red porch paint has leaked on the pantry floor in the basement. The reddish pool looks like blood. The house is bleeding, I think to myself. Pat is having trouble swallowing. I'm flying to Buffalo tomorrow and will take her in for an esophagram. Meanwhile, there's the usual weeping, which triggered a nosebleed this time. The left nostril. Blood all over my sweater and pants.

The wind is whistling outside my window. It's disturbing—such a desperate sound. All around me the world is collapsing. The poor flowers, their little heads drooping in the cold like hung men. If they had voices they would sound like dwarfs lost in a copper mine. The forsythia has flowered and the lilac's buds have opened but we are enduring lows in the teens. Can they stand a week of bitter cold? Impossible to leave out the word *bitter*. Such a reality requires a store of hardiness. Without resilience, doom. But this is not what the forsythias are thinking; they still dream of spring, with only me as witness to false hope and ambassador to ruin.

For lunch today I slurped down leftover soup. At one point I saw little drops of water break the creamy surface. Drip, drip, drip. Like rain. What the hell? I wondered. I looked up at the ceiling but there was nothing. No trickle. I realized then I was crying. I hadn't noticed. A man is a silly thing. One day he will be devoured by darkness, and then he will be no more.

I should be waiting for your call from school. I look at my watch. It's twelve thirty. You said you'd call before one and ask for a pickup. I'm still waiting for your call. When it comes I'll hop in the Saab, buckle my seat belt, drive south down Gilbert Street, pull into the EPB parking lot, and there you'll be, waiting curbside by the back entrance, a big smile on your face. You're happy to see me, glad for the pickup. It's a lonely building, especially on Sunday. You're pleased to have company again. Who knows, at any moment everything can change. This is in your smile. Me too, I smile gratefully. You always fill my heart. We'll drive up the hill to the co-op for our weekly shop. I will have brought along the green bags and the two lists you jotted down, one for you and one for me. It will be busy on Sunday afternoon. We'll divide up and meet back at checkout, me and my bell peppers, Parmesan cheese, capellini, olive oil, soy milk, toilet paper, toothpaste, gingko pills, and peanut butter cookies; you and your tofu, unsalted butter, eggs, brussels sprouts, carrots, and bok choy noodles. I love your lists, the elegant handwriting. Sometimes I'll get in trouble for going rogue, selecting an extravagantly priced cheese or the double-fudge chocolate cake. The dog is waiting for us at the back door when we return. He too is glad to see us. He dances in circles, delighted to see the food bags. Oh boy, he says.

For a while we lived such lives each day. We had good jobs, fine friends, warm families, a humanoid dog, lots of travel. It didn't seem unreal, our happiness, but it seemed charmed, almost as if someone had cast a kindly spell on us. We figured this is what good love means, what it does. It opens doors and windows, makes glad the eye, warms the heart. Tasty pasta and long companionable walks. Down deep, though, we wondered what would happen if the spell broke. The humanoid dog, Milo, was the secret link. As long as we kept Milo from harm, all would be well. The charm didn't lift, not right away, but lasted for twelve years, almost half our time together. Remarkable really. And for this we should both be deeply grateful, if only it were that simple. Our yard daffodils are about to bloom even though it's cold and bleak.

One night as I made pasta, you suddenly began dancing in the kitchen after a bit of wine. Tom Waits on the radio singing the theme song from *The Wire*. *When you walk through the garden, you've gotta watch your back.* You started shaking it, swinging your hips this way and that, drawing circles on the floor. Waits is singing, *You gotta keep the devil way down in the hole*, and I'm beginning to feel aroused seeing you revolve, wheel, and turn around. But there's a bottle of olive oil in my left hand and the red peppers are hissing at me. Milo the dog thinks something important is happening in the kitchen and joins the party, following your movements on the dance floor. *He's got the fire and the fury at his command*, says Waits. You're channeling his kinetic energy and you're spinning and swirling. There's no stopping you. Milo's big eyes are even bigger. Mine too. The band is pulsating bluesy and it's creeping under your skin, that raspy voice, the rising and falling bass line, the funky sax, all gospel and blues.

Milo is as rapt as a dog can be. This is it, he thinks. In Tom Waits he's found his god. "I bark my voice out through a closed throat, pretty much," Waits has said. "It's more, perhaps, like a dog in some ways." Yes, Milo thinks. Not like a dog but the one true dog, the first dog, the dog of dogs. Having found your groove, you dance as if nobody is watching, rocking on your hips, whirling like a genie who has just come out of a bottle. The peppers hiss and the zucchini fizzle. The linguini bubbles over. *You gotta keep the devil way down in the hole*, Tom Waits says again. You are in the moment and the moment is shaped by a wild fleeting body so glad to be alive that the kitchen shimmers. I am so distracted by this ecstatic Claire—and the dog who has found religion—I overcook the pasta and scorch the veggies. Such a noodle head. Who saw this coming? I suddenly feel guilty for hibernating in my head. I want to turn and spin outward toward the edge of perception where weird things happen. But time is always bearing down on us.

Four inches of snow today, a nice cozy blanket to keep the crocuses warm. The sparrows are squawking above a chorus of snow blowers, as if to raise a pointed question. You would have been impressed but not surprised. Always a fatalist, you wouldn't glove up for gardening till early May. Over a foot fell in parts of Iowa, record-setting. Two feet predicted in the Northeast. Large numbers of flight cancellations likely. Amtrak shutdown. Spring arrived a month earlier than usual, in mid-January in certain parts of the country, judging by first leaf reckoning. Some plants that bud early are in for trouble, vulnerable to a snap frost. But now it's only fifteen degrees. Below twenty-four degrees, you're going to see 90 percent loss of blossoms in weaker plants. That's what they're saying about the cherry blossoms in Washington coated in ice.

This untimely spring screws with the minds of farmers. February was the second warmest on record, with mean temperatures eleven degrees above normal. Ill-tempered March is making a mockery of last month's false spring. We are all reeling now from a skewed sense of things, a faulty timetable. Who would have guessed at this moment we could revert back to winter so quickly, as if the warming trend was meaningless? Hadn't we a week of seventy-degree weather? T-shirts were unfurled, shorts unrolled, sneakers put on. Bags of mulch were piling up at the nursery. A real snowfall seems so perverse, unruly. Troublesome. In outer space, there are no seasons, Space Boy says.

Your favorite bird is back, the cedar waxwing. A flock arrived yesterday, swarming in the crab apple trees, spearing berries. All day long they eat berries, though in shifts. One group feeds first and departs, followed by the next. They're voracious but don't compete for food, unlike robins. It's a pretty bird, milk chocolate head and shoulders, with grayish wings and tails, lemon-yellow underbelly, and a crested top. I can see why you were crazy about this bird. Its tail feathers are yellow-dipped and the tips of its secondary wings are brilliant red—and the waxwing is masked like a little thief, a witty look for a delicate thing.

I took several photos with my big lens. I'd mail you one if I knew your address. A mild day. Maybe the weather is turning. Up and down the street shrubs are showing signs of life, little buds unlocking, tiny green leaves hazarding out into the ambiguous March air. The brutal freeze of last week left scars, though. The damaged buds are gray and sometimes black, like cigarette butts.

There I was in your closet the other day snooping around. I felt like an intruder rummaging through your things. What I found on the top shelf was a storage bin filled with items from your past, before we met. Photo albums, diplomas, notebooks, letters. Lots of letters. Quite a compilation. Mostly *Par Avion*. Letters from whom? I wondered. Here's one from David, November 2, 1977. Stamped *München Stadt weltberühmter Biere Mit Luftpost*, addressed to *Ms. Claire B. Sponsler, 7129 Wallace Ave.*

I shouldn't be prying like this but it can't be helped. What are the rules pertaining to the privacy of the dead? You're only twenty-three years old when you receive a letter from David of Munich, who writes to persuade you to stay an extra week in Germany. There's a lot to do here, he says. David also writes that he will be able to travel to Florence and Rome *with you two vagabonds*. Who, I wonder, are you traveling with? Maybe to Greece too, if only to keep you out of trouble, he says. As you read this letter,

I'm walking in the misty rain. I can't see moonlight because of the clouds. I know it's there somewhere. I can feel it. I'm in Oregon. It rains forever in November. David of Munich, meanwhile, is plotting an enterprising agenda. *I envision a week in München, a couple of days in Berlin, a trip to Vienna, and then to Italy and Greece. I would like to go to Prague but I fear it might not be well received by you and Toni.* Toni must be the other vagabond. Curiouser and curiouser. This forty-year-old letter will outlast all of us, thanks to its high cotton content. It reveals a more civilized time.

Several letters from Munich are stashed in your box. I learn that you are writing David a few times a week. Also that David, apparently, is a thirty-year-old American studying in Germany. He's lonely in Munich, suffering longish bouts of melancholy, and has trouble enrolling in antiquity classes he longs to take, like Greek Vase Painting, since they fill up fast with German students. He is proud, though, of his German translation of Book VI of Virgil's *Aeneid.* Who would have guessed the classics are so big?

Here's another mysterious letter writer, Brad, a first-year graduate student living in Irvine, California. His letters are tedious but zealous. There is this interesting moment in one: *Claire, it was you who said that men all have one thing in common—lust. There is much truth in what you say.* Apparently Brad has more on his mind than Herman Melville and laments his inability to sublimate. He wishes you were there, at least to entertain him with your cheerful disposition and ready wit, as he puts it. This letter is postmarked November 8, 1977, which means you received letters from David and Brad on nearly the same day.

Young men writing long letters to you. Not exactly tormented young men but men eager to display their inner lives, their Dostoevskyan aches and pains. *I'm so lonely and blue*, writes one, *that I want to write about being blue but that will only make me bluer.* He also wants to enroll in a Sanskrit class. Jesus, Sanskrit. Another is having androgynous dreams, he says, on the eve of grad school. But he's looking forward to Arthurian Romance. They write faithfully and earnestly. You are their Guinevere.

I was never a letter writer then, which may have disqualified me from wooing you. My mind was savage, regardless of how bookish I had become. I worry that it still is. I loved bizarre rituals. When I turned thirty, for instance, I drove to the Pacific Ocean with the poems of Wallace Stevens and Dylan Thomas. Who does that? I was in Yachats. The tide was far out so I walked across the black jagged rocks and climbed into a sea cave where I read out loud "The Idea of Order" and "Poem in October." *It was my thirtieth year to heaven*, I sang in my mock BBC voice. I was hopelessly literary, like your suitors, but I was foolish, realizing only too late that it was high tide.

Time had passed me by. The grinding water returned with a vengeance, filled the cave with sea. I lurched this way and that, fell into the bubbling ocean, and was dragged across razor blade rocks now submerged beneath the mad sizzling foam. I may die, I thought, on my birthday. The undertow was unimaginable. Stevens and Thomas disappeared in the riptide, were dragged away like screaming women in Homer. I clung to rocks I couldn't see but was jerked farther out by retreating waves that raked me over saw-toothed edges. I was pulled underwater and wrapped my arms around a serrated rock. I lost my shirt and my pants were shredded when I finally emerged, like Odysseus in Phaeacia. Maybe I should have been a letter writer.

I had long hair and a mustache. I was a real Guido back then. You've always preferred the Oppenheimer look.

I hope you forgive me for eavesdropping. As executor of your estate, I suppose I'm required by law to leave no stone unturned. Nosy Parker, as you called me. I wound up with a migraine last night. What will I find next? We never exchanged letters ourselves. Our marriage was postepistolary. When apart, we swapped down-to-earth e-mails. Wouldn't it be ironic if reading through your private letters—there are so many—blew my brain up. Anything seems possible.

Let me add to the list of suitors, as I read through a stack of letters from Daniel L., a graduate student in the classics program at Cincinnati. His letters begin in late 1976. This guy is not Dostoevskyan and yet you'll be dating soon. He writes prosaic letters capturing bits and pieces of the everyday. It's December and his granddaddy chokes on a crumb after dinner in Maryland. He's coughing horribly and unable to talk, D. writes. Later he's off to see a movie, Wertmuller's *Love and Anarchy*, which he finds painful and ruined by a bad ending. In the next year, you'll become a couple, and the letters will start flowing. In another letter, D. visits his father, a rabbi on staff at St. Elizabeth's Hospital in Washington. While waiting in the hospital library, he says, he becomes wrapped up in Virgil's "Fourth Bucolic." What is it with these guys and Virgil?

In this letter, D. is reading the *Ajax* while staring out the window, thinking about his future in classics and with you. The very act of reading, he writes, makes him think of you. What a compliment! How come I never said anything like that? I should be ashamed of myself. Not really. D. closes with eagerness to see you again.

Here's one from fall of '78. We just returned from Delphi, he writes, and awaiting him were your two wonderful "missives." Holy cow, you're writing letters to a guy just back from the Temple of Apollo. This is like a fairy tale. Sort of. And his parents are affluent, cultivated, enlightened, charming, well-located. In another letter D. says he's had many little adventures in Athens. He could spend a long time telling you about them. And I said, out loud, Anything but that. Shame on me. At least D. writes you.

By this point, you and D. have been a couple for three years. Yikes, I'm getting a little jealous. But you're only twenty-six and need to sow your oats. (Is that the right phrase?) I'm still jealous. I shouldn't be doing this, it's so invasive, but I can't stop now. *Tempus fugit*, as D. says. Someone needs to read this.

Frigid this morning but I'm sitting on the front porch steps, back against the brick wall. Brilliant sunshine overhead. The ides of March. So-called spring break. But for the birds it's quiet. Young people walk by. An eighteen-year-old in his stride, black nylon jacket, white earbuds. Inside of his head, he doesn't look up. Across the street a well-groomed young woman marches south on Gilbert. Perky and determined, eyes straight forward, her gaze biblically fixed on what lies ahead. Here comes an older guy in ill-fitting dungarees and a gray jacket. He walks along steady but can't hide his wavering. Something is faltering. Coffee cup in hand, he waits for a voice to urge him on. On the other side of Gilbert a hipster ambles by briskly, puffing on a cigarette. Black beanie, sunglasses, skinny pants. An air of self-importance. If Milo were here, he'd be by my side, and we'd bear witness together. He was happiest when I behaved like another dog. You enjoyed porch sitting too but weren't afflicted with a wandering eye. The birds are chirping and tweeting overhead. Chickadees, sparrows, cardinals, and robins. They are restless, darting from tree to tree, up in the large oak across the street, and the maple next door, now in our crab apple. The sun is deceptively warm. I listen to the birds and then nod off. Behind me the sparrows are fluttering in the flowering quince. The quivering wings send a chill up my spine. A robin perched in the maple tree scans our front yard for food. Scattered on the snow are hundreds of red crab apple berries. Down she flies, but try as she does, the berry won't go down. Three times she snatches the berry in her beak and shakes it down her throat. But back it comes.

If I were to tell you tonight that you look stunning, you would blush. You have shy eyes, pretty blue eyes behind which you can't hide. They reveal everything. And so if I were to say, Tonight you look stunning, your cheeks would redden and your eyes would sparkle. Behind those fair eyes is a keen mind, but it is a shy mind and self-effacing. How I love your mind and your demure eyes. An impeccable mind. Here we are standing in line to pay a sales tax on our used Honda. I want to fib about the purchase price but I can't because you are beside me. Not that you would mind. To save a few bucks, why not? The aura you evoke wards off my lie. Yes, you have an aura. A likable word from the Greek meaning *breeze, breath*. I feel your breath on my neck, a warm breeze, and suddenly my little fib seems stupid. I feel like a shifty Sicilian, which I am. I think you like that about me, my craftiness. Shifty but sincere, sometimes fierce, and usually inventive. You are drawn to these Mediterranean *gifts*, as you call them, tongue in cheek. I less than you, but I admire this side of my nature more for having been with you.

You would prefer to hide your charm behind a professional smile. Do you remember when, on request, I took a photo of you in the alley? It was a dazzling day in mid-April. Sparrows were going out of their minds. A bank of red tulips had just bloomed along Mike's front porch. The photo was for the department's newsletter. I snapped two dozen, one of which looked really good, a medium close-up that captured the vivid you-ness behind your eyes, the inner Claire. Of course you loathed the photo. That won't do, you said with spirit. You're kidding, I said. Looks good to me. Not really. You look lovely. No I don't. I look stupid. How's that? If you wouldn't mind, lend me your iPhone, you said. For what? I asked. I'll take my own photo. You're kidding, I said. So you took a dozen selfies and chose the one with the widest smile, the one that looked least like you. But it was a professional look, I guess, portrait of an academic woman in command. You found a way to hide behind that man-made smile. I hate to break it to you, but we used my picture for your obit photo. I will confess to a degree of perverse pleasure in doing so. I hope where you are now you will see why.

I'm rummaging through your memorabilia. I have here a certificate of special recognition from Shroder Junior High School in Cincinnati. The certificate places you in seventh grade. You have just been honored for having placed first in a competitive short story contest. I didn't know you were a storyteller. You kept things like this from me. I've looked high and low through your carefully archived pamphlets, notebooks, photo albums, letters. My curiosity has been sparked. As far as I can see, sadly, the stories you once wrote have not survived, except for one, in a chapbook called *Reflections* published by the English department at Northview Junior High School in Indianapolis. You had just moved from Cincinnati to Indianapolis at the end of eighth grade. Your father, a train man, continued to bounce around the Penn Central network. This was move number six or seven. Levittown, Atlanta, Chicago, Valparaiso, Denver, Indianapolis, Cincinnati. Here you were in Hoosier country.

You would come back for graduate school, but right now you are about to tell us a story. Your tale is called "The Shell," and if you knew I had this in my hands I'd be sentenced to a penal colony. You're very shy about these things. You're worried, it's just a guess, I'll make fun of you. Well, no. It's a lovely story, if not moving. It's hard to imagine you're only fifteen when you write this.

It goes like this. Tim, an old mariner from a small New England village, returns from fishing with a tiny load of clams, but has also snatched a large, pearly white conch shell. Other fisherman stop by the old man's catch to admire the shell, wondering about its value on the market, but old Tim refuses to peddle his conch. *"I'm no sellin' it at all,"* the old man said sharply, peering at the others from a battered, careworn face. Tim lives alone, having lost his wife Elizabeth. He tells the fishermen that his prized conch shell is *for 'lizbeth.* But it's really meant for Mike, a neighbor and friend who has been down on his luck and health. With a wife and children, Mike could use a hand.

So old Tim delivers his sack of clams and prize conch shell to a family in need, and explains how he, once an eminent man from elsewhere, came to this small and poor village to marry a woman, Elizabeth, who was herself, like the shell, a prize to behold. *A man can wish for but one love in his life,* says old Tim.

This is where I tear up with every read. A very strange and lovely story. The other kids write about cowboys, the American flag, critters, rockets, cigarettes, little green men, fallout shelters, *Star Trek,* on being short, on being fat—you about a widower who sets his heart on doing good, who gives away a marvelous shell. What would make a fifteen-year-old girl choose such a protagonist—a solitary widower? Baffling. You live in a perilous world. Race riots in Pennsylvania. Charles Manson on the prowl. Men are on their way to the moon. And yet here you are with a battered old New Englander in a beat-up dory. Once you think about it, I guess, everything looks strange. Take me, for instance. At the very moment your protagonist hauls his sack of clams up the hill, I am standing still on a small, paved runway. It's 1969 and I have a thirteen-foot fiberglass pole in my hands. I'm looking down the runway at a black and yellow crossbar elevated twelve feet above the ground. I'm a high school pole vaulter and I can't shake a feeling of absurdity. It will never leave me. Sooner or later I have to jump, I think to myself, and that's the story of my life.

CHAPTER TWELVE
THE SUN
(THE SPECTATOR)

Our sun is 4,500,000,000 years old. That's a lot of zeroes.

—NASA

S till no sun, blustery, cold, and wet. Somehow, the daffodils got back on their feet. Four days ago, the fallen stocks looked like the slain of Guernica. Now they're standing plumb straight. The force that through the green shoot drives the flower—a sheer act of will. But whose? Invincible. I never would have guessed. I had already called the undertaker. My daffodils died, I said, before their time, murdered by March. He said, What?

Outdoors, dead leaves scatter in the wind, desiccated leaves that dance across the alleyway. The sound is like wads of paper, something discarded. They hang around, oak and maple leaves. With nowhere to go they bunch and huddle and then disperse in gusts of wind. They seem to play a part in winter.

Abrupt change. It's so mild today the birds are losing their minds. The sparrows are flapping their hearts out. The starlings are just above the treetops, swarming back and forth between Mike's walnut tree and the oak across the street. They can't decide where to stay the night. My neck is sore watching. They drop in sync into the upper branches of the oak, a potential sleeping site. But one bird twitches just enough to trigger flight and airborne realignment. What makes them change their minds so abruptly? Attraction, avoidance, occluded sight, paranoia? The twitcher must be a prominent actor. At last they settle in the walnut tree with great noise. Murmurations (new word) is the fancy term for their gregarious chatter. All these years and I've never taken notice. Mesmerizing how the birds form a self-organizing entity, angling together as though programmed for a common purpose. Later at night they gossip about their less skilled partners, those who screw up the bank and roll. The glossy black bird with a star field on its plumage. On average, half the population of starlings dies in its first year.

In class yesterday, I stumbled on the word *disorientation*. I said *dis*orientation instead. The roof of my mouth got stuck on *stor* like a wad of gum and so there was an accidental ellipsis in the middle of the word. I added a glottal. To make things worse I was keenly aware of my mistake. I marveled out loud, much to the amusement of students. It was an Oliver Sacks moment. Cerebral stress? Crossed wires? The introduction of unwanted speech sounds is kind of weird, more typical of children. Interference from somewhere, as if my brain were being hacked in midsentence. In apraxia, messages from the brain are disrupted on route to the mouth, and so you say *chicken* instead of *kitchen*. Where does my brain go from here?

The sudden warm spell has triggered the premature sprouting of bulbs. In the yard, crocuses burst through the ground yesterday and have begun flowering, just as temperatures have plunged below freezing, little white petals, upright and unwary. They have no idea what awaits them. The shrubs along the railroad tracks at school have been fooled too. Little buds are opening up. I can see their green skulls, miniature heads of lettuce. With lows in the twenties forecast for the next four days, those tiny blossoms will die back. All in a day's work. It was seventy-five degrees two days ago but it's snowing now. As the saying goes, if you're not having ups and downs you're probably dead.

I am running out of words. I hope you'll understand. There's a point beyond which language won't go, like a dog that sniffs danger. It's where I feel beside myself, literally, as though there was someone alongside me at this moment who is the saddest thing in the universe. Right here beside me. He won't speak because he is heartbroken. He's like the older brother I never had, so heartbroken he can't speak, he will never speak. His mind is full of violins. He coexists alongside me in this place. He will not speak. He looks like William Blake's Isaac Newton, someone in need of a hat. He is the only company I have here beyond the last word.

We never said goodbye, you and me. There were no final words, only your remark about chopped fruit. Why don't you ever chop fruit for breakfast? you wondered. How strange, I say. Never in twenty-four years did I chop fruit for breakfast. Maybe once. I wish I knew. And then you went upstairs. It was a sunny day in late July. In your mind, you were going over what needed packing for Cincinnati. We could take our time, you thought, see what the plumber has to say about the leak. How could you know it was the last time you would ever climb these stairs, your bare feet on maple, hair bouncing, morning light streaking through the stairwell window? You thought you were taking on morning yoga, that's all, plotting the day's options, but we would say no more to each other.

Your head will explode. We had our last cup of coffee, our last morning chat. We wondered about delaying our travel a day or two. You looked at me, your coffee raised to your lips, and didn't see me for the last time. This was our life and we were in the middle of it. Like murder but something worse. It was beyond the last word and for that reason made all those other words between us, all those naive, innocent, lived words, strange and magnificent in their ignorance. Is it because of meaning that we die? We lived a bright life together and had words and smiles and dreams. And then luminous no more, as sudden as a gust of wind. Those words and smiles, tears in rain. I sit beside my sad friend. Neither of us talk. He is nameless. His eyes are cellos.

Out my window the sky is cheerless. The bare trees sway back and forth in wind and rain while birds take cover.

When I close my eyes, I see you and me on the highway and it's very sunny. We're on our way to Chaco Canyon in New Mexico. It's so bright and hot, in fact, we squint. We're on break from summer teaching in Santa Fe. We travel up into the badlands of high-desert country, follow Route 550 past San Ysidro, then across twenty-five bone-jarring miles of unpaved washboard road into Chaco

Canyon. It's so weird here we don't say a word, just stare out the car window at desert things. Fantastic rock formations. Miles and miles of lonely sagebrush. The sandy, dusty brown landscape seems vast and muted, except for the twisted yellow petals of the creosote bush and the lone mesquite tree, grazing cattle and sheep. No sign of human life, otherwise, and so luminous as to be blinding. We hide behind sunglasses and brimmed hats, guzzle bottled water. I keep talking about flying saucers—out comes the *New Yorker*.

Chaco Canyon is remote, halfway between Albuquerque and Navajo country in Farmington. It's not easy getting here. You wore a straw hat, green and purple scarf, your black long-sleeve top, khakis, and Nike sneakers. So strange this abandoned landscape is, you say, with red-and-ochre sandstone ruins. But you love it here despite the sun.

We take cover from the blinding light in the visitor center, where we learn about the Anasazi people who built these canyon structures, town houses, and kivas. We read that fields of maize, beans, and squash once flourished in the arid canyon, and thanks to irrigation canals there was enough food and water to support an ancient culture. Now there's just cottonwood trees, empty arroyos, and kangaroo rats. Shall we go back outside? you say. Must we? I say. With the sun directly overhead there is no shade for cover. Still, we walk close to the mesa wall, surprised by Indian paintbrush and narrow-leaf yucca. You have the guidebook in your hands, leading the way up the trail. This place seems pretty weird, I say. And it's hot. You nod stoically. The stillness only makes the canyon feel hotter, you say. Even before you say so, the words are in my head. How did that happen? Later you will write about the silence of the canyon: *If there's a place in the US that you'd expect would be quiet, it's Chaco Canyon. Many miles from any city, far down dirt roads, its ruins rest silently under the desert sun. Chaco is a place one hears, not listens to.* For once, you were free of stress.

The Anasazi quarried the large cliffs and built their great halls from dark-brown sandstone. We're at site number four. It's an apartment complex, enough space for one thousand dwellers. You rub your hands over the small, finely wrought pieces of sandstone, elegant rectangles. Layers of large stone alternate with finely cut sandstone, like books plunked on top of one another. You are fascinated. We stand together in the center of a dwelling space once occupied by the *ancient ones,* a people who vanished mysteriously one night, leaving behind a thriving city as sophisticated as Chicago or San Francisco. One day six thousand people are milling about under the Chaco sun, weaving baskets, playing flutes, tending squash—the next day gone. A massive retreat by the thirteenth century. But where? Why? Imagine Manhattan suddenly bereft of New Yorkers one fine morning, entirely empty.

I've lost my lens cap. Worse, my water bottle is empty. You lend me yours. Someday, I say, we should go on a normal vacation, maybe to Bora Bora or something and walk on white sand, snorkel in an azure lagoon, sip rum as the sun sets. This was your idea, you reply. Besides, look at this, you say. Behind site number four on the cliff wall are petroglyphs of six-toed feet. Six-fingered hands as well. You explain, thanks to your guidebook, that the people of Chaco didn't have a written language but communicated mostly by rock art. What does the six-toed foot say? I ask.

We hike to the other side to see Chetro Ketl and its kiva complex. We'll climb twenty feet down the entrance-way to the great kiva and enjoy the cool shade of the large, round, subterranean room. It's very quiet here. We whisper as though others are nearby. You are behind me as we climb back up the narrow stairway. To those watching, we might look like Orpheus and Eurydice. On our way back, we ask an official at the visitor center about the six-toed rock art. He sends us off to the museum curator, a perky and bright-eyed lady, Faye Something-or-other, who explains that there was a relatively high incidence of polydactyly, as she puts it, in Native American populations at that time. According to skeletal remains, some ancestral people even had double thumbs.

On our way out of Chaco, the road seems more deeply rutted. How can that be? you say. It hasn't rained. It's a mystery, I say. Everything is a mystery here, you say. We pass a Ford van that has pulled over. We stop to ask if we can help. Not unless you have a spare cooling-hose clamp in your back pocket, a burly guy in a cowboy hat says. It shook loose a mile or two back. He gives our Honda a once-over and smirks a bit. No one drives a Honda to Chaco.

I enjoy being at the wheel when you're navigating, listening to you fill in the empty spaces with your voice. We're on Route 64, taking the northern road back to Santa Fe. Off toward Blanco we go, with a stop at Trujillo's Country Store (more a tavern than a store) for bottled water. Lots of it. We're running low on ChapStick too. Dusty-looking fellows with bloodshot eyes tossing back bottles of Corona glance your way as we leave. I can't resist looking myself. Somehow the Honda has not fallen apart. We cross the San Juan River, the first body of water since standing by the Pecos River days ago. Supposedly, you say, this river is famous for trout fishing. How about that, I say. Blanco disappears in the wink of an eye under the crazy sun, a whiteout.

New Mexico is second only to Wyoming in the number of natural gas leases on federal lands, you read. Lots of orange rocks, sage, piñon, outcroppings. We're driving toward Dulce. As we near the boundary of the Carson National Forest, there's a sign for the monastery of Our Lady of the Desert. Desert monasticism is a thing in New Mexico, you offer. Benedictines, I think, you say. Affiliated with the diocese of Wollongong in Australia, believe it or not. How about that, I say. Wow, look out your window.

Lulled by the unchanging forms and colors of the high desert terrain, we don't see this coming, the sudden alpine changeover. There's juniper, ponderosa pine, aspen, cottonwood, and high peaks. How did we wind up here? It's as though we were transported. Where are we? you ask. Sign says *Carson National Forest*. Route 64 takes us through the Jicarilla Apache Reservation and close to the Colorado state line near Dulce. Apart from the Wild Horse Casino, not much happening here. What seems to draw the most attention is northeast of town, allegedly underneath the Archuleta Mesa. If you take River Road out of town, I say, crossing the Navajo River, you'll run out of pavement and find yourself head to head with the forbidding granite walls of the mesa. You're not paying attention, but I continue. And supposedly if you stick around until nightfall, which we won't of course, you'll see mysterious lights in the sky and who knows what else. The *New Yorker* is back in your lap. My story, I see, doesn't rouse your interest, but I'm stubborn. Rumors have long circulated, I say, that under the Archuleta Mesa the military maintains an extremely secret, multilevel facility dedicated to research on extraterrestrial beings and technology. You look up long enough to remind me to keep my eyes on the road, as I'm gesturing enthusiastically.

That's a whopper, you say, and I laugh when you give me your classic ground-control-to-Major-Tom look. Alien folklore and New Mexico seem inseparable, you say wisely. Indeed they do, I agree. But this is one of the better-kept secrets in the canon, I say unironically. You are ignoring me, your eyes glued to the *New Yorker*. Cattle mutilations too, I say weakly, but I'm losing credibility fast. You know, *The X-Files* borrowed material from the Archuleta Mesa story. I may as well be talking to my burrito.

Back in Santa Fe, you're catching up with your e-mail, lots of director stuff, and I'm in the arroyo out back. I'm tracking two butterflies dancing in the air. Courtship, I think. I've read that butterfly mating is serious business. When the male butterfly recognizes a female of his own species, he quickly pursues and begins wooing. I would have you join me, but it's such an ephemeral moment. Two butterflies, both alike, the smaller with two dark blotches (sex spots) on its midwings, the bigger nearly white as snow. Round and round they fly, under piñon branches and over cacti needles, wings vibrating hundreds of beats per second, tirelessly in pursuit, the larger (the male) hounding the female, dappled and indifferent. Cabbage whites, both, *pieris rapae*. The larger is hot in pursuit, but the female Pieridae has already mated, rising and hovering like a hummingbird—no, yes, no, yes—again and again sending maddeningly mixed messages. With each spiral the larger Pieridae closes on the smaller, but the erratic female double-crosses the erotic male, zigzaging with a flawless sense of timing. What can he do—this winged creature—but pursue, his radial veins now bulging like pneumatic tubes, his femur twitchy, his forewing aquiver. A precise rumble rises from his mesothorax, which for a brief moment confounds the female who now zags rather than zigs, and the male—how could he miss this chance, that giant compound eye, all six thousand lenses focused on this one moment, on the female's brilliant oviducts?— attempts a midair mount, his claspers twitching anxiously, but instead he is overcome, surprised—confused actually— by a surplus of airborne fragrance. There are too many scents. Was ever a butterfly in this humor wooed? Such a charmed moment. How is it possible to hold onto these things once the spell is broken?

Sunshine at last. The light-devouring shadow of Mordor has moved on. Spirits lift, smiles return. There are flies even.

CHAPTER THIRTEEN
NEPTUNE (THE RANDOMIZER)

The problem is that everything's moving.

—Pseudo-Heraclitus

Who would have thought the old man had so much blood in him?

The morning we left for France, Perry took a picture of you, me, and Milo on the front porch. It's the middle of January and snow has fallen. I'm holding the dog, you're holding me. Happy family smiles all around. Milo needs a haircut but looks frisky and bright. He's staring at the snow, waiting for a crumpled oak leaf to move. You lean toward me, I lean toward you. We are on the same bias. Married fourteen years. There's a chemical bond between us. I know I'm infatuated, that's my fate, but you can plainly see this in the photo. We're traveling to France together but you will return to snowy Iowa alone in two weeks. I'll teach in Montpellier for six months. For the first time we'll be apart. I'm nervous. You seem fine.

You are used to international travel. What will it be like without you? Can I make do in a strange land on my own? I can't even speak English. This dawns on me in line at the illycaffè in Charles de Gaulle Airport in Paris. What am I doing here? For six months, no less? Have I lost my mind?

Psychologists say single people lead more fulfilling social lives and experience greater growth than married folks. There was a time before we met when I believed that, when I sneered at marriage. I would grin cynically at couples walking down Connecticut Avenue in Washington—any married couple. Marriage seemed for the emotionally frail and spineless. I was arrogant back then, delighted with my singularity. What a hypocrite I turned out to be. Twenty years later, here in France, I'm afraid of being alone. You don't know this, nor do I for that matter, because I still think I'm unerringly self-reliant. Two weeks pass quickly and you're on a flight to Chicago. I'm alone in a tiny apartment by Antigone that is barely twelve-by-twelve feet. Not everyone speaks English in Montpellier so I'm taking lessons three times a week. I have no wife, no language, no dog, no nothing. Just holes in my soles. My shoes are leaking in the rain. It rains every day—where's the sunshine?—my feet are soaked.

I don't feel unerringly self-reliant anymore but I steel myself up. Totally new this feeling of helplessness. What's happening to me? I wonder. I fell in love, I got married.

We Skype. Milo looks fluffier in my laptop camera and sleepy. You're hidden in a big woolen turtleneck. Together, you both look like sheep from County Mayo. Tired of shoveling snow, you say. There's record snowfall that winter. You run through your week. Are you okay? you ask. I'm smiling like a monkey. Yeah, just glad to see you. I talk about the weirdness of the French university system. How's your French? you ask. Not bad, I say. Frankly, I find the language thing daunting, but I don't let on. The lessons are a help, I say instead, but my French vocabulary is itsy-bitsy. Everyone laughs when I speak French. Kind of unnerving. And these are southern French, you say, just imagine if you were in Paris. No kidding. How's your apartment? Well, it's really a dorm room. Across the hall American coeds just moved in. From Missouri, I think. You laugh. They're loud and boorish, I say. Watched a fishmonger yesterday at the market selling trout from the back of a Toyota pickup. He nets the live fish and flops it into a holding tank for fifteen seconds and then bludgeons it right between the eyes with a cudgel. Whack—voilà. Merci beaucoup, you say. Poor trout. I've been told the best way to sound French, I say, is to impersonate Peter Sellers's Inspector Clouseau. That gets a laugh out of you. I'm still smiling like a monkey. Milo has fallen asleep.

Market Square Park is alive with children and birds. The black kids bouncing basketballs, the white kids climbing up and down slides and monkey bars. Two little boys scream at the top of their voices as a baby squirrel tiptoes toward them. The little creature is looking for its mother, so it draws near anything bigger that moves. These boys are scared out of their minds. I'm worried one of the kids will squish the tiny squirrel so I draw it away from danger. It hops toward me thinking I'm mom. Meanwhile, I see another baby squirrel on the basketball court with the black kids. Like his sibling, he's heading for trouble, toward bodies and balls in motion. I rush over and lure baby squirrel number two away from the hoop. I wonder where Mom is, I say out loud to the kids. I don't know where she is but his dad's probably in jail, just like mine, says one of the boys. Baby squirrel number two jumps on my sneaker and declares me Mom. He then climbs up my pant leg. I'm home, he says.

Last night's heavy winds have knocked out a squirrel nest. No sign of adults. Dogs, cats, hawks, little kids aplenty. One can only hope. Advice for caring after orphaned baby squirrels involves building a simulated squirrel nest, setting it high up in a tree, and then using a squirrel caller to summon the adults. Waldo returns again and again. Don't know how he survived a hundred-foot fall. We put him in a shoebox and fed him warm milk and mushy bread. He lasted two days. The woodsmen in your family got a laugh out of that.

It's time to weed the yard and I'm struggling with unknowns. What looks like a clump of violets is thriving in the backyard. I haven't seen this before. The cluster seems invasive and is making me nervous, with ground-level blossoms completely cloaked by a thick canopy of heart-shaped leaves. No pretty blue flowers, just sickly pale pink underneath. A little creepy. Is this a weed or something rare and wonderful? I need your garden smarts: That's a weed, get rid of it, you would normally say. So I got rid of it, the entire patch. After checking online, I see that I uprooted not a weed but a unique cluster of African violets, probably a gift.

MidAmerican Energy hired a landscaper to drop off two variegated dogwoods and three hostas in return for the slaughter of flora by the contractors. Reparations for war crimes. I've planted two of the hostas in the alley bed and the dogwood out front. By the way, I managed to resuscitate the red twig dogwood (whose limbs were slashed by the pole people). Back in February, I seated the dogwood's remains in a barrel of dirt. It was just a plant carcass and the dirt was semifrozen. The sky was dark and gloomy. The squirrels were depressed. Even the swallows. Hoping for anything seemed stupid. Two weeks ago, lo and behold, new growth. The long sleep of grayness is over and the madness of greenery takes possession of everything.

It's early spring and you are wondering if it's time to work the garden. We've been Iowans for fifteen years. I'm ready to dig holes. I've got my shorts on. First time this year. It's sunny and warm, I say. Let's plant. I'm raring to go. You're more circumspect. Hold onto your pants, you say. We have to wait for the soil to dry out before digging. You squeeze a handful of soil and it sticks together in a clump. Too wet, you say. Gardening 101. Okay, I say. You're not used to my gardening zeal. You spirit me away to a nursery before I change my mind. We walk through rows of shrubs, trees, grasses, perennials, herbs. My eyes wander. I like the gaudy flowers. You remind me to stay focused on the shade-loving shrubs. The perennials won't solve our problem. It's not color we need. We need something to stay alive, you say. It's got to be hardy and love the shade or it won't grow in our yard. Okay, I say.

We have a difficult yard, a tormented yard, surrounded by black walnut trees, toxic things that block out sunlight and poison nearby rivals. Every October we toss the wilted remains of May's new plantings into the compost. Rhododendron, viburnum, cotoneaster, potentilla. All dead or languishing, like foliage along Love Canal. We could always plant carrots, you say. Root vegetables, they're pretty tolerant of black walnuts. How about zebra grass? I say. I love zebra grass, I add. We're in the ornamental grasses aisle. The feather reed grass looks so robust I want to take home a dozen. Bet the stalks make great cut flowers, I say. Growing grasses in the shade is challenging, you say. What about bamboo? I say. I love bamboo. Bamboo would make a great screen along the fence, you say. But zone five isn't terrific for bamboo. Even if it were, you say, bamboo is invasive. It's fast-growing and could take over the whole neighborhood. It's impossible to get rid of.

How about this? I say, pointing to a butterfly bush, festooned with stalks of fragrant color, lavender and magenta. This provokes a good laugh. Quite the show stopper, you say. Certainly great for butterflies. We're in an aisle called *America's most beloved shrubs*. We pass the privets. How about this? I say again, pointing to a hydrangea with enormous white flower heads. I love hydrangeas. I think I'm wearing you down. You crouch to check out the price. Only twenty dollars. Maybe so. This is not your first choice for shade-loving plants—that would be hostas or boxwoods—but I can see you'd like to reward my zeal.

We return home with a half a dozen plants and shrubs. A week later we're ready to sow. You're the mastermind so I follow you around the front- and backyards with a shovel. You're happy to have company, not to be alone in the dirt. It has taken me awhile to freely lend a hand, I'm ashamed to write. Gardening is not in my blood the way it's in yours. This is complicated work, I had no idea, and maybe that's why I'm beside you with a shovel. I'm drawn to complexity, or so I think. Truth be said, though, I love being by your side. Simple chemistry. Dig here, you say, tracing a circle around the hydrangea pot. About six inches down. *Va bene, capitano,* I say, and plunge the shovel into the soft soil. Slithering in the loose dirt are worms, mealy bugs, ants, and centipedes, their world suddenly upside down. I like getting my fingers dirty, working the moist soil like pizza dough. As a kid, I once put a handful of soil in my mouth, me and Rusty Baker. Took half a day to swallow. What came over us? My mom thought I was nuts. I came home with sludge oozing down my lips. What's that on your face! she screamed. Dirt, I said, confused. But the sound coming from my mouth didn't sound anything like that because dandelions had already sprouted in my windpipe. I was too embarrassed to tell you this earlier. The hydrangea is root-bound so I unravel the tangle of tubers and set the lollipop plant into its hole. You return with a water bucket, soaking its soil. We spend the afternoon thusly. After two years of this, I'll actually know what I'm doing, sorta.

It is more civilized, said Seneca, to make fun of life than to bewail it. Whatever can happen will happen, over and over again. We must endure our going hence, so it is said. I hide my grief but people still walk up to me gingerly. Sadness could be contagious. It's hard enough to remain buoyant in the bubbling sea of life. You can see that my endocrine and cardiovascular systems remain on the blink. Even now my sentences are wavering as though locked in some kind of chrono-synclastic infur ibulum. Our short stay in this world—blink-of-an-eye short—is a cycle of unimaginable moments. I dreamt of Milo last night. He is in a brown baby seal outfit and is having the time of his life. He's all wound up as I rub his sides, and I'm wondering if Milo has really turned into a seal or is just wearing a costume.

The real challenge out here is finding one's way around deep space. A message from Space Boy. It's been awhile.

I think he's miffed I made fun of his memoir. Is this another journal entry? I radio back. I'm using star sightings, radio signals, and the sun's gravity to plot a basic trajectory, he says. Thought you'd be interested. Sure, I radio back. Technically speaking, you must be on the threshold of interstellar space, I say. Think so, says Space Boy. The problem is that everything is moving. How's that? I ask. The Milky Way itself is ripping along at an average speed of 514,000 miles per hour, not to mention other celestial bodies in motion. And some orientation points, like Pluto, have a weird orbit (the weirdest in the solar system)—the random results of chaotic interactions. I didn't know that, I say, and I've watched a lot of *Star Trek*.

Three years after France, it's your turn to spend six months elsewhere. You're staying in Chapel Hill on a fellowship at the Humanities Center near Durham. It's late January again but with less snow. I give you two days to adjust to your new digs and then call. Milo is in my lap this time. I hear your voice and I feel inexplicably sad. I don't know why, I say, but I'm feeling strangely sad. So am I, you say. It's overwhelming, you add. I feel engulfed. Me too, I say. It's like we'll never see each other again. Yes, you say. What's happening? I don't know, you say. Maybe we shouldn't do this anymore, spend time apart. I agree, you say. This is really weird. I don't like it, I say. When can you visit? you ask. In a few weeks, I say. I fly out to see you twice. You fly back once. We forget the bewildering sadness. You like your apartment in Chapel Hill and so do I. You're downstairs making coffee. I'm dressing. Be careful on the stairs, you call up. Unbelievably slippery. I don't hear you. I have wool socks on and tumble down the stairs. You scream. I'm okay, I say. Boy, those stairs are really slick. I spend the rest of my visit limping around Chapel Hill. You are convinced, from this point on, that something terrible will happen to me.

I took care of the taxes, you'll be glad to know. I apologize for not helping more when you were here. Page after page of tiny inscrutable text and empty boxes, ominous blanks, and forbidding dotted lines. I'd rather jump out of an airplane. I mean it. Once tax-related documents—all those 1099s and W2s—began arriving in the mail, I wanted to curl up in a fetal position. I can't even write my name on a form—once I see it as a form—without needing counseling. A phobia exists, by the way, related to filling out forms. Scriptophobia, I think. I know this sounds lame but it's a fear that something bad will happen as a result of completing a form. Same thing with questionnaires, surveys, applications.

I recently opened up a new account at a nearby bank. Two managers were present to witness my trembling hand while the dreaded application form awaited my action. They exchanged furtive glances. I needed a drink after that. I steeled myself for the taxes. I actually took two Advils and a beta blocker. I had no choice. I gathered all household information, the bloody tax documents, set everything in order, and attached a detailed note of explanation to Margo Grady, the paralegal lady who has been handling our estate. *Dear Margo, enclosed you will find in detail a list of numbers and dates that mean absolutely nothing to me but may be of some relevance to the task at hand.* If I had greater resolve I would liquidate everything and enter a monastery. I would make scented candles.

Margo loves her work, apparently. She talks excitedly about tax forms, 1090 this and that, can't get enough. Her office is stacked high with client folders she has resolved for decades. Life shows through in her face. You would like her. I should add there is something slightly askew about it, her face. A tiny part of it seems offline. Maybe basal ganglia trouble. I checked her hands but saw no tremors. Anyway, I can't believe I did this. I bet you can't either. I am so restless my name won't stand still.

I'm finding things out about you that are news to me. I'm writing this down so it sticks, like reclaiming a part of my wife that remained off limits. After you finished your MA in classics, you traveled with Susan Stites to Europe. This was the first of many trips abroad. I have a notebook you kept from that tour. Very orderly. It's among your memorabilia. You drove in bad weather from Cincinnati to Toronto, it says. This was in late August of 1979. You're twenty-five years old. From Canada you flew to Heathrow. You had a steak dinner and later a large breakfast, you say. Your inflight movie was *Young Frankenstein*. Your ledger skills are in evidence here. The notebook begins with a five-page list of purchases. Earphones on the transatlantic flight to London ($2.50), a bus to Victoria Station (60 pence), dinner at Wimpy's (68 pence), Italian phrase book (10 pence), bus to Stonehenge (80 quid), ice cream (10 pence), ticket to the Louvre (25 francs), candle at Santa Croce (100 lire), another ice cream cone, chocolate and käserbrot (3 marks), beggar (1 mark), map of Hamburg (2.90 marks), sweater (19 marks), two nights in hotel (44 marks), ballet ticket (2.60 marks). I can't help noting all of the chocolate and ice cream. Ice cream cones will remain a prized travel item for both of us. Remember Teddy's at the Dun Laoghaire pier? That cone was to die for. You would later blame your sweet tooth on me, and I believed you. I feared I corrupted a pear-eating virgin. But I see that young Claire also likes her donuts and double-chocolate nuggets. Here's a relevant line item: Little Debbie's Chocolate Cookies (1.50 marks)—cookie rings with caramel and coconut.

On arrival in London, you had a "disgusting" meal at Wimpy's and then visited the British Museum for a quick look at the "classica," as you folks called it. Something must have disagreed with you, maybe the Wimpy's burger and chips or the decapitated figures from the Parthenon, because you woke at midnight and didn't fall asleep until four. It was a fitful first night and you kept turning the days events over in your mind. Much later, you will wake at midnight and read the *New Yorker* on an iPhone tented under sheets and blankets. I'll pretend not to notice the glowing light. The following day brings nice weather. After a large breakfast you're walking the streets of London. *Hard to get used to jaywalking,* you note. You stop at Trafalgar Square to send a telegram but fourteen words will cost £2.00 ($15 today), so you settle for a postcard and stamps.

At the National Gallery, you and Susan plant yourselves on a bench before Botticelli's *Portrait of the Young Giovanni de Medici,* who looks like your sister's husband. Back from the museum, you stop for a bite to eat at an Italian restaurant near Trafalgar Square. *Not too expensive so we went inside. Sat near two middle-aged women from St. Louis. Embarrassing. Had cannelloni and honey dew melon. Melon delicious.* You're in your midtwenties and have spent the day gazing at masterpieces. Just when you thought you had arrived, scrunched together are two round-faced lovelies in Bermuda shorts with giant shopping bags jabbering about Harrods in an American midland accent. Absolutely cringe-worthy. Wisely, it's off to Stonehenge the next day, a good whiff of Druid air, but first must confirm reservations at the YWCA (£7.00 split two ways). Your frugality is masterful, always. Crowded on Basingstoke train. A woman with a giant German shepherd sits down beside you but doesn't talk. You know now not to smile at Brits. Such a grumpy lot. Change at Salisbury. Bus is late. Walk to the Salisbury cathedral with soaring spires. Magnificent inside, you note, especially the choirs and stained glass windows. Splendid day, mild and sunny. Lovely countryside, rolling plains, cows, horses. Back to London.

Wait, London so soon? What happened at Stonehenge, that massive monument on the chalky plain of Wiltshire? Did you rub your hand on a Heel Stone? Did you feel the ground tremble? *Mum's the word.* On to Paris but first one more peek at the Egyptians in the British Museum. The gilded sarcophagi and Ramses II and the King's Library. Train to Dover, boat to Dunkirk. No Chunnel yet. Lots of delays. Finally, train to Gare du Nord. Not sure how the metro works here. Worse, can't find your hotel. Good night's sleep and then—yum, yum—café au lait and croissant and jam and butter in the morning. And then the Louvre.

And so it goes. From 1977 to 1983, you'll travel to Europe repeatedly. London, Paris, Marseilles, Hamburg, Venice, Florence, Berlin, Munich, Naples—over and over again. It's all written down neatly in your notebook—Claire's splendid orderliness. In 1982, you'll spend a year at the University of Tübingen, another foreigner among thousands of international students. Was this pent-up wanderlust or eagerness to escape the dreary middle-class trap you had been born into? You would say the latter.

You're not the meandering type, like me, but I'm wondering now. I never traveled abroad back then. I was broke and afraid. Where would I stay, what would I say? In my naive mind, Europe might as well have been the moon, so unreachable. I would later ask you, How on earth could you afford flying to Europe every summer? You told me your grandmother gave you two thousand dollars every year. That was quite a sum of money, I said. Yes, you said. That's some grandma, I said. Yes, you replied.

Here's a picturesque postcard of a Benedictine abbey in Bavaria, where the monks are known for making a special kind of schnapps. *Dear Family*, you write, *We've been having a very active stay. David's two close German friends, Johannes and Hans-Georg, have led us on a round of restaurants, coffee houses, and bars. Hans-Georg has been especially thoughtful: yesterday he drove us around Bavaria looking at baroque churches, gorging ourselves at every eatery we saw.* (There's that David again.) This is young Claire keeping Mom and Dad in the loop—you send them cards almost every other day—but I wonder, did you try the schnapps? How could you not drink the schnapps? The monks, I understand, experiment with indigenous herbs and precious-juiced flowers, like Friar Laurence. Down the hatch. I love your handwriting, by the way, so steady and legible. The slopes are fluent and the loops consistent. So graceful. It calms my perturbed soul, even now. My handwriting is gnarled and eccentric. I should be kept in the attic. By the way, what's with all the boys?

Today I passed a stack of three-by-five cards at Staples and flashed back five years ago to an early September afternoon when I stopped by your office to say hi. You are flipping through a pile of index cards just retrieved from students in your medieval culture class. I sit down next to your desk. What are these? Index cards are mostly obsolete nowadays, I say. I ask students to tell me a little about themselves at the start of class. Three-by-five bios, you say. No kidding? I like that, I say. Let's see what you've found out. I point at an index card. Who is that? Carrie from Des Moines, you say, whose dad works for Wells Fargo and whose mom is a realtor at Coldwell Banker. Boy, that's pretty nosy, I say. Sometimes, students volunteer stuff. It just comes out, you say. What else? Carrie writes for the school newspaper and can speak French, you read, and her favorite novel is *The Hobbit*. Where does she shop? No laugh—you take your index cards seriously. Like little snapshots, I say. Something like that, you say. It helps me remember the person behind the name. That's a lot of cards, I say. Forty-two students, you say. Do you save these? Of course not. Why would I? I worry there'll come a time, I say, when I won't remember a single student's name. Dementia and all. If it ever comes to that, you say, just shoot me.

The red chicken with white polka dots has returned. It's standing in place beside Hickory Hill Park, glad to be outdoors after weathering winter in someone's cellar. I can sense the impatience of all things, especially green things. This fowl is dead still but other birds are busy. Were you here you'd point out the checkered black-and-white downy woodpecker feeding upside down on a locust tree across from an Aston Martin. This one is a female without the bold red patch on its head, you'd say. Dormant for five months, the organic world has come back with a vengeance. Ample rain and sun. Heat wave in middle of May, three days of ninety degrees.

And wouldn't you know it but the air conditioner didn't

work. Reports of the collapse of the vulnerable parts of the West Antarctic ice sheet appeared in the news today. The flow of ice into the sea is getting faster and faster. So green and aromatic here. The Oriental poppies bloomed earlier this week, and our backyard peonies are surfacing. Last night's thunderstorm rubbed out the wispy orange petals. For years the peonies never blossomed. Making up for lost time. Melting ice fields are far away.

How long have we been in Iowa? I ask. I don't know, you say. It's been thirteen years, I say. You shoot me a critical look, as if I just told a lie. You don't want to know the number. Same with your age. You don't want to know the number. You know, I say, our anniversary is coming up. I always keep track of that. June 17. You're amused by my sentimentality. Do you know how many years? You ignore me. You don't want to know. It's our fifteenth wedding anniversary, I say. Should we celebrate? You roll your eyes. You don't share my interest in the past, which is admittedly nostalgic. I can't blame you. I also sense a bit of denial on your part, but I think your refusal is more intelligent than my nostalgia. I think you were (maybe still are) more here than me. Anyway, we have been in the Midwest, speaking of hereness, longer than anywhere else in our lives as adults. It's home now, even if it doesn't always feel that way. We don't fight it. There's subliminal resistance but that happens anywhere.

We've resigned ourselves, partly because of summer travel. It's wired into your genetic code and now it's in mine too. We always travel in summer. The emptiness makes us restless. This year we are on our way to Santa Fe. We just left Milo in Cincinnati with your mom and dad. It's a long, tedious drive, especially through Missouri. But we're traveling with the third edition of Stern's *Roadfood*. We're on Interstate 44 in the middle of the state. I don't like it here, I say. All these goddam pickups going ninety miles per hour. What happened to the laid-back farmer? The frenzied traffic makes you nervous too. You thumb through the state of Missouri in *Roadfood*. Mostly St. Louis and Kansas City entries, you say. Beef and barbecue joints. Looks like something interesting in Rolla, though, in fifteen miles. We've been on highways since eight this morning. In all, 460 miles. What did you find? I ask. A Slice of Pie. My eyes dilate. There's nothing like a good piece of pie on the road. They have over two dozen different kinds of pies, you say with a devilish grin, not to mention lunch entrées. It says here the servings are big.

I step on it. We get off the highway and wander around Rolla until we find A Slice of Pie. Not a memorable town, you say. Not at all, I say. Kind of depressing, you say. We drive past a Kroger and Wendy's, some churches and collision shops. You're pointing out the window—it's across from Ozark Wellness. The whole town feels industrial, I say as we sit down. Even though there's no industry, you say. I can't believe my eyes. Over a dozen lip-smacking pies in the glass case. This must be where pies go when they die, you quip. I laugh. Diane, I say, four thirty p.m. Dining in the town of Rolla, five miles south of nowhere. It's eighty-four degrees and overcast. This is a running joke. We like David Lynch. We check the menu. Half order of chicken salad, you tell the stressed-out waitress. I'll take the coconut cream pie, please. We watch other diners. These are not tiny people, I say. They're loving their food, you say. That didn't take long. Here comes the waitress. Your chicken salad is huge, and so is my slice of pie.

We could feed a village, you say. At least. Holy cannoli, if this is what they call a slice. I guess the book wasn't kidding, you say. You nibble on your chicken salad, leaving more than half behind—it's that big—while I finish my so-called slice of pie. Damn fine food.

We're back on the road. You're driving because I keep nodding off. I feel bloated. At least five thousand calories. There's gallbladder pain too. I could go into a coma. We night over in Joplin near the Oklahoma border. The next day the sky darkens. Oh boy, I say, this looks menacing. We're somewhere between Tulsa and Oklahoma City. Ahead, the apocalypse waits for us. Boom goes the thunder and then the rain. The rolling hills, the oaks, crape myrtle, pine trees all disappear. It's just you and me and the hairy sky. Winds are whipping the car toward the shoulder. A burst of lightning to the west. Up ahead a tractor trailer has flipped over in the ditch. We pull off the road and wait out the downpour. We hold hands we're that scared. The winds rock the car back and forth.

This is a dream and in it you are dressed in professional garb, a nice-looking pantsuit. You want me to take new photos of you which I am to "resend," though I don't remember where. The *resend* sticks in my mind. I pause to whisper in your ear how deeply in love I am with you. This brings a smile to your face. On Planet Claire, you say, there are no photos. Photography belongs to the world of time. You must be visiting, I think, making a house call. Maybe you've forgotten what you look like. Where do I send your photos?

Sometimes when the sadness comes, I feel like a bug trapped in amber, in a honey-colored, thick gummy casing. I can't turn my head or close my eyes. The sky is no longer blue and the street is silent. I can only hear myself think, though it's not me but a fossil. I'm a fossil, petrified remains, and my thoughts are resinous and sticky. They cling to my fingers, memories of you and me, leaning on a railing over the River Liffey, they cling to me. Whisper in my ear that you are near, please whisper in my ear that you still love me, that you are near, that you forgive me for being among the living.

Each morning over coffee, we read the paper and chatted in snug soft chairs. Behind us, the bookcase. On your lap, the dog. Atmospheric morning light filtered through the north window. We rested our feet on the coffee table and for forty-five minutes the universe seemed to configure itself around us. Mornings that began this way aroused a profound sense of well-being. We had lively conversations. We talked about work to be done around the house, upcoming meetings, zany ideas, travel plans, *New York Times* articles.

Every once in a while, however, I would talk about literature. These were not my best moments. My whole demeanor changed. I'd sit up straight for added volume, clear my throat, and search for words. Suddenly unspontaneous, as if typing sentences in my mind before speaking. You tried to ignore me but it was impossible. You gave me threatening looks, rolled your eyeballs, buried your head in the paper. It was the only time your tender blue eyes turned unfriendly. I think they even changed color. But I couldn't help myself. I became a blowhard. I was possessed. I underwent a kind of paroxysm that turned me into a talking head. The dirty look you gave me was a thing of beauty. As soon as you saw me struggle for the right word, you knew I was lost. Your chair is empty now, but this memory fills my mind with delight.

Shrubs and trees are leafing out with abandon. Neighborhood parks are aswirl with dogs and kids and watchful adults. Everyone sees the green light. Wish I could feel a bounce in my step. It's just not there. Filled six lawn bags with winter debris. Dead leaves, candy bar wrappers, cigarette butts, ancient plastics, fallen branches, coffee cups, bony twigs, rusted metal. Can now see the hostas spears pushing through the soil. Life will out. Things coming up from the ground and out from under rocks, from the darkness into the fragrant light. Here among the brown-gray detritus, I see you everywhere and nowhere. You are here and not. But I will kiss you just the same.

I've reset the patio blocks. The chipmunks dug deep and extensive tunnels in the middle of the yard. The patio stones sank into the ground. I emptied a fifty-pound bag of pea gravel into the underground burrows. In another year, the stones will sink again. The chipmunks are indefatigable. The back porch is rotting out, so I've hired a carpenter to rebuild the entire structure. You would like him. He's garrulous and methodic. He told me all about himself. "I hate to paint," he said, "but I don't mind doing it. That's what I tell everyone." He's my age but has three kids under ten. "My friends think I'm an idiot," he said, "but I don't mind." While attaching the tongue-and-groove floorboards, he fielded several phone calls. "My kids won't leave me alone," he said. "They can't figure anything out for themselves. *Dad, can I have a tuna fish sandwich?* My eight-year-old calls me up in the middle of a job about lunch. *Yes*, I tell him, *that's what tuna fish is all about*."

Dreamt we sat together on a crowded bench. You held my hand. You were coming back, not literally but in some kind of symbolic way. You were coming back symbolically. I don't know what that means.

On my walk, lots of tree debris. Crab apples losing yellow leaves as though October, black walnuts bombing the alleyway with nuts. The sycamores have been the messiest. When the breadth of the sycamore expands, the brittle bark cracks and comes loose. It's like a snake molting, routinely casting off a part of its body. The jumbles of peeling bark, scattered widely, look like the remains of torn-apart books. I picked up a fragment of bark and wondered at it. Quite beautiful and fully textured. My first impulse was to write on its inside, a poem or something. I've become so dorky.

Early this morning I blacked out in the bathroom. Woke up on the floor. How'd I get here? I wondered, flat on my back. Last I remembered I was upright and peeing. My head was killing me, my neck too. I had slammed my skull into the wall. I was in a daze all day, could hardly move my neck. Should be more careful with my metaphors.

My first neighborhood walk in weeks. To my surprise, the wolf is gone on Pleasant Street near the park. The foxes too. The wolf's platform is now a bare stump. A large red dumpster sits in the driveway. On one side of the porch a pile of old kitchen cabinets, through the front window scattered debris. No one will see me stopping here. The little deer must think it queer. Mildred's husband died and she has moved away, into a condo, though not without her wolf.

Down Cedar Street a black-eyed Susan winds its vine stems around a mailbox. In the park, an old woman gathers nuts at the base of a shag-bark hickory tree. Her blue slacks are rolled up. She works diligently, cracking nuts, filling her white bucket. I draw near. She looks up. Howdy, I say. Have you come to pick the nuts too? she says. No, I say. Her bucket is nearly full. What will you do with your hickory nuts? I ask. Mostly bake things, she says, cookies and cakes. I make them for the neighbors. Her name is Jo Ann, Jo Ann Burton, an eighty-two-year-old from Coralville, comes for the nuts. Brown eyes, gray hair. Her face is wrinkled, her legs too. She's old but lively, full of spunk. A large crow caws in the tree above us. Where do you live? she says. On the other side of town, I say. Out for a walk? Yes, I say. That's good. I walked three miles this morning, she adds. Always good to be walking. Yes, I say. The crow overhead is rattling and clicking now. The bird seems impatient. I thought hickory nuts were too bitter for eating, I say. Nonsense, says Jo Ann. It's a myth hickory nuts are only for squirrels. The meat has a mild pleasant taste and is dense in nutrients and contains healthy oils and antioxidants. You have no idea.

I keep alert for narrative arcs, but grief is beyond any shape I know. If anything, it resembles a spiral galaxy. Its meaning is far away. I keep orbiting around that awful moment, like a man trapped in space. Round and round I go. Your death. It's misery to look, misery not to. I keep circling around that in a succession of irregular loops, like a man trapped in space. It was a death without warning. Why no signs? The worst kind of end, a failure of meaning. The immeasurable scope of your death. I can hear myself breathe, my lungs whispering. I dwindle, I could vanish. Such a comedy my disappearance will be—you don't know what you're missing. Hearing, it is said, is one of the last senses to go. The point about beauty is to see it. I saw you and still.

CHAPTER FOURTEEN
CENTAURUS (THE TRAVELER)

*The Boomerang Nebula is definitely the coolest
place in outer space.*

—Space Boy

I am thy husband's spirit, doomed for a certain term to walk the night and by day to read the daily news. I skip over the sport scores and go straight to disaster. The extreme skier Matilda Rapaport died in a hospital in Santiago, four days after she was buried in snow in the Chilean Andes. The cause was brain damage from oxygen deprivation. She was buried for at least half an hour before rescuers, alerted by a film crew, dug her out, unconscious. Compare that to Genelle Guzman, who fell from the sixty-fourth floor of the World Trade Center, was buried under a ton of rubble for over twenty-seven hours, and yet came out alive. Such is life.

Recently, a young girl was hit with a stone thrown by an elephant in a Moroccan zoo. She died hours later. Astonished zoo officials said this kind of mishap is rare, unpredictable, and strange. One of the elephants picked up a stone with his trunk and just hurled the rock at a seven-year-old, who was propped up on her dad's shoulders the better to see. The girl was struck in the head, which bled and bled. Elephants sometimes get bored in captivity, the reporter said.

So alive you were, never dying. You were alive and then the blackness which exploded in your head like plutonium. No one could see you bleeding. Metamorphosed on the spot in a plutonic instant. Sheer luminous darkness. Your aneurysm erupts over and over again in my own head. Words veer left and right, breaking free of verbal thrombosis.

Just the other day lightning killed a herd of reindeer in Norway. All at once. Their bodies were strewn about like dead men in combat. A field of carcasses, morbid and bizarre. The odds of being killed by lightning is 1 in 300,000. Multiply that by 323. I peek at the randomness of the universe but bury it under layers of stupidity. The mind cowers before the unforeseen, as though surrendering to ignorance. A herd of reindeer electrocuted by a thunder cloud. I can't assimilate that. Nor your death. The implications are too radical. The arbitrariness of the universe can't be computed, my brain whimpers. What if life has no meaning? it thinks. What if life were a nonlinear dynamic affair with chaotic behavior?

Since you left, I keep looking for signs, anything that might make the randomness of the universe seem meaningful. That was your job, to connect the dots. I'm good at detecting anomalies, you at normalizing the data. We were an exceptional team. But now I'm vulnerable to worry—physics says existence is improbable—and sometimes think that life is so unpredictable I don't want to leave my bed. It's gotten to the point where spaghetti no longer tastes good. To imagine the universe is not extremely random requires a leap of mythopoeic magnitude.

Or at least marriage. For me that option is up, contradicted by death. Death is a terrific contradiction. It's the opposite of marriage, building a home, finding confidence to exist. We did all that. But these activities only work in a reasonably predictable universe. We stake a lot on a problematic assumption, but what's the alternative? A head-scratcher. Lost at sea is what I am.

The Tyrrhenian Sea was calm and the sky cloudless. We stood in line at the Porto Di Mergillina. *Due biglietti per Palermo, per favore,* you said at the SNAV counter. I'll get the tickets, I said. Not necessary, you said. You were suspicious of my French and Italian and preferred to take charge on occasions like this. By myself, I was likely to get it right. But I knew you were monitoring me for unforced errors, and sometimes I felt jinxed.

Anyway, we boarded a hydrofoil that would take us to Sicily, with an overnight stop in the Aeolian Islands. It was not a large ferry but a fast one. On board were mostly Italians, some going only to Lipari, the largest of the Aeolian Islands. As we pulled away from the dock, the bunched-up apartments above the Bay of Naples grew smaller. You pointed to Capri, shrouded in haze. Before long the sea was empty. The boat's giant turbine roared as we climbed the rolling waves. You were fascinated by the submerged wing-like foils lifting the hull above the water. As the boat lurched on heavy swells, we sat back in our seats. You read the Lonely Planet, I gazed out the salt-stained window at the undulating sea.

You were scanning overnight options in Lipari, where we'd stay and eat. I was lost in thought, always the absentminded traveler. If it were up to me, we'd be sleeping under picnic tables and dining on earthworms. The hydrofoil droned on. Those passengers not smoking in the open were dozing off in the cabin. Everyone was awake when we passed Stromboli, the first of seven Aeolian islands. An active volcano, the magic mountain draws all eyes. No one wants to miss the show. It's May of 2007. Stromboli is quiet now but will erupt in two years, a few short but energetic bursts, ranging up to 1,500 feet in height, containing ash, incandescent lava fragments, and stone blocks. You press your nose against the window. We both crowd to the back of the ferry with the others. The volcano seems to have come from nowhere. It's just there, an eccentricity of nature, with its steep slopes and forbidding profile. It says here, you point out, that the volcano has been in continuous eruption for twenty thousand years. Gee whiz, I say. You can see smoke coming out of its crater every twenty to forty minutes, the book says, you say. Some folks hike all the way to the top. You're kidding, I say. No. But you need a tour guide. Then you can get really close to the rumbling. You would like that, you say. I would, for sure. The ferry has cut its speed so we can get an eyeful of volcano. That's some volcano, I say. Nearly five hundred people live in the village beneath it, you say. Not a lot to live on here. No, you say. Is that a black beach? I ask. Yes, you say. You're looking that up in the book. Volcanic pebbles, you think. How about that.

We're both hungry when we land on touristy Lipari, surprised by Roman sarcophagi lying around everywhere. We check into our hotel and then head to the archaeological museum up the hill, on the advice of Lonely Planet. More sarcophagi and a Greek cemetery. Lots of amphorae. They make me thirsty. At dinner, I spill olive oil over my new shirt. Such a klutz, I say. You smile. Palermo is not a thing of beauty, you say later. We're in Sicily at last. That's for sure, I say. Palermo has a thick atmosphere of decay—crumbling baroque villas, lugubrious banyan trees, and monsoon clouds. A bit seedy and dangerous, you say, but atmospheric.

We walk to a market near San Domenica Piazza where a fisherman boils a live octopus. It's very purple, I say, the octopus. What did you expect? you say. Well-heeled tourists are snapping pictures with their Nikons and Canons, giant zoom lenses. I'm jealous. The vendor is burly but a maestro with a large fish knife. He pulls the octopus out of the salty boiling water, slices off its legs which are then cut into manageable pieces. You are mesmerized, drawn to squid and octopi. Your lips aren't watering but your eyes are bigger. The vendor quarters its head, garnishing the cuts with slices of lemon. I am aghast. You are tempted— but for the long line. Looks irresistible, I say. You smile.

I'm on the back porch where you liked to sit and gaze at the garden. Little green aphids are crawling up my arm. They're hardly visible but tickle. I'm reluctant to blow them away. If not for birds and insects I'd be alone, more so than St. Francis, who had an entire order to himself. It's baffling how easy it is to feel that way—alone, or left behind. I've always felt like a stranger but in the past it produced a reassuring feeling, as if I were original. It's not like I was some kind of Meursault, psychologically detached from the world, but I liked thinking of myself as an outsider. Marriage normalized me, which was a good thing. Now I'm that stranger again and feel isolated, as though on a country road without a home in sight.

I did meet someone a short while ago, you'll be relieved to hear. She's an artist and quite lovely. Her work is compelling and so is her life story. After all this sulking, I find myself intrigued. She's more sociable than either of us, which is instructive, but doesn't live nearby. This means I travel a lot, and this gives me plenty of time to ruminate. I like that word. Cows do this all the time, ruminate, but stand still. I'm moving seventy-five miles per hour when I ruminate. Mostly I've been ruminating about life. Where am I in life? I ask myself. I actually say this out loud in the car. You'd be amused. *I have no idea* is always my answer. It's not a productive dialogue, but I don't want to be alone—you taught me that.

I have a few more letters to read. It's 1986 and both Jane and Susan have written condolence letters regrading Phil. Who's Phil? Anyway, you've been dumped by Phil, they say. My sympathies. Guys suck, for whatever reason. I'm a total dickhead myself in 1986. Glad we haven't met yet or I wouldn't be writing this sentence. That same month, you ask your ex-boyfriend D. how to know when you've met the right guy. He says, Well, you'll just know. Wise D. Here's a letter from J., who laments your move to Washington in the fall of 1988. We're catching up, by the way. I've just passed you in the hallway at George Washington the day J.'s letter arrives. You're wondering about me, the brooding guy whose office is right next to the chair's, and I'm wondering about you, the new girl who, for a medievalist, seems pretty cute (though nerdy). You've only just arrived in your small Toyota with a cat and a pile of theory. Meanwhile, J. is writing from Indiana and wondering how your romance might have played out had you not left for Washington. He's missing you. It's impossible for me not to speculate, he says, about the intimacy we enjoyed. I don't like the sound of that, but what can I do here in the future, helpless? I'll meet this guy in a couple of years in Bloomington and feel an instinctive mistrust. (My prophetic soul.) We're in a booth at a hippie restaurant and I have a stack of buckwheat pancakes—they're really good—and I can't help but watch the way he looks at you with those dark, possessive eyes. Skinny, restless fellow. I'll later ask if you two were involved. You'll say no. Clever girl.

I was never much of a letter writer myself. I couldn't muster the insistence to say what these fellows say. Such long and thoughtful letters. Who can guess what you wrote to keep them coming? I'm relieved I'll never know. The girls in your archive, by the way, write better letters than the boys, with less to prove.

Truth be said, I did write before I met you but they were baroque love letters that were more like LSD trips. Efforts that surprised me. Crazy metaphors flew out of my brain. I didn't know there was such a gonzo voice inside. Glad you were spared this Hunter Thompson. I locked that guy up. I can sometimes hear him yowling. I didn't have the heart to throw my letters away, though, but I dreaded the possibility that you might stumble on them, so I hid them so artfully I haven't a clue where they are today. Someday a stranger will find these and have a good laugh. Or maybe not.

I see your image in the words of others, striking, smart, and attentive. Each guy had his say, described his struggles, his desires, the books and movies he liked, ambitions. I knew little about you in the years before we met. Now a younger you sits beside the ylang-ylang tree in my mind. Epistolary Claire, with many friends and overseas adventures, open to the world. Letters of a traveler. When shall we two meet again?

My oyster eyes are awash in memories. You are at the kitchen counter in a fur-lined brown sweater, your favorite stay-at-home wear. Your right index finger curls around a pen. Beside you, a red bag of tangerines. It's midwinter and sunny outside. The blind is half-closed. Your back is straight but you are tilting toward the left. For balance, your other hand is propped on the counter, your middle finger pointing at a paragraph as though guiding the writing on the page. I see you now in a classic posture, the *Editor*, deep into reading. I can't tell if you are vexed or inspired. Just single-minded, resolved. Whose text? I wonder. Yours? Mine? A student's? So quiet and Zen-like, you remain this way for hours, your eyes locked on someone else's thoughts. Milo is asleep on the sofa. I am putzing around. The wind rattles the window. Every now and then I take furtive looks your way, amazed by your stillness, such terrific focus. Frightened even. Suddenly your blue pen is set in motion and another annotation takes form in the left margin. If it's my writing, you're flagging the ninety-ninth digression. Or yours, more theory and less description. A colleague's half-finished line of thought. A student's ungainly sentence.

Thoughts should be orderly, that's what you think. Writing should be lucid. Always so reliably bright and clear-minded, tireless and determined to illumine what we ourselves refuse to resolve. I still cringe every time your blue pen takes action in my mind. I know what that means. Where's your topic sentence? you will ask me, and I will look at the targeted paragraph and just scratch my head. Abducted by aliens, I offer lamely. No kidding, you say. I have an aversion to the topic sentence, I'll add. It's like a serotonin deficiency. I was born that way. You will go about your business, meticulously supplying the missing idea or realigning a crooked sentence.

You never complain about these half-baked texts. It was a gift, what you did for us—what you did for me. How you always covered for others, amending our boo-boos. I don't think it was easy to live life so conscientiously. I would have died a long time ago. That's my best paragraph, I would cry in despair. What do you mean *it doesn't fit?* Of course I knew it was off-topic but the idea of irrelevance was so unthinkable to me. Everything is relevant. You simply ignored me and suggested I walk the dog. For you, editing was like refinishing an armoire, stripping away mind gunk. Sooner or later, something interesting would show up.

Dreamt my heart was bleeding. Was taken to intensive care for shortness of breath. I was hooked up to monitors—just like you. The medical staff was alarmed. Why are you short of breath? I don't know, I said. The ranking nurse said my heart was bleeding. That doesn't sound good, I said, critical-condition-like. Once the medical people understood my heart was the culprit, they ignored me. I was prepared to die but wondered where the doctors were. They all left. I said to myself, I guess this is it. I don't mind dying but where are the doctors? Staff unhooked me from vital-sign electronics and wired up another patient, a younger man. I was no longer in need. And then I got better. Apparently there is nothing you can do for a bleeding heart. Broken hearts must mend on their own, if ever.

Julian Barnes lost his wife unexpectedly. It was cancer. Suddenly he was alone with grief. Few friends really understood the meaning of his loss. He found it necessary to keep talking to his wife, constantly, as if she were an imaginary friend. *You constantly report things,* he says, *so that the loved one "knows." You may be aware that you are fooling yourself (though, if aware, are at the same time not fooling yourself), yet you continue.* Why let death end the conversation?

I'm thinking of getting a tattoo with your name on my right upper arm. No dates, such as in 1954–2016. Don't want a tombstone. As it is, I'm towing a body behind me—that's what it feels like to lose you. Your imaginary body is tethered to my shoulders by an invisible harness. Wherever I go, you go. Ironic, we're still inseparable. I find this consoling but also a little weird, in a Tom Stoppard way. It's not that your body is heavy in any literal sense—it isn't—but the resistance is enormous. The drag is massive, though not in this dimension. This comes from elsewhere, Planet Claire maybe, where there is no gravity as we know it but hidden variables. When I die, I'm sure the joke will be on me. I can almost sense its irony from here, not as a misgiving but as a kind of unknowable humor, a joke never before told. Death for me will be different than for you. I do think a tattoo would be fitting. Just your name. No frills, hearts, or dragons. And on my left arm, a tattoo of an untold joke, my death.

Centaurus is a large constellation in the southern sky. It's also bright, especially Alpha Centauri, its most popular star. You can see it with your naked eye. It's the closest system to our own, only 4.4 light-years away. Not only is it close, so to speak, but it holds an 85 percent likelihood of hosting a habitable planet, some place to take a shower and get a bite after a long drive. Maybe the newly discovered exoplanet Proxima b in the neighborhood of Alpha Centauri. The Boomerang Nebula is farther out in Centaurus. Way out. Space Boy says the plan is to take his chances on Proxima b, rest up, and build a new set of exciter equations, focusing on phase transitions and anomalous-burst drive. What do you mean by *exciter equations*? I radio back. Dark matter has a different profile out here, he says. Lots of hidden variables in interstellar space—so it's a trickier business formulating the correct tickle sequence. That sounds really weird, I radio back. You have no idea how much energy is hiding in dark matter, he says. Space Boy seems to have recovered his spark.

How are things down there? he asks. Do you really want to know? I radio back. No, he says. He'd rather talk about his spaceship. He says it's not the coolest of designs but Claire would like it. *Is this the first time he has uttered your name?* My ship looks like a Chuck Taylor High Top. I pretend otherwise, he says. Punch it, Chewy, I say to the empty seat beside me.

It's a relief Space Boy's search goes on with renewed zest. Extreme isolation can warp the mind. I worried he would hear phantom footsteps and see whirling lights, that sooner or later he'd be crouching on all fours. I've become dependent on his radio messages, though I hide my interest. He can be so cocksure. Maybe that's what it takes to find you. I'm such a doubter, but so are you. Even Milo was a doubter, a four-legged skeptic. No matter how famished, he'd sniff suspiciously at his chow, as if assassins lurked nearby. At least someone in the family is a high-flying go-getter. Space Boy is a real gambler. I like that.

We're at the kitchen counter and I've just rolled three ones. YES, I say with too much enthusiasm, and scribble *1,000 points* on the score sheet. You give me a dirty look. I'm behaving obnoxiously. You needn't gloat, you say. It's your roll, I say smartly. You shake the dice in your right hand and flash me the evil eye one more time, just in case I missed the first. Of the six dice only one is a score. You set the five aside and roll again. Five sixes this time. Holy shit! I say. 2,400 points! Not fair! You're smiling a big smug smile. I'm suddenly behind. Your turn, you say. I rub my hands together and pick up the dice, shaking longer than usual. They make a rattling sound that evokes pure randomness, possibility, and dread. I can feel a paradigm shift. The probability of rolling five sixes is one in ten thousand. Something has changed that is trending upward for you and downward for me. I feel star-crossed. My confidence is crippled.

I roll. A scratch. I moan in agony. Not one dice scored. I lose my turn. You're not doing a very good job of concealing your glee. You take a sip of your wine and then roll three fives and two ones. I flinch. Shit, I say, truly wounded. Seven hundred more points in your column. I rub my hands for dear life, scoop up the dice, and roll again.

The game goes on this way. With one flip of the wrist, you roll three sixes and two ones. Eight hundred more points in your column. I roll three hundred and fifty—lousy score—which now I take because I have to ride out this ill-fated run. You take another sip of wine and then flick your wrist. Three ones and three fives. Unbelievable, I groan in dismay. 1,500 points plus another roll. You're unstoppable! I roll four hundred. It's the best I can do. I feel doomed. Don't lose hope, you say. You never know what the next roll may bring. Sure, I say, utterly dispirit- ed. Easy for you to say. I'm getting clobbered. The game's not over yet, you say. I'm listening for a note of falseness in your voice but don't hear it. You really mean it. Luck is believing you're lucky, you say. Luck is luck, I say. Either you have it or you don't.

Sometimes bad luck hits you like a Greek tragedy, Werner Herzog says, and it's not your own doing. That's what this is like, a Greek tragedy. It makes no sense, but losing by a wide margin is crushing. We've both remarked on this, how playing dice feels uncanny, as though an abbreviated form of existence. It feels like life, you say, being down and fighting off despair, strategizing a come- back against the odds, finding faith in little scores (three hundred and fifty points), and knowing when—the timing needs to be perfect—to go for broke. A bad roll, you say, isn't really bad in itself. It's the despair that follows. De- spair makes a player edgy, you say, and this anxiety blinds one to the unexpected. True, I say. Dice is nothing if not about the unexpected. As if to prove the point, I go on to score 2,900 points to your 1,250. You win in the end, but this little twist of fate seems (for the moment) to restore order to our fragile lives. The wizardry of chance. Blind luck, you say.

My mind wanders. Is it from sadness or is it just me? I'm at my grandmother's house, a second-story apartment on the south side of Buffalo. She's making minestrone soup. Grampa is at Bethlehem Steel and his scary dogs are restless. Sunny outside but it stinks, the steel mill being upwind. On the corner above Caruso's Bakery a billboard displays a woman in a blue dress smoking a Lucky Strike cigarette. What a splendid smile, I think. Remember how great cigarettes used to taste? she says. Grandma doesn't smoke but everyone else does. The lady in the blue dress is mesmerizing. If I could, I'd light up right now. The sound of schoolkids carries over rooftops. A giant bus roars down South Park Avenue.

It grows dark outside early, the streetlights blink on, and a sudden downpour hammers the row of houses on North Division Street. A lone Ford creeps eastward, turns right on Culver Road. Outdoors, people have scattered. North Division is empty now, save for the wind and rain. From the kitchen, the sharp chopping of vegetables, a reassuring sound. One onion, two carrots, one leek, two zucchini, one potato, tomato paste, parsley, oregano, one can cannellini beans, one can kidney beans, one cup Parmesan, one cup small shell pasta. Chop, chop, goes Grandma's knife. The pot simmers beside a gallon of olive oil. In the oven, fresh bread.

I feel my mind stumbling through time. Not you, who slipped out of the body before its ruin. Your death is implicit in me. I am breathing, in and out. This feels desperate, a certain unsteadiness. You who no longer breathe the air of this planet are beyond desperation. No more sleepless nights or burnt toast. Saliva pools behind my lips. An old man who has not been born. I'm terrified. I am nowhere and I'm reading Alan Watts. Just be alive, he says. So here we are at the threshold of the incommunicable— the kingdom of spirit—you and me and Alan Watts.

Summer has begun and soon a year will have passed

without you. I have yet to shake off the sensation of losing not only my wife but a largish chunk of me. What's truly scary is that Space Boy's flight across the universe is beginning to seem real, as if this were not an elaborate trope. I can't explain that. Maybe that's the fate of people with only forty-four billion neurons. They believe everything they read. Anyway, I rented a truck in June and traveled to the Southwest. I wanted to revisit New Mexico and go fishing for UFOs in southern Colorado. The perfect diversion. I was back in the so-called real world but hardly acting the part.

It was a long drive through the Great Plains. A vast emptiness so immense it paralyzes the imagination. Nebraska is like that and so too Iowa. I drove the length of both, through field after field of corn and soy, across the treeless Platte River floodplain. Vacant cattle ranches as far as the eye can see. Peopleless grain elevators. No one in sight but lone pickup trucks, as if the whole country had disappeared, leaving behind a moribund infrastructure. From Nebraska, you can almost see the Pacific. There's nothing to stop the eye. Except for the capitol building in Lincoln, it's a horizontal state. Little soars. Even the birds seem borne down by example. Clear light and calming vistas, maybe, but the void seems to swallow up anything that walks on two legs. Tribes of Native Americans, European trappers, fur traders, migrant workers, a whole history of wandering erased by unthinkably wide and flat space. When the Union Pacific rumbles down the tracks it seems a ghost train. Here in this bright-green void I was at home, serene even. For the first time in a year I didn't feel like jumping out of my skin. Such terrific emptiness.

This was a survival test. (Survival isn't an academic

skill.) Almost a year after your death, I would revisit the sunny, arid Southwest, travel the same highways we once drove together—by myself—wandering through a place in memory filled by your voice and smile. I rented a large Ford truck, obscenely big, packed it with camera gear. I was up to my old habits. Nebraska was easy. Colorado was another story. I crossed the Nebraska border near Julesberg and down through Ovid and Sterling I drove, then Fort Morgan and Hudson.

The Ford climbed up the sparsely populated High Plains. Suddenly, the sky darkened and it rained and the wind howled. I didn't mind the bigness of the Ford then. But I looked to my right and saw the empty passenger seat. For seven hundred miles I'd forgotten I was alone, that you weren't there. You and the *New Yorker*. The emptiness of the Great Plains had consumed me and I felt beside the point. It was liberating. Your not-thereness stabbed me in the chest. I swerved into the on-coming lane, hit the brakes, and then corrected myself. Lordy. I pulled off onto the side of the road. Lucky I was the only misplaced person on this forsaken highway. The rain pounded on the sunroof. I got out and walked around the truck, as though looking for a flat tire. The wind snapped at me. I felt spent, despised. Blow, winds, shatter me. I felt like roadkill, something not fit for living. But I didn't mind, felt enormous relief, in fact. I wanted to lie down on the shoulder of Route 138 but didn't want road grease on my pants.

I have a crush on Portland, I tell you after our return from Oregon. Oh really? you say. We've been talking lately about alternatives to the Midwest. I love the nearby Cascade range and the Columbia River gorge is an eyeful, I say. You don't say anything. I go on. It's a bicycle town, which is pretty cool, and it's youthful. Plus it's a friendly place and fairly progressive with lots of interesting neighborhoods. Frankly, I was hoping for more effective public transportation, you finally say. I've always heard wonderful things about its light-rail system, but you can't go anywhere without a car in Portland, and all the highways are congested. Don't you remember? Actually, rush hour is really bad, now that I think about it. How could I forget? From what I've read, you say, Portland traffic is the twelfth worst in the country, almost as bad as Seattle, and you know, you say, how you griped about driving around there? I don't have a leg to stand on. But the craft pubs, I say sheepishly, they're great.

It's August and we've just unpacked. You're looking at a seashell you brought back from the Pacific coast. It's a pretty nautilus. You've rallied from your acrophobia. The mountain dread is gone. Milo is due at the vet's for dental work and cyst removal. We're confident this cyst, like the last one, is benign. Milo likes going to the vet. The treats are big and there are other dogs and cats to watch. A routine visit. Still, the vet always makes us a bit nervous. He may be kind with a good touch, but he also looks like someone who harbors dark secrets. He'd make a good Lloyd in *The Shining*, you say. I agree.

We leave Milo behind and go about our late-summer business. Food shopping, weeding, my turn to clean the bathroom. Three hours later a phone call from Dr. Gray. I take the call because my ears work. Good news and bad news, he says. My heart drops to the floor. I know what's coming. The cyst was benign and removed, but we found an unusual growth, says Dr. Gray, in Milo's throat, just to the side of his laryngeal pharynx. His what? It controls the opening to the esophagus. The area is inflamed and doesn't look right to me. I've taken a biopsy and will send it to the lab. No one here does this kind of examination so the tissue sample will have to go to Chicago. I don't want to be morbid, he says, but usually this is not a good sign. Meaning what? I say. Well, this could be *cancer*. Jesus, I say. In the worst-case scenario can you remove it? I can't even say the word *cancer*. Well, no, he says. Given where it is, the affected tissue is inoperable. Holy shit, I say, loud enough for you to hear.

Thus begins the Milo Death Watch, as you call it. Dr. Gray, who has now become Dr. Doom, refuses to offer any hope. There is no chance of surviving this, he says, I don't want to kid you. The tumor is malignant and aggressive, and because it's right next to his adrenal gland it's probably all over the place by now. How long does Milo have? I ask. My voice is so shaky I can't make out the words. Maybe two months, maybe only one. And just like that our lives have changed in some unalterable way. We are baffled by this, how the impending death of a pet can seem so world-ending. But that's what if feels like. The life we lived and loved for twelve years—the Milo years— is coming to an end. Then I tell you about my Milo dream two weeks ago.

We are visiting my mom, who lives on a busy street. We're about to take Milo for an afternoon walk but he runs toward the street before I can leash him. Oh no. We both shout Milo! That's when a shiny red 1958 Thunderbird drives up the curb and stops suddenly on the sidewalk. A young man in black races out of the car, grabs Milo, and then drives away. In the dream, we're astonished. It's a beautiful classic, I say of the T-Bird. You're unimpressed. I don't think a Thunderbird is a good sign, you say, beautiful or not. Besides, it's a raptor. A big one, you add. No, I say, it doesn't look good. I google *Thunderbird*, of course. Google says for Native Americans the Thunderbird animal totem carries souls to the other side, provides them with strength and comfort.

One can only hope. Who doesn't need that?

I watched a video on YouTube yesterday in which an alleged alien was interrogated by government agents from Project Blue Book in 1964, the operation launched in 1952 to investigate high-profile UFO cases. No doubt a hoax but nevertheless spooky. The creature was gaunt, hairless, large-eyed, with an extended skull, and spoke in a gravelly voice. He said that time travel is possible by traversing space, that this universe is only one of many, and that death as we know it is merely a construct. He also says he is from the future.

You were in high spirits when we returned to Iowa. Dublin lifted your mood. You even took me out to the local pub for a late-afternoon beer. We sat on high tables. Sunshine flew in through the tall windows. This is a first, I say, a late-afternoon beer. Not exactly a dark and brooding Irish pub, you say. Beggars can't be choosy, I say. Your smile is full of sunlight. We compare beers. Mine is the "Martian," a whiskey-barrel-aged ale. You're drinking an IPA. Boy, this tastes good, I say. You take a sip. Not bad, you say. I try your IPA. Not bad, I say, but kind of insipid. You're not crazy about hoppy beer, you say. It's good to be home, you say. That rain was a bit much, I say. What was your favorite moment in Ireland? I ask. I'm always asking questions like this. It's a stupid habit of mine, as if any moment in isolation can be meaningful, but you're a player. You liked the Arran Islands best, you say. Why? The stone, the flat sea, open sky, the silence and vastness, the sea light. How about you? I was pretty fond, I say, of the walk from Bray to Greystones. A four-and-a-half-mile cliff walk three hundred and fifty feet above the glittering sea, with a clear view of the Wicklow Mountains. I stop repeatedly to photograph seabirds circling below. The trail is narrow and I will climb over the rail to get a good angle. Afraid I will fall over the edge, you grab me by the waist. Remember how you held onto me? I took several fake photos just so you would cling to me. I could feel your happiness. I have a photo of you walking ahead, with your straw hat on and five-dollar backpack. You are naming the wildflowers, yellow gorse and red valerian. The brightly colored blooms are stirring in the summer wind above the blue Irish Sea.

When you walk around an island, I've read in an Irish poem, you do not return to where you started out. The poem is called "Clare Island" by Macdara Woods. It's easy to say nothing remains the same, but it means more than that.

In a dream, we are both traveling, vaguely in a hurry. I stumble on a brown paper bag, an old folded bag with many crease marks, like a reused lunch bag. Inside, five or six letters in their envelopes. Mostly saved letters. We are in a hurry and don't have time to examine the letters. Still, I grab one, overcome by curiosity, reach in, and pull an envelope out randomly. It's addressed to you and me, as a married couple. There's a check for two dollars. That's right, a two-buck handwritten check. The brief letter says this is a holiday rebate from the cable company. The date is—and this is the interesting part—1979. That's over ten years ahead of schedule. I wonder what the other letters say.

The Boomerang Nebula is impossibly far away. That kid—what gumption! I try to imagine myself in Space Boy's seat, spiraling toward Planet Claire. I've watched enough *Star Trek*. I try to let go, try to pretend I'm surrounded by solar winds and magnetic clouds. Out the view screen, I'm seeing a multitude of random objects, and the instrument panel is beeping. Red alerts keep sounding off. Icy body portside. What's an icy body? I say aloud to Space Boy, but he's taking a nap. It's not very pretty, the ice body. Weird, actually. Looks spongy and rather desiccated. Avoid impact. Beep beep. Maybe if I stare long enough at the portside ice body I will learn something about coldness—or is it farawayness?—whatever.

It's electrifying out here, though I don't think Space Boy would use that word. He'd say cool or weird or mind-blowing. I can see how vertigo is a problem, though. Rumors are that the speed at which you move through space affects movement through other dimensions, like time. At 98 percent of the speed of light, Space Boy's little ship can generate enough corollary energy to harness the force of a small black hole, if one can be found. I guess that's what this little gizmo on my left is, a crazy gravity detector. I know a thing or two about gravity. Small black holes populate the universe. My next move, I have a hunch, will require a terrific leap of imagination, an act of pure whimsy. The pyramids of Giza—impossible structures— were burial mounds built by ancient sadness, so improbable in the dune-covered wilderness. What I'm looking for is a closed time-like curve, a path that will take me to the past.

After a string of mind-boggling loops I would come knocking on your door in Bloomington, Indiana. There'd be a stunned Dave Bowman look on my face. My Omega Moonwatch would read 1984. *Terms of Endearment* has just won five Academy Awards. Over seventy inches of snow has fallen in Red Lake, Montana, but it's a sunny day in Indiana. I'm standing on the large porch of a big old house on West 4th Street. I knock. Hi, is Claire here? I say. A tall woman with long hair answers the door. Her name is Marcy. No, she says, Claire's in the library. Can I hang out on the porch until she returns? If you want, says the tall woman, but it might be a while. I sit on a porch swing and instinctively take out my cell phone. It's quite the veranda. There are sparrows in the crab apple and a guilty-looking mutt across the street. Some guy is watching me through a crack in the tie-dye curtains, amazed by my gadget. There's no signal, of course, but I put on my earbuds and listen to music. Why not? I think. Three hours later my phone is dead and I have no charger.

The sparrows are gone. Still no sign of you. I'm not surprised. Maybe you met up with your reading group after the library. Who are you reading now? You're a theory-head and your group is counting on you for clarity, because you can cut through the crap. Maybe you went out for dinner at Uptown Café but I doubt it. Not on a Wednesday night. You're too frugal for that. Besides, you're saving money for travel. Then where are you?

Everyone has left by now. The tall, dark-haired woman set sail a half hour ago and so did the guy who looks like Iago. He gave me an odd look before mounting his bike. No one here now but me the Traveler. The temporal-typicals have scattered. You know, I don't think anyone locked the door, so I'm lured by the idea of waiting in your room with the cat. I'm sure there's a cat. Ulysses. Your room is on the second floor. It's cramped and has a sloped ceiling but is very tidy. There's a Günter Grass poster on the east wall. Theoretically, the cat doesn't know me yet, but he jumps up on my lap like an old friend and begins purring. Good cat. I stroke his furry back. I know your room by a neat stack of medieval books and two or three *Par Avion* letters lying around, letters I have already—and this is so weird—read.

What will I say when you finally return home? Hi, we need to get you to the hospital immediately. I may seem like a perfect stranger—or worse—but trust me. You have a slowly bulging artery in your brain that needs to be repaired or you're dead in thirty-two years. The words surge out of my mouth like a storm. A look of terror crosses your face. Who is this crazy man!

What happens next, of course, is that you call 911 and the Bloomington police arrive on the scene. And that would be a nice bit of dramatic irony, all things considered, me the subject of a 911 call. But this does not happen because I decide to be more subtle. Who are you and why are you in my room? you ask with annoyance. You're not afraid, just vexed. You look me over. I've inhabited my younger mustachioed self. I have on loose-fitting jeans, a blue crew-neck sweater, and a button-down white shirt. Penny loafers too. Not very hip. My head is full of curly hair, which is making me dizzy because I haven't felt such a mop in years, but at least I fit in. I don't look like a futurist. I have a nice smile. (It helps to come from the future.)

At this point in the story everything is ironic, so profoundly funny (the letters, the cat, your helpless theory, my mustache), that I want to roll around on your moth-eaten carpet and laugh with the cosmos, as Kierke-gaard once advised. Because that's what I feel now is how comic this is. I'm holding the laughter back, which evokes a very nice smile, a very genuine smile. Your eyes are moving quickly, up and down, left and right. You're not sure what to make of me. Ulysses jumps down from my lap and curls up at your feet. Ulysses, you say, who is this man? Ulysses doesn't let the cat out of the bag, but I think he knows me somehow. Maybe cats aren't trapped in time the way we are. As Einstein said, the separation of past and present is only an illusion, though a tenacious one. It's my turn to speak but I don't know what to say. I've come all this way and I'm tongue-tied.

Hi, I'm from the future, I say. In eight years, you and I will marry. This startles you. You take off your denim jacket and sit on the edge of the bed. You haven't called the police yet, thanks to the cat who is in my lap again. What are you doing here? you ask, now concerned, maybe for my mental health. We haven't met, I say. Really, I'm from the future. I show you my phone to prove it. In a few years we'll meet. You're beginning to think I have Asperger's syndrome. You like almost-handsome, intelligent men with interesting flaws. I seem on the high-functioning end of the spectrum but obviously delusional. Are you all right? you ask. Maybe you should lie down. I just want to get my hands on your precuneal artery but I'm beginning to feel nervous because I don't think you're supposed to intervene in the past when time-traveling—there are protocols.

You're obviously baffled—how not? There's no plausi-ble idea for this, for me. I'm beyond theory. I'm beyond the pale. On Planet Claire, this is standard operation. There, time isn't. I want to tell you this but it's such an extraordinary paradox I'm afraid I might vanish, and what would that accomplish? So I look into your eyes and I say, without moving my lips—aliens everywhere do this— *Remember me.* There will come a time when you will repeat these same words, and that will be a moment of such utter strangeness we will both be hurled out of our minds.

In a dream there's a gate change. This is an end-of-summer dream, just the other day. It comes over the PA system. Our flight will be leaving from gate 331. I look at my watch, wondering where you are. You're late. The walk to gate 331 is not a short one. I look around and there, suddenly, you are, walking toward me with shoulder bag and purse. A gate change, I say. In another terminal. We should get moving. You look good in your stylish gray blouse, your wavy hair. Diamond patterns. You've been busy. We walk together toward the plane—we can see it in the distance. Gate 331 is not your typical boarding area. The gate is not inside anything, nor is the plane outside. These concepts don't exist, inside and outside. It's also dusky but not because the sun has set. Night and day aren't night and day here. It's the light of the dark-black night. I know where we're going, and the strangeness of journey's end doesn't phase me. We're visiting Planet Claire, you say. Just a visit, I say. Yes, you say, just a visit. We're going on a plane ride, you and me, you say—just a visit.

~~~

AFTERWORD

~~~

As I write, California is on fire while Americans struggle with a pandemic that has killed (at this point) 200,000 people. That number is likely to rise significantly. There are a lot of casualties out there. During a plague, death is contagious. This radical fact has serious consequences, especially as it applies to loss and sorrow. Grief is no longer posthumous but anticipatory. Perhaps even contagious. No one's ready for that.

Viruses are the most prevalent life-form on our planet. They live everywhere in nature, and many if not most are symbiotic. They are swimming in my bloodstream now. I find myself rethinking my body, its boundaries, and the nature of intimacy.

Do germs grieve? Odds are they don't care. Cellular replication is a form of ecstasy, if anything the opposite of sorrow. The ancient Greek word (*ékstasis*) means moving out of one's mind. Grief is all about relocating one's mind and body in relation to a missing subject. We care and that's why, as a species, we grieve. We struggle to offset that displacement. I suspect there's a migratory aspect to grief that more conventional accounts sidestep. Perhaps this is why the bereaved are so restless. Oedipus became a wanderer in a story that begins with a plague and ends in grief.

According to germ theory, it's all about proximity. It's not what you are—such a distraction—but *where* you are. I recently remarried. Lucky I am to be near someone I love and care for. To find tenderness and passion in another, after the journey of grief—how strange and unexpected. The nearness of life is a great mystery. I think germs understand this better than we do. In death, there is no nearness. If sorrow deepens the capacity for love, the collective sadness that awaits us may be a great challenge but maybe also a lucky chance.

Acknowledgments

I would like to thank Carl Klaus, Patricia Foster, Kerry Howley, and Jan Weissmiller for their invaluable insights while reading early drafts of this book. It's hard to imagine moving forward without their keen suggestions. Splendid writers and good friends. Ann Hood, the editor of this imprint, played a crucial role in bringing this manuscript to print, as did the staff of Akashic Books, who are remarkably perceptive readers. Ann is a compelling writer with terrific instincts, and I can't thank her enough for her guidance during the final stages of this book. Special thanks to Marcy Rosenbaum for her archival help and to Claire's medieval colleagues (Kathy Ashley, Jody Enders, Carol Symes, Theresa Coletti, Kathy Lavazzo, and Jon Wilcox) for their encouragement and insights into her scholarship. Thanks also to Rina Yoon for her support, and to my colleagues in English for their good cheer and inspiration. I would also like to thank Johnny Temple and Johanna Ingalls specifically, the publisher and managing editor of Akashic Books. Lastly, belated thanks to Poppa Clair, Jean, Beth, and Lauren for taking care of Milo while Claire and I dillydallied our summers away.